MERCHANTS AT WAR

Survival Tactics For Armed
And Unarmed Merchants

To Jack,
You're a great human being
and it's a pleasure
working with you. I value
Your friendship.
Best Wishes Always,
Paul Caparatta

MERCHANTS AT WAR

Survival Tactics For Armed
And Unarmed Merchants

Paul Caparatta

VARRO PRESS
Kansas City

MERCHANTS AT WAR

Survival Tactics For Armed
And Unarmed Merchants

Paul Caparatta

VARRO PRESS
P.O. Box 8413 - Shawnee Mission, Kansas 66208 USA

Printed and bound in the U.S.A.

Caparatta, Paul.
    Merchants at war : survival tactics for armed and unarmed
merchants / Paul Caparatta.
    p. cm.
    Preassigned LCCN: 98-60175
    ISBN: 1-888644-99-0

    1. Robbery--Prevention. 2. Retail trade--Security
measures. 3. Self-defense. I. Title.

HV6652.C37 1998   658.4'7
                             QBI98-10833

TABLE OF CONTENTS

IMPORTANT WARNINGS AND DISCLAIMER! READ THIS BEFORE YOU CONTINUE!

The author and the publisher of this book disclaim any liability, including liability for negligence, for any personal injury, property damage, or any other loss, damage, cost, claim, or expense including claims for consequential damages that the reader or others may suffer from following any of the suggestions, advice, or methods of instruction provided in this book. The reader of this book recognizes and accepts this disclaimer of liability by the author and the publisher, and the reader ASSUMES THE RISK of using firearms and/or attempting to defend him/herself or others from criminal attack. This DISCLAIMER OF LIABILITY by the author and the publisher and ASSUMPTION OF RISK by the reader is made and communicated in part because of what is described below:

YOU NEED TO LEARN THE LAWS OF YOUR OWN JURISDICTION(S). The laws regarding self-defense and the use of deadly and non-deadly force vary from state to state and country to country. Obviously, the author does not know the jurisdiction(s) in which you live, work, or need to use force in self-defense. Accordingly, the discussions in this book about the legal standards for the use of deadly force in self-defense are intended as a general discussion only, for the purpose of beginning your education on the subject. While these discussions present a fairly representative picture of the law in many parts of the United States at the time of this writing, it is incumbent upon you to learn and abide by the specific laws, definitions, and legal standards of the particular jurisdiction(s) in which you may be armed or may need to act in self-defense. Legal information of this sort can and should be obtained from your own attorney, county prosecutor or state attorney general's office, law library, law enforcement agency, the handgun license section of your local police department or in the personal protection firearms courses taught by qualified schools and instructors in many parts of the country. A growing number of states print pamphlets explaining their firearms and self-defense laws for distribution to individuals seeking to obtain concealed carry permits. The National Rifle Association can also provide state-by-state information on certain aspects of the law related to firearms. Having once obtained this knowledge, it is also important for you to stay abreast of changes in the law as they occur.

READING AND FOLLOWING THIS BOOK IS NO GUARAN-TEE THAT YOU WON'T BE SUCCESSFULLY PROSECUTED OR SUED! An infinite number of variables are present in every deadly force confrontation, and the judgments and decisions you may have to make—often in a split second, and under high stress—may not be clear-cut. The many variables, judgments, and decisions will be examined and evaluated afterwards by the police, prosecutors, judges and juries to determine whether your actions were justified civilly and criminally. No one, including the author, can offer you a foolproof formula, guaranteed to pass legal muster, that tells you when to shoot or when not to shoot. Your application of the concepts discussed in this book are beyond the control of the author, as is your interpretation and understanding of what you have read. Whether you follow any of the suggestions found in this book, or the advice of a panel of experts, you may nevertheless find yourself criminally prosecuted and convicted, or successfully sued in civil court, for your actions—even if you acted with the best of motives and intentions, and have followed the law to the very best of your ability. Using force against others, including mere display of a firearm, even in self-defense, has these potential consequences, which is why it should always be viewed as a last resort, when you are convinced the consequences of not acting are likely to be even more extreme!

ATTEMPTING TO DEFEND YOURSELF IS DANGEROUS!

Regardless of how skilled you become with a firearm (or any other form of self-defense), or what tactical measures you take or advantages you believe you have, the fact remains that attempting to defend yourself or others in the face of a violent criminal act is extremely dangerous. You or other innocent people may be injured or killed if you resist. On the other hand, you or other innocent people may be injured or killed if you take no action. No one, including the author, can tell you in advance whether it is better for you to resist or comply in any given situation. That decision is yours alone. Only YOU are in a position to evaluate your own abilities, the situation in which you find yourself, and the risks which you face by either resisting or complying. Hopefully, you will make your decision by weighing all the information available to you at the time, in light of the knowledge, skills, and judgment you have been able to develop on this subject in advance of that moment. The purpose of this book is simply to provide you with some—not all—of the data you may find helpful to factor into this equation. Other valuable data, theories, and information exist in other books and texts and which are the protected properties of other publishers, writers, and firearms experts.

FOLLOWING THE TACTICS SUGGESTED IN THIS BOOK WILL NOT GUARANTEE YOU WON'T BE HURT. While following the author's suggestions as to tactical store layout or other aspects of advanced tactical planning will hopefully improve your chances of deterring or thwarting a criminal attack, there can be no guarantee, and so the author makes none! Every crime and every place of business involves unique variables and unknowns, and so no self-defense plan or store design is foolproof. The suggestions in this book are intended simply to provoke your own thoughtful consideration of the factors that may apply to your own situation.

Firearms cannot be relied upon to stop a felon/robber, with 100 percent certainty, from performing or continuing the felonious act which puts you or others in jeopardy and which prompts you to shoot. The author makes no claim or guarantee, expressed or implied, that using any recommended firearm or ammunition will succeed in preventing you or others form being harmed or killed. For example, the presence of adrenalin, alcohol and certain prescription and illegal drugs, alone or in combination, in a felon/robber's body, can temporarily block the pain and incapacitating effect of bullets and allow a felon/robber to continue functioning long enough to inflict serious or mortal injuries upon you or others even though the gunshot wound(s) he suffered are ultimately fatal.

HANDLING FIREARMS IS DANGEROUS, AND YOU CAN'T LEARN IT ALL PROPERLY FROM THIS — OR ANY OTHER — BOOK. GET HANDS ON INSTRUCTION FROM A QUALIFIED INSTRUCTOR BEFORE YOU START! Firearms are inherently capable of causing death or inflicting serious bodily harm, which is why they are useful in self-defense. The reader should not attempt to learn to shoot a gun just by reading this book— any more than he should learn to drive an automobile or skydive or scuba dive, just by reading a book. For your own safety and that of those around you—as well as for the efficiency of your learning process—you should first attend a hands-on personal protection firearms class taught by a qualified, certified instructor of that subject. Your class should include both classroom instruction and live firing on the range, and should at a minimum cover firearms safety, general knowledge of how firearms and ammunition work, basic marksmanship skills, how to safely and properly load, unload, fire, reload, clear malfunctions, clean and store your particular firearm, fundamentals of self-defense shooting techniques, basic tactics such as use of cover, and the laws of your jurisdiction relating to firearms and self-defense. Basic classes of this sort are offered in most parts of the United States through shooting ranges, gun clubs, police departments and the NRA. Several sources of excellent hands-on instruction are listed at the end of this book. Some states have organized and mandated such classes as a requirement for issuance of a concealed carry permit, but attending such a class would be a good idea even if you only plan to keep the gun in your home or place of business, rather than carrying it concealed on your person. Even if you have owned or used firearms for many years for recreational purposes, you are best advised to attend a personal protection-oriented firearms class before embarking on this new discipline, as many of the techniques and much of what you will need to know to proceed safely may be different. Some activities, such as learning to draw a loaded gun from a holster, are particularly dangerous without proper, professional, hands-on instruction in advance. The information on gun handling techniques and the suggestions for developing your own shooting skills presented in this book are intended to SUPPLEMENT — not substitute — for what you learn hands-on in your class from your instructor.

Furthermore, it is the author's position that all federal, state, and local laws regarding the ownership and use of firearms as well as laws regarding the use of force must be obeyed. Nothing stated or written in this book should be construed or misinterpreted to mean that the author advocates, advises, or suggests that any law be disobeyed, ignored, or circumvented.

DEDICATION

For my wife, Denise, and our sons, Joseph, Paul and Craig.

And especially for my dear friend,

Charles J. Boedigheimer,
Deputy Inspector, Transit Bureau,
New York City Police Department,
who had to leave early....

ACKNOWLEDGEMENTS

The author wishes to acknowledge, with grateful appreciation, the many firearms instructors and law enforcement officers with whom he either shared or acquired knowledge, skills and ideas throughout his career. First, the late John Babernitz, the U.S. Customs Service firearms instructor who taught the author which end of the gun to point down range and who provided the author's very first exposure to professional firearms instruction. Along the way were firearms instructors, too numerous to mention, of the New York City Police Department, The New York City Transit Police, The Nassau and Westchester County Police Departments, Conrail Police and the Hempstead Police Department. On the federal level were the instructors of the FBI at both Camp Smith, Peekskill, NY and Quantico, Va., the Drug Enforcement Administration, The Alcohol, Tobacco and Firearms Division, U.S. Customs Firearms staff at the World Trade Center, and, of course, the firearms instructors of IRS:CID, both in Manhattan and in the national firearms task forces.

Along the way were some truly gifted and knowledgeable individuals such as Detective David Lendzian, NYPD, Special Agents Harry P. Clark, Ken Harper, Richard Bird and Wayne Santoro, IRS:CID, Special Agent Stanley Wojis, BATF, Jim Cirillo, NYPD, and the superb firearms instructors of the Smith and Wesson Academy, under the very capable direction of Robert Hunt, a gentleman of the highest order, each of whom gave unselfishly of his time and knowledge and was instrumental in assisting the author in attaining his current level of expertise. Special thanks go to Jeff Cooper, perhaps the world's leading authority on defensive handgunning, who made time for the author to insure technical accuracy of the most relevant and widely quoted and taught lesson plan ever offered to anyone who carries a gun for a living.

Special thanks also go to Emanuel Kapelsohn, a nationally recognized firearms and Use-Of-Force expert and much sought after expert witness in firearms related legal matters, for his time, guidance, and technical assistance with this book.

ABOUT THE AUTHOR

Paul Caparatta began his law enforcement career in the Fall of 1966 with the Criminal Investigation Division of the Internal Revenue Service. He had just completed his first training school when a draft notice arrived in May of 1967. Caparatta spent the next two years as a military policeman in the U.S. Army. This included a full tour of duty in the Republic of South Vietnam.

He returned to civilian life and the Criminal Investigation Division in May 1969. As a result of showing more than a passing interest in firearms, he was given the task of arranging for firearms training for the Manhattan District Office, more so because he was still in a trainee status than because of any management belief that he was right for the job.

Caparatta arranged for training through the New York City Police Department's Firearms and Tactics Section, being managed at the time by Lt. Francis McGee, perhaps the era's leading expert on police firearms training. Caparatta seized upon every opportunity to obtain knowledge from Lt. McGee, McGee's successor, Lt. Tom McTernan, and the many other skilled firearms instructors who manned the NYPD outdoor range at Rodman's Neck, New York. For there, in the Bronx, near the Throgs Neck Bridge, perhaps a 45 minute drive from Caparatta's lower Manhattan office, sat the mother lode of firearms lore and knowledge.

Special Agent Caparatta read every scrap of pertinent information he could find dealing with firearms, gun related crimes such as robberies and shootings of law enforcement officers and use-of-force. He was also quick to cultivate casual friendships with the firearms instructors of a number of police departments and all of the major federal agencies in his area.

Caparatta took a special interest in retail robberies because of the high probability that one of his agents would be present when a robbery occurred or would possibly walk into a robbery in progress. This became apparent in 1969 or 1970 when a jeweler with a ground floor shop in New York's landmark Woolworth Building was robbed, ordered to the floor, then executed with a bullet to the back of the head. Caparatta had planned to visit the jewelry store that morning and missed being involved in the robbery by about 15 minutes.

Caparatta credits the Firearms and Tactics Section of the New York City Police Department for providing the initial skills and knowledge that formed the basis for his own firearms training program. He went on to participate in national firearms task forces that modernized and reshaped firearms training for the Criminal Investigation Division, nationwide.

Caparatta has attended more than ten formal, firearms related academy courses and has authored more than 20 magazine and news articles on the subject. He is a guest on TV talk shows when the subject matter is firearms or gun control. He is called upon by the Video Production Unit of the New York City Police Department for technical assistance and has even acted in several professionally made police training videos. He is also an equipment and set advisor for several movie production companies.

Special Agent Paul Caparatta served as his division's senior firearms instructor from 1969 until his retirement in May of 1995. Today, he is Director of Law Enforcement Sales for DeSantis Holster and Leather products. He also provides private firearms instruction, specializing in discreet instruction for celebrities and high profile VIP's. His activities include assisting lawyers defending police officers and conducting tactical audits for merchants in his area. He is a member of the International Association of Law Enforcement Firearms Instructors, and a Life Member of the National Rifle Association.

PREFACE

In early 1995, a fellow special agent stopped by my desk to tell me that a personal friend of his, a pharmacist, had recently been shot during the commission of a robbery. His second hand description of the events disclosed that although a licensed handgun was available and was used, no plan existed to defeat a robber nor did the interior design of the store assist the pharmacist in any way. If anything, the store layout facilitated the crime. Unfortunately, the pharmacist was wounded and the gunman escaped.

This robbery caused me to reflect upon many other merchants whom I knew and who had been robbed, shot, injured, and sometimes killed during robberies. It also heightened my concern for the safety of my teenage son who, at the time, was working part time in a local pet store. That the pet store owner was licensed to carry a handgun gave me no comfort or relief whatsoever. He wasn't trained. Worse, he often departed early and left it to my son to close out the register, set the alarm, and lock up for the evening.

One evening, while picking up my son from work, I studied the counter and cash register area and imagined how I might defend myself and my son if this was my store and I suffered a robbery. Despite my skill with a handgun and knowledge of the law, I concluded, rather uncomfortably, that my chances of prevailing were between slim and none. Everything was wrong. There was no cover, no time to react, nothing to keep a gunman out from behind the counter. It was a tactical death trap - as deadly as wearing a noose while sitting in an electric chair set in a snake pit in the middle of a minefield. The only option available was total, unconditional surrender and compliance. This caused the tactical half of my brain to kick in:

Change this, change that, do this, do that, heighten this, move that, block this, and so on.

I began making notes for a possible article for a gun magazine. Or, perhaps I was subconsciously motivated by my son's comment that he'd someday like to own a pet store. One note led to two others, and one page of notes soon filled a writing pad, as my thoughts multiplied in a geometric progression. This exercise lasted several months. If my son ever opened his own store, I would ensure that every conceivable variable and percentage was stacked in his favor. He'd earn the first black belt awarded for total merchant preparedness. His store would be the first to be designed along tactical lines with the thought that it may someday be necessary to have - no, make that win - a gun battle in it. I would be the general contractor. The store would be built my way or not at all. The architect, carpenters, and merchandising experts would all learn a new way of doing things.

Thus was born the concept of tactical store design, a concept in which the physical layout, features, and properties of a store are surreptitiously arranged in such a way that it can help the merchant defeat the robber rather than helping the robber defeat the merchant. Consequently, if tactical store design catches on, I'll take the credit for it.

I soon realized that a magazine article simply wouldn't do. I had more than enough new, original, and never before published (to the best of my knowledge) material to write a book, the book you are holding in your hands. While hundreds of excellent books exist on use of force, self defense, and the shooting disciplines, by authors with impressive credentials, it occurred to me that none addressed the particular tactical needs of the armed merchant, of which there were many thousand. This is how my book differs from the others: While the legal aspects are generic and apply to all use of force situations, the tactics are drawn from the vast amount of knowledge available but tailored to be user specific. I believe I've broken new ground. This is new information.

I am familiar with the attendant circumstances of ten separate merchants who were robbed. Sadly, I did not know a single merchant who prevailed. They all lost their encounters. Four paid with their lives. The common thread in all these merchant defeats was the absence of physical and mental preparation for an armed encounter beyond merely owning a gun. When push came to shove, these merchants lacked the training, commitment, knowledge, judgment, tactical sense, resolve, and tenacity it takes to win at life's ultimate challenge, an endeavor where the loser usually pays with his life or suffers a debilitating injury. I cannot stress enough the need to take this information seriously and act upon it. Human nature being what it is, some of you will shrug your shoulders and do nothing. In time, you'll forget what you've read, even forget where you put the book, or who you loaned it to. And then it will happen: sudden, swift, frightening, and without much warning. Afterwards, if you survive, you will think to yourself, "I knew this might happen to me and I did nothing about it."

Of course, there will also be merchants for whom the information, thoughts, and ideas contained in this book prove instrumental in defeating an armed robber. If so, both I, and the publisher, hope you'll share the details with us.

One thing is certain: An armed robber can only face two kinds of merchants, one who presents a pillar of resolve, confidence, resourcefulness, and determination, or one who reacts like a trembling mound of Jell-O. You can be a victim or a survivor. The choice is yours.

INTRODUCTION

"He that suffers his life be taken from him by one that hath no authority for that purpose, when he might preserve it by defense, incurs the guilt of self murder since God hath enjoined him to seeek the continuance of life, and nature itself teaches every creature to defend itself."
—From a sermon delivered in Philadelphia, PA in 1747, according to Jeffrey R. Snyder in his paper, "A Nation of Cowards."

While there can be a million variations, there are but three kinds of gun battles: best, second best, and worst. The best kind of gun battle is the one that can be **avoided** through proper planning and a survival oriented mindset, proactive security measures, awareness, and constant alertness, all of which we'll examine in this book. The second best gun battle is the one you win, whether or not you hit your adversary. If you cause your attacker to break off the assault and flee with nothing more than a ruffled ego and acute sphincter muscle failure, you have won! The worst gun battle, of course, is the one you lose. The small business owner is on the endangered species list. He is under constant assault from shoplifters, dishonest employees, the advent of the super stores, and the ever present threat of the armed robber. Of all the threats facing the merchant retailer, it is the crazed gunman who is most feared. He's too unpredictable. Full and rapid compliance with his demands does not guarantee our safety. He may kill us anyway.

According to the U.S. Labor Department's Bureau of Labor Statistics, during 1992, 1,004 people died as a result of workplace homicide, of which 82 percent were attributable to robberies and miscellaneous crimes. Further, at least six percent were police officers who died in the line of duty. Another four percent of the homicides were attributable to domestic violence that carried over into the work place, and eight percent were the result of customer and client violence that had nothing to do with robberies. So, if you're hard nosed about taking back defective widgets, someone just might kill you as a result. There were 175 homicides occurring in grocery stores alone during 1993. Based upon statistics available from the U.S. Department of Justice, over 125,000 robberies of various stores occur each year.

Incidentally, I will only quote a few statistics in this book. You already know that armed robbery is a serious occupational hazard. You don't need endless bar graphs, pie charts, piles of numbers, ratios, etc. to document or prove the obvious.

This book deals with armed confrontations. Large numbers of merchants are already armed and countless more are arming themselves, legally or otherwise. Unfortunately, many merchants are of the impression that buying a gun and storing it under the cash register is all that's necessary to insure personal security. In a recent survey conducted in New York, it was found that as many merchants as felons had died in shootouts during the period studied. Also, a distressing number of innocent bystanders had been wounded or killed by both merchants and felons.

As part of a study for one of the nation's largest convenience store chains, Athena Research Corporation interviewed 181 armed robbers. The study, first reported in the October 1996 issue of *Security Management Magazine* and summarized in the May 1997 issue of *Police And Security News*, found that robbers like to target stores near easy escape routes and with easy access to cash. Most robbers would target a store if they believed they could get at least $200.00. Stores with drop safes were a deterrent to robbery because of the small amount of cash usually available. Forty percent of the robbers lived within two miles of the convenience store they hit and one third of the robbers interviewed had committed at least five or more store robberies. Over 60 percent of the robbers stated they had an accomplice during the robbery serving as a driver or in-store look-out.

The study also found that the number of people or victims present didn't matter much as the robbers felt they could manage up to about a dozen people with their guns. Unarmed security guards had little deterrent value. Armed store personnel served as a deterrent but most of the robbers felt that either the victims would not actually shoot or, if they did, would not be able to hit them. It was also found that store clerks who resisted were 50 times more likely to be killed than those who offered no resistance and did not make any sudden moves. Injuries and deaths suffered by cooperative clerk/victims were attributed to the robber being "nervous" or high on drugs.

In most instances, resistance is ill timed, impractical, and motivated by the wrong emotional triggers. That is, shopkeepers who lash out against impossible odds because they are outraged by someone trying to take their possessions are almost guaranteed to be seriously injured. Outrage, shock, and disbelief, three strong emotions, could account for instances of shopkeepers taking on gun or knife armed thugs with nothing but bare hands, a broomstick handle, or baseball bat. In many instances, the injured and killed are store employees who may feel some obligation to at least make an attempt to safeguard their employer's assets.

That victim/resisters are 50 times more likely to be killed is neither surprising nor an argument against resistance as cooperative victims are also injured and killed. Rather, it illustrates that in order for resistance to work for the storekeeper, it must be tactically correct, it must never be an emotionally motivated knee-jerk response, and most of all, it must be effective.

Merchants, even gunshop owners, do not fare as well as they should during confrontations. To understand why this is so, it is necessary to understand the interrelationship and interdependence of a number of mental and physical elements that separate the winners from the losers. They are, in order of importance, **mindset, knowledge, judgment, tactics, marksmanship, and firearm.**

Merchants die as a result of felonious activity for the same reasons that law enforcement officers die: one or more of the above mentioned critical elements necessary to win a confrontation was missing.

Consequently, it is necessary to examine each critical element separately as well as how they interrelate to each other. Assuming equal ability and mental commitment for both the robber and the merchant, it is the merchant who will most likely lose because the robber is the initiator. Self defense is a **reaction** to a felonious act. The robber most often enjoys the element of surprise, aided in part by the fact that most merchants don't expect to be robbed by each and every customer who enters his store. In tournament chess, white always opens first. Black must react to the opening move. Consequently, white continues "acting" while black continues reacting until such time that white makes a mistake and black can seize the initiative. Statistically, most chess players win more games playing the white pieces, merely on the strength and advantage of being allowed to move first. The merchant must seek to overcome the disadvantage of having to react by stacking every possible and conceivable advantage in his favor. This is the reason for this book.

Tactically speaking, the merchant enjoys an advantage over the law enforcement officer: the merchant is on his home turf. He knows every nook and cranny of his store. He must only prepare for one type of felonious emergency but with predictable variations. He can even make changes to the store's physical layout to make it more defensible for him. The police officer, on the other hand, is constantly on unfamiliar turf and often must deal with many unknowns, thus complicating the tactical considerations necessary to win a confrontation.

In practical terms, there isn't much difference between a police officer and the armed merchant or homeowner besides the obvious facts that the officer has police powers granted by his state, is usually much better trained, and must be prepared to manage an infinite variety of felonious emergencies. However, a gun battle is a gun battle. That is, an armed merchant who elects to defend himself must be as proficient as the uniformed officer in mastering the elements necessary to win an armed confrontation. There are no shortcuts. Second place isn't good enough. Thus, a failure to recognize and appreciate the need for tactical planning and to be mentally prepared for a confrontation in which someone may die can land both the officer and the merchant on the embalming table.

I would like to stress, right from the beginning, that gun battles must be avoided if possible. You might be wondering why I'm saying this if this is a book about armed confrontations. The modern police firearms instructor devotes the bulk of his training time to teaching his students how to avoid shootouts through proper mental conditioning, planning, and tactics. We recognize that confrontations often degenerate into shootouts because of poor tactics or a lack of understanding of the dynamics of the confrontation. That is, the law enforcement officer most often provides the opportunity for a felon to attack. He doesn't recognize unmistakable warning signs that, if noticed, could have saved his life or avoided the need to employ deadly force. Or, he enters an adversary's kill zone (we'll define and examine kill zones later in the book) flat footed and with his brain in neutral. Consequently, I will devote a portion of the book to proactive measures you must take to reduce the likelihood that felons will target you or your store. Remember, felons also have a tactical sense: they tend to avoid people who make themselves difficult targets.

In reality, whether we live or die depends more upon the person holding the gun, particularly, his mindset, than on the gun itself. I know of several merchants who rushed to scrap their revolvers in favor of the 9mm pistol, then lost faith in the 9mm when the FBI adopted the short-lived 10mm cartridge. Then the .40 S&W made its debut and quickly gained a firm foothold in the law enforcement community, causing many private citizens to join the stampede for the latest refinement in handgun/ammunition technology. Despite their awesome armament many of these merchants can still be defeated with nothing more than a slingshot or a finger in a pocket.

Magazine reviews of new handguns or cartridges tend to deal with the new product in a vacuum. Product quality or suitability is emphasized but it's up to the owner to integrate it into a comprehensive defensive plan. Consequently, far too much emphasis is placed upon owning the ultimate defense handgun as though it is the gun that will save us. To complicate matters, there are even regional preferences with regard to defensive firearms. For example, single action, custom made pistols based upon the U.S. Government, Model 1911, .45 caliber semi-automatic appear to be especially popular in the Southwest, while the newer, double action semi-autos, especially in 9mm, enjoy more popularity in the Northeast.

The armed merchant must also be intimately familiar with the laws regarding the use of force in his state of residence. Remember, you may have but a heartbeat in which to respond in order to win. Hesitation caused by not knowing the law, specifically, not knowing whether deadly force is legally justified, or making the assumption that you will automatically go to jail for shooting someone can cost you or a loved one his or her life. This is quite a legal dilemma created, in large part, by lawyer/politicians and jurors who watch too much television and thus think they're Perry Mason. If you act a second too soon, you may be charged with a criminal act such as reckless endangerment, menacing, or manslaughter. But, if you act a second or two too late, you'll find yourself under a sheet.

The merchant who shoots an armed robber can expect to have his actions measured against a very tough legal yardstick. The wise merchant, knowing this, will be mentally and legally prepared for both the physical encounter and its legal aftermath. The unprepared merchant, one who shoots a shoplifter, an irate customer, wildly slings lead in the general vicinity of a fleeing felon, or who makes irrational or unfortunate remarks to arriving police officers, can expect to find himself nailed to that legal yardstick.

It is my intention to cultivate a survival instinct in my students based upon a winning mindset, knowledge of the law, an understanding of the importance of judgment, knowledge, and tactics and, in many instances, minor changes to your store's interior to stack the tactical odds in your favor and to reduce the number of options available to the felon.

There are four parts to an armed confrontation:

1. Early recognition of the warning signs that a robbery is about to occur;

2. The confrontation itself, whether or not shots are fired;

3. The immediate aftermath of a confrontation, or the point when the firing (if any) ceases. You may have suffered an injury and the robber has either been defeated, is in the act of fleeing or has fled.

4. Scrutiny of your actions by the police, district attorney, the grand jury and attorneys hired by the robber or his estate in an effort to win a civil judgment against you. In some locales, you may also face legal harassment from social activist groups, particularly if you and the person you've shot are of different ethnic groups.

This book will assist you in winning all four parts of the confrontation. You need to hit the grand slam. A single just won't do. For example, a justifiable act with an illegal handgun renders you vulnerable to a successful legal attack, both criminal and civil. Not only do we want to save our lives but we also want to save our life's savings. If you are an armed merchant or plan to be one, this book is required reading. If you are armed outside the law, I cannot stress enough the need to be in compliance with your local firearms ordinances, whether you agree with them or not. Keep this in mind as you read the book.

You may decide, after reading this book, that armed defense is not right for you. Perhaps it's best to comply with the robber's demands and hope for the best. That's okay. This is a book about saving lives. In many instances lives may be saved by not resisting, particularly if you are not willing to become thoroughly proficient in shooting, are unable to fire a handgun at another human being no matter what, and are not willing to harden your store against robbers. Also, even though you are armed, there will be many situations where armed resistance would not be practical. This is where the element of judgment can save your life. As you will see, resistance cannot be half hearted. You will be fighting for your life. There is no second place. It's the gold medal or nothing.

Life would be much simpler if robbers adhered to some sort of bandits' code of honor. That is, if you comply, they won't hurt you. Unfortunately, the newspapers are full of stories about shopkeepers who complied with a robber's every wish yet were summarily executed anyway. This is perhaps the greatest dilemma facing the merchant: deciding whether or not to resist and trying to second guess which robbers are content just to take your cash and which will also rape your wife or a customer, then shoot you for kicks. While we are all familiar with the terms "mass killer" and "serial killer," the FBI unit that assists local police departments in tracking serial killers has added a new term to our vocabulary: the recreational killer. While mass and serial killers are often motivated by some twisted demon eating their brains, recreational killers kill purely for fun. And speaking of serial killers, authorities estimate there are perhaps 50 serial killers roaming the country at any given time. Unfortunately, these individuals must eat, buy gas, stop to use the facilities, and buy cigarettes or liquor. This means that they must interface with you, the merchant. Hopefully, if you cross paths with one, he's having a good day.

Robbery isn't the only motive of felons. Some go on shooting sprees where the objective is to both rob and shoot people. On April 21, 1994, four youths, aged 17 to 21 years of age went on such a shooting spree in Suffolk County, New York, robbing two separate Dairy Barn Stores and a Texaco station. They killed one store manager and wounded two clerks. Perhaps the most tragic example of mindless violence in recent years occurred on December 19, 1995 when a mentally deranged individual invaded a Bronx, New York shoe store with the intent of robbing it. He studied the store for weeks, deciding in advance not to leave any witnesses. Almost immediately he opened fire, killing four customers and the wife of the shop owner. Just two weeks prior to this incident, eight people died in a Harlem, New York retail outlet, including the arsonist/gunman, following a landlord/tenant dispute with alleged racial overtones. If, after reading this, you're still of the opinion that you cannot fire upon another human being, even in the face of overwhelming provocation and justification, may I respectfully suggest that you close your store and return to the planet from which you came. Self defense is legally recognized throughout the free world and is even permitted or condoned by the major religious faiths.

The author was personally acquainted with 10 merchants who were robbed, of which four were killed in their places of business. Nine merchants offered absolutely no resistance while one made a feeble attempt at self defense with a .25 automatic that malfunctioned after the first shot (a gunshop owner who should have known better!) One survived a major abdominal wound, another survived a gunshot wound but suffered a stroke and died shortly thereafter. Yet another merchant, unharmed during the robbery, suffered a series of strokes and was forced to give up his business. A pharmacist, interviewed for this book, suffered a gunshot wound to the jaw, requiring considerable reconstructive surgery. He too gave up his profession rather than face the onslaught of robbers.

As previously mentioned, merchants have a less than admirable record in defending themselves. This is understandable because the merchant is not trained nor is he mentally conditioned for a felonious emergency. Being prepared for an armed confrontation is more than going to a shooting school and receiving a wall certificate. Preparedness is a daily and ongoing commitment. Winning an armed confrontation is also a matter of skill and luck. **The more skill you have, the less luck you'll need.**

Robberies can occur at any hour. However, the 24 hour convenience stores are favorite targets of robbers. Robberies also tend to occur close to closing hours when the cash register should be full and you are mentally and physically exhausted. You've got your mind on closing the store, setting the alarm and getting home to food and family. You're not paying attention to little warning signs that can buy you precious seconds in preparing to manage a felonious emergency on your terms. You may not realize that a robbery is occurring until you're staring down the barrel of a gun. Even then, some felons have to whack the merchant across the head with the gun to obtain his full and undivided attention and compliance with his demands. The robber may not appreciate that you momentarily may not comprehend what's happening or that you become immobilized with fear. Any perceptible delay in your response can get you shot.

The more valuable the target, the greater the security precautions needed to safeguard it. But, the larger the target, the more tantalizing it becomes. The robbery team willing to go for it will be more intelligent, better organized, more professional, and willing to take great pains to study your security in the hope of uncovering the weak spots. If they find the chinks in your armor, they will attempt the robbery. Firearms cannot and should not serve as a substitute for reasonable security measures, particularly those recommended by your local police, various merchants' associations, and the security firm that patrols the mall where your store is located, if applicable. The possibility of a deadly force confrontation can be reduced by constantly reviewing and upgrading security procedures.

Lest there be any doubt or confusion, it is not the purpose of this book to convince you to go out and buy a gun, nor to convince you that armed resistance is the only way to respond to the robbery plague. In most instances, you already own a handgun and you have decided you will use it if necessary. Hopefully, the information contained in this book will help you use it in a tactically and legally correct manner.

I will touch on many topics which, in and of themselves, are often the subject of books devoted entirely to that subject. Some of these include the criminal mind, tactical and evasive driving, training and use of protective dogs, handgun selection, combat or defensive shooting, hostage situations, laws relating to physical force, domestic violence, workplace violence, proactive security measures, handgun safety, home defense, etc. It is incumbent upon the reader to do additional research or avail himself of the many specialized security courses and schools if he wishes to obtain in depth information on any particular topic.

I am somewhat dismayed at the large numbers of credentialed "certified protection professionals" who make pronouncements on every aspect of physical and personal security but stop well short of even broaching the subject of physical force. The very best proactive security precautions can be circumvented by stealth, force, or license. When that happens, where's their plan B? These experts can't bear the thought of actually having to shoot somebody . Therefore, they would prefer that you don't shoot anyone either. In fact, one nationally known security expert, with at least one respected book to his credit, proudly takes credit for disarming a large security force when he assumed management control of it.

A comprehensive security plan must have both a proactive and reactive aspect. To be sure, the well prepared merchant or businessperson will have all his proactive and reactive ducks in a row. That is, he will do everything reasonably possible to avoid becoming a target. However, when a gun is called for, nothing else quite suffices. After reading this book, you may better understand why some citizens terminate a crime and are hailed as heros while other citizens, in remarkably similar circumstances, face prosecution and whopping civil judgments. Of course, the greatest variable of all is the jurisdiction itself. The unevenness with which the laws are applied across this once fine nation truly defies logic. Add to this the fact that attorneys much prefer jurors who are seemingly brain dead. Any juror who displays even the slightest awareness of what's going on beyond the confines of a Tupperware container is quickly removed for fear he might ignore perception and emotion and apply logic and common sense to the facts at hand. If you consider the entire deadly force/self defense issue as a legal minefield, then consider this book the mine detector! Plan B follows.

CHAPTER ONE

PROACTIVE CONSIDERATIONS

Being prepared for a felonious emergency also involves avoiding them in the first place. You have smoke detectors in your home and you educate your children on what to do in the event of fire. But, you also make sure your house doesn't catch fire! The same concept applies in robbery prevention.

I've observed a wide disparity of preparedness among merchants. Those operating in neighborhoods with enough violence to rightfully classify it as a war zone have sometimes found it necessary to curtail business hours while others have transformed their establishments quite literally into fortresses. In some instances, particularly the mini convenience/tobacco/candy outlets, all transactions are conducted through a tellers' window. The customer remains in the street while the merchant remains barricaded within.

Moving away from the inner city, preparedness falls off considerably as complacency begins to rear its ugly head. It's quite difficult to remain prepared for a rare occurrence whether you are a merchant or a police officer. In an incident that occurred near my home, several individuals were traveling on Merrick Road, Long Island, a secondary thoroughfare running into New York City. Perhaps on impulse, these individuals decided to rob a Kentucky Fried Chicken outlet in an area that rarely witnesses violent crime. Moments later, two employees of the restaurant were shot dead despite offering no resistance.

My point is, if you're a retailer, there is no such thing as a safe neighborhood. On Memorial Day 1995 and a five minute bike ride away from the Kentucky Fried Chicken killings, the manager of a shoe store was shot and killed during a holdup. Each and every merchant must take reasonable precautions to insure that if they're targeted for a robbery they will have the resources at their disposal to lawfully terminate the robbery in their favor.

There's no need to construct a moat around your store and stock it with hungry alligators. Reasonable precautions fall about half way between none and paranoid. For example, even though at least one elephant handler is pancaked each year by an angry elephant at a domestic zoo or circus, equipping each and every patrol car with a firearm capable of handling a large animal emergency would be sheer lunacy. Thus, for the merchant operating at zero preparedness, much of what follows may seem excessive. Following are proactive recommendations which can greatly reduce the likelihood of having to confront an armed felon.

Most large police departments have anti-crime units which may have suggestions and guidelines that, if followed, will reduce the likelihood your establishment will be targeted for an armed robbery. Information on robbery prevention may also be obtained from your insurance company, trade associations, and perhaps the local chamber of commerce. Trade magazines also contain periodic articles on robberies and their prevention. Regardless of how well you think you're prepared, no sane and prudent person wants to engage in an armed confrontation that could have been avoided.

The Crime Prevention Division of the New York City Police Department suggests the following:

Do not keep large sums of cash in the cash register. Registers bulging with cash do not escape notice. Often, word gets around that so and so's store is a gold mine and the cash registers hum all day. Also, it isn't a wise idea for patrons to see you periodically removing fistfuls of cash which you then squirrel away somewhere in the back room. If the bulging register is an inviting target, belief that there's also a mother lode somewhere in the store will surely invite an armed robbery.

And speaking of back rooms, an intelligence gathering technique used by potential robbers is to make a small purchase with a large bill that you cannot cash with the register contents. If you go somewhere else in the store to obtain the necessary small bills to offer change, you have disclosed the existence and location of additional cash. Always have enough cash in the cash register to cash a one hundred dollar bill. This may put a bit more cash at risk but avoids disclosing a cash horde to a stranger which then makes you a more inviting target.

If necessary, make several trips to the bank daily. If you are blessed with trusted employees it would be a wise idea to have them assist in making deposits, provided employees are randomly selected and they do not adhere to a time schedule. Do not approach night depositories if someone is lurking in the area. Avoid the depository and, if necessary, call the police.

To this list I would also suggest that you not bring cash receipts to your home. Take them to the bank or leave them in a commercial duty safe and make sure your employees do not suspect that you keep large sums of cash at your residence. In the New York City area, hardly a week goes by that a store or restaurant owner is not ambushed at his residence. Sometimes these robberies go bad and innocent family members are either taken hostage or slain. For example, in the summer of 1995, thugs invaded the Valley Stream, NY, home of Myung-Kuk Chun, owner of a cosmetics firm, with the intent of committing a robbery. According to an article in *Newsday*, a former employee of the firm believed her employer brought cash receipts home each night. She allegedly shared that information with her boyfriend; accomplices were recruited and a plan was hatched to locate the family home and rob them there. Apparently, Chun's 24-year old son resisted when the robbery team invaded his home and he was promptly shot to death.

Some ethnic groups seem to have an innate distrust of banks and prefer to deal in currency. I'm also aware that many owners of cash businesses underreport their income and, therefore, do not deposit skimmed receipts to their business bank accounts where it may be easily found by the IRS. Trying to avoid banks, the IRS, and audit trails can easily make you a more inviting target to robbers.

If you're swimming in cash, the wrong element will soon know it. Robberies that are business related but occur at a residence often involve a loose lipped employee who may or may not be in on the robbery. Human nature being what it is, those loose lips may be your very own. Most businessmen cannot resist the temptation to brag about how well they're doing and how they're screwing the IRS.

These steps may help reduce the amount of currency lost during a robbery. However, you should not assume that following these precautions will automatically keep you from being robbed. The felon may not know of your multiple and varied daily deposits and may assume that the day's receipts are either in the cash register, in the ubiquitous cigar box under the register or in your pocket. With regard to the cash register, it is a wise practice to situate the register in a manner which prevents customers from seeing its contents. In the chapter on tactical store design, we will take an in depth look at cash register location.

Back rooms should be closed off from public view so that a potential robber does not know who or what is back there. Generally, felons don't like to deal with too many unknowns or situations in which they cannot gain immediate control. You can enhance the illusion that someone else is in the store by leaving a radio or television on in the back room just loud enough to be heard in the store. Later we'll discuss converting the back room into a safe room as a further step to insure your personal safety.

Stores should be well lighted and the area around the cash register should be easily viewable from the street. This means avoiding cluttering up the windows with sale signs or posters. Felons feel more secure if their actions cannot be observed from the street. You may recall the Seacrest Diner incident. The diner, located in Westbury, NY, a respectable, middle class area, had no windows. On May 29, 1982, five armed robbers invaded the diner, quickly gaining control of employees and patrons alike. Two robbers stationed themselves at the entrance to intercept arriving patrons who could not suspect a robbery was in progress. In addition to robbing the diner and the patrons, the patrons, particularly the young women, were forced to strip and commit sexual acts with each other. One individual was shot. Shortly after the robbery, extensive renovations were performed which removed much of the exterior masonry facade, which was then replaced with large, plate glass windows.

Remember, the robbery you're trying to prevent may occur outside the store. For this reason, you are at risk when going to the bank and also when opening or closing the store. At that time, most of the lights may have been turned off and a robber may assume you're carrying most of the day's receipts. You must be particularly observant of anyone loitering near your store. If you become suspicious of one or more individuals, call the police or mall security, if applicable. Do not challenge the loiterers on your own. Just because you have a handgun tucked in your waistband does not make you a police officer.

Other retailers in the area face the very same risks as you. Retailers should form informal security cooperatives. Assume for the moment your establishment is one of four such establishments on a street corner. If all of you have similar closing hours, you may agree to try to close at the same time, thus making it more difficult for a robber to isolate you and force you back inside the store. I would like to add here that even though you're armed, if you observe suspicious activity at a neighboring establishment, you should call the police rather than become directly involved. With regard to the security cooperative, it is not necessary to set up a formal organization with officers, elections, dues, Roberts Rules of Order, etc. Simply get together for a cup of coffee and agree to be a bit more alert and to watch out for each other. Six, eight, or 10 eyes are better than two. If you sincerely believe you were the subject of intelligence gathering by a potential robber, let your neighbors know. Also, you and your business neighbors will subscribe to different trade publications, depending on the nature of your businesses. You may agree to share relevant articles dealing with retail security matters, including robberies.

Teach yourself to be "tail conscious." Someone may be following you to ascertain your daily movements or to find out where you live or do your banking. Keep an eye in your rear view mirror when leaving the store, especially if carrying a sum of cash. If you think you're being followed, either make four consecutive right turns or pull over at a convenience store and observe the actions of the suspect vehicle. If your suspicions are confirmed, call the police from where you are or drive to the nearest police station. Do not challenge the occupants of the suspect vehicle. If you can, obtain their license plate number without making it obvious you're doing so.

While on the subject of vehicles, do not allow yourself to be forced off the road. Ordinary citizens get forced off the road because they're afraid of damaging their cars, and their entire motorist history has been devoted to avoiding collisions and subsequent lawsuits. Consequently, you have been programmed to avoid accidents, even if it means bringing your car to a halt. It may be necessary to incur some property damage in order to escape because fear of damaging your automobile can result in damage inflicted upon your body. It is quite common for the manager of a fast food restaurant to be intercepted in the parking lot or on his or her way home, brought to a halt, kidnapped, then forced back to the restaurant to open the safe. In the absence of a traffic dispute, complete with obscene gestures, if someone attempts to force your car off the road, it usually means he has felonious intentions or he's out of Grey Poupon mustard.

In the most common cutoff maneuver, your adversary will be on your left and he'll try to force you to the right. Instead of turning your wheels to the right to avoid contact, make a sudden right turn and flee if there are intersections present, avoiding cul-de-sacs and dead ends. Another option would be to brake hard, allowing your adversary to momentarily pull ahead of you, then make a left turn or "U" turn if these options are available. With the "U" turn, you must be able to do it in one motion. There won't be time for the back and forth maneuvers required in a narrow street. Acceleration is also valid provided you do not exceed the speed at which you can still maintain control of your vehicle. If you're the type who likes to stay 10 miles per hour under the speed limit (in the left lane, of course) chances are you do not have the driving skills necessary for a high speed escape. The point is, you need to be highly aggressive if you're going to avoid being halted, then possibly shot. While I can't offer any statistics or proof, it is probably safe to say that the instant your adversary senses you're on your way home from a demolition derby and you're no pushover, he'll break off the assault and look for someone else. I have merely touched upon some of the driving techniques which may be used to escape a hostile vehicle. There are many others I could share with you, but they must be learned, not in a book, but in a school dedicated to evasive driving and surviving high risk motor vehicle escapes.

Most times, felons or robbers will steal a vehicle if one is needed to commit a crime. Consequently, they don't give a wit about property damage. Therefore, they'll ram you, cut in front and jam on the brakes, or do whatever they can to stop you. And what if they have two vehicles? A skilled driver can easily evade two motor vehicles. With a two vehicle assault, most likely, they'll try to box you in by placing one vehicle in front and the other to your side. The aforementioned evasive maneuvers will also work against two motor vehicles with the one exception that accelerating out of the trap may not be an option.

As you can imagine, a robber becomes quite upset when you defy him. Consequently, if you execute an evasive maneuver, he may be inclined to start slinging lead at you. The best weapon available to you is the gas pedal. Use it to escape. Any damage you inflict upon your vehicle is less serious than the damage your adversary plans to inflict upon you. But your chariot is brand new? You can repair or replace the vehicle but you're only issued one life.

Be aware that fleeing from a suspicious vehicle does not authorize you to cause injuries to innocent people. You are legally responsible for your actions whatever the provocation or emergency at hand.

Firing at a moving vehicle is extremely hazardous to innocents, besides, it's also a waste of ammunition. If your adversary succeeds in bringing you to a halt, you will now enter an armed confrontation with some or all of your ammunition exhausted. Trading shots, Hollywood style, also places you on treacherous legal ground. A bit later in the book we will discuss the obligation to retreat and how it affects your justification for using deadly force. At this point you should try to picture yourself executing evasive maneuvers. You must rehearse them in your mind. When driving, imagine that a nearby vehicle is an adversary. How can you escape? What options can you identify in an instant?

Despite your best efforts, what should you do if you're forced to a halt? Whether you're armed or not, immediately exit the vehicle on the side opposite your adversary. If the lead is going to fly, you need to get your own automobile between you and your adversary's gunfire, if any. One thing you should not do is remain seated in the automobile and wait for your adversary to decide what to do with you. If you flee on foot, try to select a route that cannot be driven by your adversary, unless you're curious to know what the underside of his car looks like.

If your circumstances are such that you seriously believe you can be targeted for a robbery, such as when it is necessary to carry large amounts of cash on a regular basis, then I recommend two types of automobiles: something very fast and nimble-footed, or something large and heavy. Today, a 3,600 pound automobile would be considered large. Please avoid the granny-mobiles and all those miserable little hatchbacks that can't get out of their own way, or anyone else's for that matter. You're dead meat in a hatchback because you're easier to reach with gunfire if the "bogey's on your tail." I would also avoid any vehicle, particularly some of the sport-utility vehicles which have been identified as especially susceptible to rollovers during aggressive driving maneuvers.

Driving is one activity where confrontations seemingly materialize from thin air. We might call it Road Rage Syndrome because that's exactly what it is. The American Automobile Association conducted a study which conservatively identified 10,037 incidents of road violence during the five year period ending in 1995. These resulted in 218 deaths and 12,000 injuries. In 70 percent of the incidents, the vehicle was used as a weapon. Presumably, other forms of assault, including firearms, accounted for the remaining deaths and injuries. Most times, initiators of violence were males between 18 and 26 years of age and often had criminal records, a history of violence, and drug or alcohol problems. Remember, the numbers above are only those which could be proven. The actual numbers are probably far higher.

A small percentage of legally armed individuals may not be as inclined to yield to an aggressive or inconsiderate driver. However, I highly recommend, whether or not you are armed, that you follow the recommendations of federal highway officials when confronted by an aggressive driver;
• Do get out of their way
• Avoid eye contact
• Ignore gestures and don't return them
• If you have a cell phone, report aggressive drivers

To this list I would add that you refuse offers (most often by hand signals) to pull over. In most instances you are legally required to retreat or withdraw from and avoid all situations which may result in use of force or an escalation of force. In the chapter on justification we'll take a closer look at the obligation to retreat, and how failing to do so when required can result in very serious felony charges against you.

If you have had an incident with an aggressive driver, don't assume it's over when you think it's over. A small percentage of these drivers can be quite persistent and will follow you until such time as they can gain an opportunity to bring violence to bear against you. Check your rear view mirror. If the person sped off and is in front of you somewhere, consider taking an alternate route to your destination. If you're being followed, DON'T DRIVE HOME!

When on foot, walk towards busy areas if you believe you are being followed. At night, be aware of your shadow as you walk past street lights. If someone is approaching from the rear, his shadow will reach you before he does. This may be the only warning you get that you're about to be robbed.

Robbers also don't like security cameras. You may argue that a security camera is easily defeated by wearing a mask. However, many robberies are unplanned, impulsive acts committed by someone who is desperate for his next fix. Security cameras will definitely reduce the number of felons willing to target your store. In addition, the video tapes, if of good quality, can prove valuable in making an arrest and obtaining a conviction.

Robberies of "name" jewelry establishments, and jewelry and precious metals wholesalers often involve more intelligent robbery teams. They may spend months planning the robbery and when they finally do strike, removing the tapes from the security cameras is high up on their list of things to do. If your business has portable inventory that could be worth a million dollars or more, you may consider installing one or more hidden cameras which may escape notice.

Unfortunately, retailers often use the video tapes over and over again. When a robbery does occur, the videos are so grainy and of such poor quality, they are of little help to investigators and easily attacked in court. Also, cameras tend to be installed too high, making it difficult to clearly see the robber's face.

The electronic revolution has produced some really small, high tech camera systems. I would advise that your video security system include at least one disguised or hidden pin hole type camera installed slightly above shoulder level, behind you and facing over the counter to the customers' side of the cash register. Since all modern cash registers require electricity to operate, you may have your security company wire the hidden camera to go on any time the cash register drawer is opened.

Having a video record of the crime makes it much easier to prove that your actions were justified. Also, the video tape will discourage unscrupulous attorneys from shading the facts to suit them. In the confusion following a robbery, weapons may disappear. In high crime areas, guns represent power. As the crime scene will not be secured until police arrive, you may indeed have difficulty proving that you were being robbed if no gun is found at the scene and there are no witnesses to corroborate your statements.

Some police departments, insurance companies, and security companies will send a representative to your store to conduct a security survey. Avail yourself of this service if available in your area. The police officer or security expert can provide valuable tips about avoiding robberies as well as other non-violent crimes plaguing merchants, such as shoplifting or employee theft. However, do not expect them to teach you how to defeat a robber with a handgun. This is a skill you must learn on your own.

If you request and receive a security survey, be sure to maintain documentation of the survey. There is a legal reason for this. For many, the confrontation is the time span between the first and last rounds fired. Instead, I want you to think of the confrontation as beginning the instant you believe you have been targeted for a robbery until such time as you have been fully exonerated by the authorities.

Assume for the moment you are a defendant in a civil action arising from your use of force. If the law is on the plaintiff's side, they will argue the law. If the facts are on their side, they will argue the facts. If neither the law or the facts are on the plaintiff's side, they will attack you! The plaintiff's attorney will seek to attack your actions by weakening your justification, your character, or both. This is referred to as impeaching your credibility. He may attempt to portray you as a Rambo type just itching for an opportunity to shoot someone such as his client, an innocent, disenfranchised victim of society. Character assassination will be much more difficult if it can be documented that you took all reasonable precautions to avoid a robbery. The written security survey, along with the name of the expert who conducted it, will prove mighty handy at this time. As you can see, we are laying the groundwork to help insure you win the confrontation, beginning to end. Conversely, placing a few unfortunate bumper stickers on your automobile such as "insured by Smith and Wesson" is just the ammunition an attorney needs to rip you to bloody shreds on the witness chair.

Dogs, particularly in high crime areas, provide a useful deterrent to some, but not all robbers. They can reduce the need to resort to deadly force. For a definitive discussion on various types of protective dogs and how to integrate a dog into your security plan, may I suggest that you read Massad Ayoob's *The Truth About Self Protection.* This book is available from Police Bookshelf, PO Box 122, Concord, N.H. 03302-0122. Mr. Ayoob points out that a trained dog can easily pre-occupy a robber long enough for you to arm yourself and fight back. During a robbery, a dog must be viewed as expendable. This may seem painful but human life comes first. Consequently, if you are justified in firing, you should not withhold fire for fear of hitting your dog. It is easier to defeat the robber while he's preoccupied with the dog than to wait for him to shoot or stab the dog, then turn his undivided attention to you.

Earlier in the book we mentioned the plague of robberies occurring at 24 hour convenience stores. Most often, a convenience store is manned by a single employee/clerk. Consequently, they make easy targets. Recently, in an effort to stem the rate of convenience store robberies, several of which resulted in homicides, the city of Gainesville, Florida passed an ordinance requiring that 24 hour convenience stores must be staffed by at least two people from 10:00 p.m. till daylight. Although this move was strongly opposed by the convenience store industry, robberies are down a reported 94 percent!

Another technique which can greatly reduce convenience store robberies, without resorting to gunfire, is to service all customers through a teller's type drawer and window during night time hours. The store clerk locks himself inside the store and no one is permitted entry. Of course, employees must be trained in the techniques an individual bent on robbery might use as a ploy to con them into unlocking the doors. A small percentage of robbers may attempt violent means to force a store clerk out of the store. I'd rather not list different kinds of forceful entries which might be tried because I cannot control who might read this book and I do not wish to give anyone ideas.

Lastly, the convenience store should be equipped with a drop safe so the cash register does not contain too inviting a target. Generally, drop safe equipped stores advertise this fact with a sign on the door to the effect that the clerk cannot open the safe. This too can reduce the incidence of convenience store robberies as the smaller the potential reward, the more likely it is that robbers will go elsewhere.

While not classified as a robbery, some store owners must take special precautions against burglaries or forceful entries. During the early 1970's, New York City suffered a major power failure. Taking advantage of the chaos that temporarily resulted, enterprising individuals drove up to a well known Manhattan gunshop and used the motor vehicle (probably a truck of some sort) to rip the protective cage from the store front. The thieves made off with a substantial number of rifles and shotguns. Fortunately, the handguns were stored in a safe. Whether or not required by local ordinances, and regardless of the inconvenience, gunshops must return all handguns to a commercial duty safe when the store is closed. In my opinion, many gun owners, including some gun stores, are not doing enough to safeguard their inventory against robbery/burglary.

In New York City, a procedure was in effect that in the event of a power failure, any police precinct having a gunshop within its boundaries, was to dispatch a patrol car to that store and the police presence was to remain until power was restored. In the incident described, a patrol car was not dispatched. There's a lesson to be learned: gunshop owners can request automatic police protection in the event of a power failure, civil disturbance, or a weather emergency.

Or, you should arrange with your security service for automatic protection during natural or man made emergencies. In the introduction I said gun battles must be avoided if possible. An indirect method of reducing the likelihood of a gun battle is to do your part in preventing the theft of firearms, particularly handguns.

A relatively new type of burglary is the "smash and grab" or "smash, grab and run." Thieves will steal a car, then run it right through the front of your store. Sure, the alarm goes off and the video footage, if the security cameras are running, is truly breathtaking, but the thieves, most often fleet footed youths, grab handfuls of whatever isn't nailed down and are gone before anyone can respond to the alarm. Gunshop owners must suffer the inconvenience of running steel cables through the trigger guards of the long guns whenever the store is closed in order to prevent their loss or possibly reduce the number of guns lost in this type of crime. It would also be wise to study your store, possibly with police assistance, to ascertain whether or not you're vulnerable to a smash and grab and what reasonable steps you may take to discourage or prevent this kind of attack. Granted, a smash and grab is not an armed robbery but take a hacksaw to a long gun and you have a weapon suited only for felonious activity. Double barrel shotguns, with the barrels cut off just forward of the fore-end, and the stock hacked off just behind the pistol grip, in violation of federal law, make highly concealable and deadly weapons often used to commit robberies.

Perhaps the most difficult robbery to guard against is one in which the robbers hope to gain access to inner offices and safes by impersonating police officers or other authority figures. This type of crime is most often perpetrated against restaurants, large retail establishments, or any business where it is known or it is assumed a safe is present. Most times, the robbery team consists of two known individuals.

Most retailers, particularly restaurateurs, often operate their business with their fingers crossed and one eye over their shoulder. They must not run afoul of food, building, and fire inspectors, sales tax personnel, EPA (Environmental Protection Administration), OSHA (Occupational Safety and Health Administration), and immigration officials, to name a few. They expect unannounced visits from authority figures at any time. Consequently, robbers often pose as authority figures to get past the sales floor or customer area in order to isolate the person likely to have the safe combination.

As a business owner, there are a number of steps you may take to reduce your vulnerability to this type of crime. First, you should establish written guidelines for dealing with authority figures and official inquiries. Then, your employees must be trained to adhere to these guidelines. When confronted by an authority figure, employees should be instructed to tell these individuals to remain where they are and to then summon the owner/manager to the public area of the store. Employees should be especially wary of individuals who insist on being taken to the manager's office or who seem overly anxious to bypass the public area. Needless to say, instruct your employees not to bring authority figures to inner offices unless these individuals are known to them from previous official visits. This tactic can force their hand and cause the impostors to give up the ruse and announce or display their true intentions much sooner. As a result, not only are you disrupting their tactics, but you may also manufacture an opportunity to resist because the robbers have made their intentions known before they were able to obtain control of you or otherwise get you within their kill zone (kill zones are defined and discussed later in the book).

A legitimate law enforcement officer will not hesitate to display his photo credentials in addition to his badge. An individual who flashes a badge only and who refuses to produce photo credentials, or claims to have "forgotten" it at home is probably an impersonator. Consequently, you and your employees should not accept a badge as identification when not accompanied by a photo ID. Remember, a drivers license, Social Security card, or "official" identification card (obtainable from vendors advertising in mens' adventure or pornographic magazines) should not be accepted as identification. The ID card must be issued by, and bear the name and seal of the issuing agency. Also, robbers, at times, are in possession of genuine appearing identification which may be forged, found, or stolen.

When you are informed that authority figures wish to see you, try to discreetly observe these individuals from a distance before going to meet them. Observe their dress. Inspectors often wear business attire, while detectives may be dressed in business or casual attire. Are their hands visible or concealed from view? Observe their mannerisms. Do they appear nervous and fidgety? Are their eyes darting about in 360 degree sweeps? Are they carrying attache cases, business folders, or some other form of document holder one would expect an inspector to have? Has one authority figure stationed himself at the entrance, while one or two others insist on going to your office? Did the visit occur at opening, closing, before, or after your posted business hours? These are some of the warning signs that something may not be right.

If the robbers had the audacity to telephone for an appointment, did they insist upon visiting at an irregular or inappropriate time? If so, you should first attempt to verify the caller's identity by calling the agency he claims to represent and asking to speak with him. If the agency disclaims knowledge of this individual, or you get to speak with the named official but he denies calling you and doesn't sound like the same individual who called you, notify the police immediately and arrange for an official "greeting" party.

If you are suspicious that the authority figures are impostors, call the police or 911 immediately. Stall for time. When calling, be careful not to exaggerate what you see because the individuals may indeed be legitimate and you may inadvertently cause an armed confrontation between groups of law enforcement officers. If the authority figures are legitimate, they may grow impatient with your stalling tactics but generally will not attempt to bully, force, intimidate, or bluff their way past the public area. Also, legitimate authority figures normally do not direct foul or abusive language against your employees or otherwise threaten them. Your employees should be instructed to call police when these forms of unprofessional behavior are exhibited, particularly when accompanied by improper identification or badge flashing.

If you meet with these individuals in the public area of your establishment, be wary if they insist upon talking with you in private or insist upon going to your office when other suitable locations may be present.

Of course, under no circumstances should you display or deploy a firearm in the absence of a specific criminal act. This criminal act may be a physical assault against an employee, such as pushing him out of the way. You must be absolutely certain you are dealing with impostors before offering any form of resistance. This is what makes this type of crime so difficult to defend against. The impostors do not make their true intentions known until you are in a position where they may easily gain control of you and your immediate surroundings. At this point, resistance is often no longer an option.

CHAPTER TWO

MINDSET

"The purpose of fighting is to win. There is no possible victory in defense. The sword is more important than the shield, and skill is more important than either. The final weapon is the brain. All else is supplemental."

—John Steinbeck

Mindset is where the confrontation is either won or lost. Mindset is the catch phrase for all the psychological factors which may contribute to victory or defeat, whether it be a self defense situation or a sporting event. If you were to ask 20 police firearms instructors to define a "combat" mindset, you would receive 20 different answers, all of which are right. In the most general of terms, mindset, as it relates to armed confrontations, is a winning state of mind or attitude that needs to be self-instilled, cultivated, and groomed until it becomes a permanent part of who we are.

Mindset May Be Divided Into Four Parts:

1. Acknowledging that you may, in fact, be the victim of a robbery,

2. Deciding in advance that if legally justified by the circumstances, you can inflict, without hesitation, such grave injuries that your adversary may die,

3. Deciding in advance that if you become involved in a

mortal confrontation, you will win, even if wounded. You will use every last ounce of will, tenacity, and blood to defeat your adversary. You will not give up and hope for mercy. You may want to commit to memory the words of General Ferdinand Foch from his book, *Principles De Guerre*, "A lost battle is a battle one thinks he has lost."

4. Understanding and managing the full range of human emotions which are likely to be present during and after the confrontation.

If you really wish to possess and understand all the mental skills necessary to maximize your chance of winning a confrontation, then bear with me. If you elect to skip this chapter, don't bother reading the rest of the book.

Most people have a psychological denial mechanism which may be called the, "Other Guy Syndrome." You witness this syndrome each time you see someone puffing on a cigarette. The smoker has decided someone else is going to get lung cancer and die, not he. The denial mechanism can be so strong some people become annoyed, rather than thankful, when you call their attention to a potential danger such as their child wandering too close to a known hazard.

People who are of the attitude that "it" will never happen to them will not take the steps necessary to be mentally and physically prepared for a deadly force confrontation. If you really wish to be around long enough to see your grandchildren graduate college, then you must acknowledge to yourself, right now, that "it" can happen to you. Don't think, "if it happens to me." Think, "when it happens to me."

Complacency is the silent killer in the law enforcement profession. People who are complacent are of the opinion that the possibility of a deadly force confrontation is so remote there's really no need to invest much time and thought to winning one. Complacency infects members of virtually every law enforcement agency in existence and has probably put more officers in their graves than all other factors combined. It will kill you too if you allow it.

You must decide, in advance, if legally and morally justified, you can perform a physical act that may result in death or serious permanent injury to another human being. If you privately know you cannot do this, or, if you wait until you are involved in a hostile confrontation to debate this, your indecisiveness may cost you your life. Felons rarely show any genuine remorse for the pain and suffering they inflict. They will pull the trigger at the slightest provocation, real or imagined. And they're real quick about it. There are rarely any tension filled delays for the mindless dialogue that Hollywood directors like to lace into their plots. As a law abiding citizen, you have learned to respect life. However, you must first respect **your** life. That means assigning it far greater value than the life of the armed individual on the other side of the counter.

It's been a few years since we lived in caves. Life was simple then. In fact, there were only two kinds of people: strong ones and dead ones. True, the need to maintain the skills necessary to prevail in mortal combat have become increasingly remote. Unfortunately, the world still contains numerous predators who have not fully evolved. If they think you've got what they want, they will attempt to take it by force, even if it means taking your life or causing permanent injury. The time for moralizing is before you purchase a handgun, not when a seedy character, wearing a trench coat in 98 degree heat, politely asks you to finish with your other customers while keeping one hand in his pocket and his eyeballs in constant motion.

Understanding emotions such as fear, panic, anger, revenge, and hatred are important because these emotions must be anticipated, understood, controlled, and managed to insure they work for you in a positive and lawful manner. Managing emotions which affect your shooting accuracy and judgment during stressful situations is of paramount importance. Post shooting emotions such as remorse, guilt, and traumatic stress must also be anticipated, understood, and properly managed.

We fight with our minds as well as our bodies. Confrontations, whether a shootout or sporting event, can be won or lost before the first ball is thrown or the first shot fired. It is imperative you develop both the conscious and subconscious portions of your mind to give you every possible advantage during a deadly force confrontation.

To a significant degree, your mindset is a product of your upbringing. Some of you grew up in tough neighborhoods where you either became fearless and tenacious or cowered in fear at every possible threat. Perhaps you had to fight off older brothers on a regular basis? In these hostile environments, your instinct for survival has to be closer to the surface. You learn to strike back with the reflexes of a cat.

On the other hand, some of you grew up in serene neighborhoods and households. School discipline was strict and little or no opportunity or need existed for school yard confrontations. You grew up with the values of responsible adults such as parents, clergy, and teachers. Police officers were your friends. Mortal confrontations occurred in other neighborhoods, far away. There's nothing wrong with growing up in a peaceful environment with the one exception, it tends to dull the senses and instincts needed for making rapid decisions during felonious emergencies. Inflicting grave injuries on another human being, without hesitation, is an apparent contradiction of your personal values.

If you spend much time in the inner cities, you quickly realize inner city youths have much sharper street smarts and survival instincts than their suburban counterparts. These people are products of their environment. You may also recall, the best professional boxers invariably came from the toughest neighborhoods. When the Irish and the Italians lived in neighborhoods with nicknames such as "Hell's Kitchen," it was they who dominated in the ring. As they were displaced from these neighborhoods by African Americans and Hispanics, so too were they displaced in the ring. These inner city boxers are no larger or stronger than their suburban or rural counterparts. What they do have is a mental edge and a stronger will to survive which allows them to both absorb and dish out greater punishment and literally fight to the death. If there is such a thing as a mean streak, it is certainly wider in the tougher neighborhoods.

For criminals bred in the inner cities, fighting for personal space and to protect their reputation and meager possessions is entirely consistent with their value system which, at best, is amoral. If someone has something you want and you are stronger than them, you take it. Often, they join gangs ruled by violence and committed to violence. Any trace of feelings for others is viewed as weakness. Consequently, it is quickly extinguished.

Please don't get the impression that all criminals come from the inner cities. Also, never assume you can predict the skin color of the person who will attempt to rob you, as many vicious felons also come from suburban and rural areas. They also come in all colors.

At this point it would be helpful to take a quick view of how we mentally manage our daily lives:

1. Conscious mind—The portion of your mind that manages most of your wakeful activity such as thinking, memory, reading, observing.

2. Sub-conscious mind—By constant repetitive practice you will produce trained skills which require little or no conscious thought. Example: Has your mind ever wandered while driving? You're suddenly at your exit and have absolutely no recollection of having driven the last few miles. Your subconscious mind was driving the car. Its programmed memory cannot be accessed by the conscious mind.

3. Sixth sense—The sixth sense is a phrase sometimes used to describe a feeling or sense something is about to happen or something is not right. It develops with experience and intimate knowledge of your surroundings. When your sixth sense detects something troublesome, you will automatically heighten your degree of alertness and attention to your surroundings or situation in which you find yourself. What would I do if? Try forming a mental picture of a possible encounter and quickly select a course of action. This training helps condition your mind to anticipate likely avenues of attack and to quickly identify options available to you. For example, if your store has but one entrance open to the public, you may formulate scenarios based upon one or more robbers entering the store through that entrance. However, if you have two

entrances, your scenarios will include robbers entering from either entrance or both simultaneously. By rehearsing likely robberies, we will acquire a learned response which will enable us to respond more quickly during an actual robbery.

The State of Mind

Jeff Cooper, one of America's most knowledgeable and respected authorities on self defense, was one of the first to understand the role your mind plays in self defense situations, and also one of the first to include mental conditioning as an integral part of firearms and self defense training. Today, it is standard training material in virtually every police academy in America. Undoubtedly, many law enforcement officers and private citizens alike are alive today thanks to Cooper's innovative approach to self defense.

Cooper assigned descriptive colors to help us understand and describe the varying levels of alertness people maintain. Although many gunwriters have since tried to "improve" Cooper's lesson plan, it is my opinion, Cooper's original lesson plan, as offered below with his permission, remains one of the single most important training texts ever offered to police and civilians alike.

Condition White: Unaware and unready. No amount of training, marksmanship, nor weapon power can help a man who is caught in Condition White. The best shot in the world, armed with the best gun, is helpless if he is mentally and emotionally unready. Most of us live in White most of the time. That is why most of us look so bad when we get into a scrap.

Condition Yellow: Relaxed alert. In Yellow you are aware the world is a dangerous place. You have no specific confrontation in mind, and, most important, you have no specific target. You are, however, alert. You know what is going on around you. You "observe everything within sight or hearing," as enjoined by Interior Guard Duty General Order #2. You cannot be surprised and, if something threatening turns up, you are not astonished. You are aware you may have to shoot to save your life today. A man in White can be easily killed by anyone who takes the initiative. A man in Yellow offers a problem to his aggressor.

Condition Orange: Specific alert. When you shift from Yellow to Orange you have a specific, probable target. You are not sure this man poses a deadly threat, but you feel he may. You maintain your attention upon him. You analyze his behavior and you watch his hands. The vital difference between Yellow and Orange is that in Yellow you say you may have to shoot today, whereas in Orange, you say you may have to shoot **him** today.

Condition Red: In Condition Red you have made up your mind to shoot. You do not necessarily shoot unless a specific act on the part of your antagonist calls for it, but you have told yourself you will if such specific act takes place.

Changing Mental Gears—Your mind can move from Condition Yellow to Condition Red in an instant. It takes much longer for your mind to go from Condition White to Condition Red because your mind must first be retrieved from the cerebral mud, identify a threat does, in fact, exist, then decide what to do about it. Often, it is too late. This helps explain why so many armed, off duty, or retired police officers are successfully robbed by muggers; their minds didn't recognize a threat that should have been recognized. If you elect to maintain a firearm for lawful self defense, you have no choice but to remain constantly aware of your surroundings. This does not mean you must become paranoid about every last person or noise, but rather, allowing your conscious, rather than your sub-conscious mind to manage your daily chores and movements. It should be evident to the reader that, in order to remain in indefinite Condition Yellow, it is necessary that a fistful of brain cells be permanently assigned to sentry duty. You may do what you like with the rest.

Control of Emotions

We mentioned emotions such as anger, revenge and hatred which must be managed in a positive manner. You cannot ever let these emotions take over. If you do, they may lead you to commit an unlawful act, and can result in criminal charges against you.

The laws of self-defense require that you act in response to a threat. Consequently, the possibility exists that you may be shot or seriously injured in some other manner by the aggressive actions of the subject. At this point, you have two choices, give up and possibly die, or fight back. The force of anger and revenge can fire you up to a point where you can temporarily ignore pain or the reality of being shot so you may shoot back and possibly defeat your adversary.

The dangerous side of these emotions is that if left uncontrolled, you may resort to excessive force with all the legal consequences. If it can be demonstrated that the amount of force you used was both excessive and motivated more by anger and revenge than the need to defend yourself, chances are you will face a criminal indictment and/or a successful civil suit.

Amazingly, the mind can will the body to die. An example frequently cited in police academies regards a police officer who mentally equated being shot with dying. Subsequently, this officer suffered what should have been a non-lethal wound in the arm with a .22 rimfire but died of his injury.

Anger and revenge can serve you in a positive manner in that if you can ignore the reality of being injured long enough to turn an apparent defeat into a victory, you can also will yourself to overcome the injury and remain alive.

Of all the emotions at work, revenge can be the most difficult to control. Let me paint a scenario: a robber attempts to rob your wife, who is at the cash register. You're in the back room and the robber is unaware of your presence. The robber panics and shoots your wife. You fire one shot and the robber falls wounded. Seeing how badly your wife is wounded, you go into a rage and fire all your remaining rounds into the robber's back. Given this scenario, it will take one heck of an attorney to extract you from criminal prosecution and a civil action. Remember, the law recognizes your right to self defense. It does not include summary trial and execution of the perpetrator.

Undoubtedly, you have heard stories of people on their death bed who willed themselves to hang on to the flame of life long enough to enable their children, traveling from another city, to see them alive one last time. Your mind has its own arsenal of psychological weapons. You may not understand exactly how they work, but, as long as you have them, use them.

Panic

Panic is one of the most difficult emotions to control. It is best defined as a psychological and physiological reaction to a sudden emergency for which you are neither mentally or physically equipped or trained to handle.

People in a state of panic lose virtually all their mental abilities, they cannot think or act in a rational manner. They can't even step out of the way of an oncoming train or exit a vehicle stalled on a railroad crossing. Unfortunately, you cannot use your panicky mental state as the excuse to ask the courts to excuse you from shooting an innocent bystander or applying excessive force to a subject.

Imagine, for example, you witness your two year old child falling into a swimming pool. You have two choices: jump in, pull him out, and administer CPR if necessary, or stand at the edge of the pool and jump up and down while screaming your head off. Early recognition and mental rehearsal of and for a potential danger helps you make the right choice when and if that danger materializes. The best way to avoid panic is to remain mentally and physically prepared for emergencies you are likely to encounter, and to rehearse them in your mind. You must avoid the mental state of denial. Denial is a pre-requisite for panic.

CHAPTER THREE

JUSTIFICATION

Most people only have an approximate knowledge of how much force they may lawfully use against another person and when they may use it. Also, they are only vaguely familiar with the legal standards which the courts will use to determine if their actions were reasonable and necessary under the circumstances. What private citizens do know is usually learned from television, the newspapers, the storekeeper next door, guys at the gun club, or the police officer who lives up the block. Consequently, their knowledge of justification is a patchwork quilt of other peoples' beliefs, opinions, hunches, and suppositions.

It is incumbent upon you to be thoroughly familiar with the use-of-force statutes in your state of residence and anywhere else you will carry or keep a gun for self-defense. Self defense laws vary from state to state and the differences can be critical. Particularly, what constitutes deadly force and the circumstances under which its use is legally permissible. These statutes are usually contained in your state penal or criminal code. Your local library may have a copy. Law school libraries and county law libraries will have copies, and most lawyers keep copies for reference.

In the introduction I discussed the elements necessary to win an armed confrontation, one of which was knowledge. Basically, you need to know, in advance, what the law expects of you. If the amount of force you use is determined to be excessive, you may face criminal and civil charges. Either way, financial ruin is a virtual certainty. A competent defense in a major felony case will almost always cost $100,000, or more if you don't happen to have a cousin named Vinny. Knowledge of the law is but one segment of the element of knowledge. Knowledge embraces the totality of mental, physical, and tactical considerations necessary to prevail in felonious emergencies.

The following discussion is intended as a general guideline and should not be relied upon as being accurate in your state of residence. Wordings and definitions and the principles of justification vary from state to state. Secondly, this book is limited to armed confrontations which, therefore, almost always involve deadly force. In your state of residence, there may be other limited circumstances in which you are not in immediate danger yet deadly force may be permissible. Since I'm not teaching you how to be police officers or armed security guards, I will confine this discussion to generic robbery/self defense issues applicable to private citizens.

At this point we have no choice but to get a bit tedious. Remember, the confrontation isn't over until you have been criminally exonerated by the grand jury, and the person you've shot, or his estate, decides there is virtually no chance of winning a civil judgment against you. Consequently, you must know the law as well as you know the inside of your store.

Let's take a look at deadly force. Using the New York State Penal Code as an example, deadly force is defined as a degree of force which creates a substantial risk of death or which causes death or substantial risk of serious physical injury. Examples of serious physical injury would include protracted illness or impairment of health, disfigurement, broken bones, or the loss or impairment of the functioning of an organ. Consequently, you may be justified in using deadly force to prevent someone from slicing off your ear, throwing acid at you, or stabbing you with a hypodermic syringe which he claims contains AIDS contaminated blood.

Interestingly, deadly force is an absolute. That is, the courts do not recognize degrees of deadly force. If you are justified in using deadly force, it will not matter whether you use a .22 derringer, a 12 gauge shotgun, a broadhead arrow, or an eighteen wheel semi. Unfortunately, some unscrupulous attorneys attempt to create degrees of deadly force by implying levels of "humaneness," as though there is a humane way of shooting someone. Thus, if you use a high tech, exotic bullet, a magnum round, or a gun with some unfortunate model name, an attorney may attempt to use these facts to portray you as someone who was not merely satisfied with shooting his client, but who had to use a weapon so "deadly" that there was virtually no chance of survival (according to him) if shot with it. In effect, they want to convince the jury that you should have shot their client just a little bit.

Although it should have no legal bearing, shooting someone once or twice with a .45 automatic is legally more defensible than shooting him a dozen times with a pipsqueak round such as a .25 auto or the old and obsolete 158 grain lead, round nose .38 Special load. The more rounds you fire, the easier it is for an attorney to portray you as someone out of control. Conversely, the better your marksmanship abilities, when combined with a potent, fight stopping cartridge, the more difficult it is to impeach your character.

More importantly, there is a subtle legal issue at play which you must understand: No one, including the police, has the written authority to kill another human being outside of a legal execution conducted by a governmental body. What the law permits you to do is to remove yourself or a third party from mortal danger. In so doing, you are permitted to apply a level of force so great that death may result. That death being incidental to your need to avoid death or serious physical injury. In effect, you are permitted to apply a degree of force necessary to stop your adversary from doing whatever it was that prompted you to shoot, even if your adversary dies as a result. Once you have **stopped** your adversary, the application of force must cease.

The phrases, "shoot to kill" or, "kill or be killed," belong in Hollywood. Erase them from your vocabulary and never utter them again. You'd be amazed at how the most seemingly innocent remarks can come back to haunt you. If your local statutes actually gave you the right to kill, as many people believe, there would be no such thing as excessive force as you would be authorized to continue using deadly force until the person was dead rather than merely stopped.

We have used the phrase "excessive force" several times. At this point, it helps to discuss "excessive " as it is one of the legal quagmires you must avoid. Paraphrasing William Geller of the Police Executive Research Forum, in a recent article he described excessive force as, "force beyond that which is necessary to accomplish a legitimate self defense purpose." In an article by Richard Abshire that appeared in the January 1996 issue of *Law Enforcement Technology*, he stated that "excessive use of force is difficult to define satisfactorily, impossible to measure, viewed with alarm by the public in light of egregious high profile cases, as much a matter of perception as of fact, and based on real world, split second decisions that must pass muster in the theater of the absurd that our legal system has become."

A common expression is, "perception is reality." In the absence of compelling evidence to the contrary, what is perceived as truth will most often pass for truth. A lawyer's interests are best served when he can carefully cultivate, in the alleged minds of the jurors, a perception of truth in place of the actual truth. "Excessive," which is not a fixed unit of measurement in any mathematical discipline I'm aware of, is one of several key legal issues which may be used to skewer you.

On occasion, you will read something in the newspaper to the effect that police have orders to "shoot to kill" with regard to a particularly heinous killer on the loose. This is nonsense. Either the reporter is being stroked by the police or someone in the police department doesn't know the law. There's an implication that if police can shoot to kill, they can also shoot not to kill. More nonsense. Police officers face the same legal scrutiny as private citizens whenever they have to shoot someone. However, there was a time when the word of a police officer was not seriously questioned and the general public was of the opinion that criminals belonged in jails and cemeteries. Rehabilitation was endorsed provided it occurred at the end of a rope. Of course, this has all changed now.

Let me repeat, the existence of use of deadly force statutes does not convey the written authority to kill. It conveys the permission to stop the adversary's felonious act that places you in mortal jeopardy, even if he happens to die as a result of your action. As deadly force is an absolute, it doesn't matter that the only force that's practical to use is so great the adversary's death is a virtual certainty. An example of this is when a police marksman is preparing to shoot a hostage taker through the head with a long range rifle. Or a woman, dragged to a rooftop and about to be raped at gun or knife-point, seizes a sudden opportunity to push her attacker off the roof to a concrete courtyard 25 stories below. In either example, is the outcome in much doubt?

When asked by an investigator, a prosecutor or a plaintiff's attorney whether or not you were trying to kill your adversary, the answer should be "no," even if your adversary died. You were not trying to kill him, you were trying to **stop** him. If you answer "yes" to the question, and assuming it was necessary to fire multiple rounds, an argument can be made the adversary was essentially defeated after being hit once or twice and the remaining rounds fired by you were an attempt to kill him. It will be argued that, in effect, only one or two rounds were necessary and the rest constitute excessive force.

Can you shoot to wound? This question often comes up during my lectures. The hypothetical situations most often raised are: if a situation justifies physical force but not deadly force, can I use my firearm in a non-lethal manner by trying to wound the adversary in the leg or shoulder or butt? The answer is a resounding **no**. Firearms are defined as lethal or deadly weapons. Therefore, discharge of a firearm, regardless of your intention, constitutes deadly force and would automatically be excessive if you are not in mortal danger.

Most people equate deadly force with the act of killing another person and therefore, anything else you do to another person that doesn't kill him outright must be some other kind of force. That is, they don't realize that a degree of force that causes serious physical injuries but not death is still classified as deadly force. With the possible exception of the most superficial of wounds, any bullet which enters the body will cause damage that meets both the legal and medical definition of a serious physical injury. You may not inflict serious physical injuries upon another person in situations where you or a third party are not at risk of death or serious physical injury.

The second question involves a situation where deadly force is justified but, for humanitarian reasons, you wish to make a deliberate attempt not to inflict a mortal wound. While your intentions may be admirable, you increase the chance of being killed and also convey the impression that, in your mind, you really didn't believe you were in danger of death or serious physical injury as you didn't consider the threat to be immediate enough to try for an immediate cessation of the hostile act. In a genuine, close quarters life and death encounter, it is not likely you will have the presence of mind to be so selective with bullet placement. We will examine statements and comments in the chapter titled, "Aftermath."

If deadly force is an absolute, can it also be excessive?   Yes. Deadly force can be excessive in at least seven ways:

1. Using it when it wasn't justified by the circumstances at hand.

2. When you or a third party whom you are defending, had a readily available and safe means of retreat.*

3. Failure to stop using it when it was clear your adversary had been defeated or had surrendered or fled and no longer had the present opportunity or intention to harm you.

4. Combat by agreement. That is, agreeing to meet and fight

---

*Other states require you to retreat except if you are inside your own home (not outside). Still other states require you to retreat except if you are inside your home or your own place of business. The reader is again cautioned that deadly force laws vary in critical ways from state to state. This book presents only a general discussion of the law. It is the responsibility of the reader to find out, in advance, the specific law of the state(s) in which he or she may need to use deadly force in self-defense. Some states do not include an obligation to retreat in their use of force statutes.

someone who has issued a challenge to fight you at a specific time and place. This is an avoidable use of force, and even if you're technically justified in using deadly force, (perhaps you thought it was going to be a mere fist fight and didn't realize your antagonist was armed), the attendant circumstances are so legally treacherous that you'll most likely be charged with a crime. Excluding licensed sporting events or legitimate martial arts training, combat by agreement is illegal in most, if not all states. Surprisingly, many merchants are indeed challenged by irate customers dissatisfied with their widgets.

5. Setting a trap. Every few years we read about some misguided soul who rigs a loaded shotgun with a trip cord with the intention of shooting a burglar or intruder in his absence. I don't know of any reasonable circumstance in which such an act would come even close to being justified. Remember, your use of force is justified only to protect yourself and other innocent people from death or serious bodily harm—not to protect mere property regardless of its value. If no innocent people are present when the burglar enters your home or business, use of a rigged gun (deadly force) cannot be justified. A burglar alarm is a better solution and won't land you in prison.

6. Baiting or entrapment: Similar to item five, this is a situation in which an individual is lured or induced to commit a crime with the intent of "legally" shooting that individual during commission of the crime. Whispering in the ear of the village idiot that you have a potato sack stuffed with cash you're worried about because you are "going away for the weekend" and the lock on the back door is "broken," then shooting him when he comes to take it, would probably subject you to murder charges if it can be proven by your conduct you intended to cultivate a series of circumstances in a deliberate attempt to bring about a deadly force confrontation.

7. Pre-emptory strike: In this instance, an individual enters your store whom you suddenly recognize as the person who robbed you at gunpoint several weeks or months earlier. You immediately draw your handgun and open fire on this individual without waiting for him to announce a robbery or produce a weapon.

The fact he robbed you in the past does not justify deadly force in a subsequent encounter. You will have an extremely difficult time convincing anyone that the mere presence of this individual placed you in mortal jeopardy. In this theoretical circumstance, you should be preparing yourself for a hostile encounter and calling the police if you have the opportunity.

Use of force statutes generally require you to use no more force than is reasonable to stop the act that necessitated your use of force.

In determining whether or not you were justified in your actions, the courts will examine whether or not you reasonably believed your adversary possessed the **means**, the **present opportunity**, and the **intent** to cause death or serious physical injury to you or another innocent person, such as a family member, employee, or customer. A judge or jury will decide whether or not you were reasonably led to believe the perpetrator had the means and present opportunity to take your life or cause you serious physical injury, and whether or not he signaled any intent to do so as to make your actions reasonable and necessary under the circumstances.

It is vitally necessary that you research the use of force statutes in your home state (or any other state in which you will be armed for self defense) because, in most instances, the law will place an additional restriction on your use of force. If you know you have a readily available means or avenue of retreat where, with complete safety, you can remove yourself and all innocent third parties from danger, the law will expect you to retreat rather than to use deadly force against your adversary.

Generally, there are a number of instances when you are not obligated to retreat:

1. When you are in your own dwelling, or, a dwelling in which you are licensed or privileged to be, and you are not the one who provoked the incident.

2. When acting in lawful defense of another person who does not have the ability or means of retreat.

3. When acting at the request or orders of a police or peace officer.

4. In any situation in which your state penal or criminal code specifically exempts you from the obligation to retreat.

5. In any situation where you do not know there is a readily available means of retreat.

6. In any situation where you know an avenue of retreat exists, but retreat cannot be accomplished with complete safety. An example of this is to attempt to turn and flee from a robber armed with a firearm. As he can easily shoot you in the back as you begin to flee, running from a robber, most often, cannot be accomplished with complete safety.

Retreat becomes an issue when it becomes painfully obvious you could have easily removed yourself from harm's way. It most often becomes an issue in all those mindless confrontations such as traffic disputes, fights over money or women, petty issues, domestic disputes, bar room brawls, etc. where you could have avoided a fight by merely driving or walking away. Quite frequently, these situations begin with verbal insults and escalate into a fight to the death. Retreat is more likely to become an issue when your adversary was not armed with a firearm. I don't know too many people who can outrun a bullet. For example, you're closing your store when a homeless man on crutches produces a knife and demands money. If you can remove yourself from danger by stepping away from him, you are obligated to do so rather than shoot him.

Now let's examine the three elements of justification—means, opportunity, and intent—in detail.

Means

In simplest terms, does the attacker have the means or capability to take life or cause serious physical injury? Most often, this refers to his possession of a firearm, knife, club, or other deadly or dangerous weapon. However, it doesn't matter whether or not the gun is real (provided it appears to be real) or whether or not it was loaded or unloaded, or capable of being fired, or even visible. If a gun is pointed at you during a hostile confrontation and the gun isn't an obvious toy, a reasonable person would believe the gun to be real and capable of causing his death or serious physical injury. Courts have ruled that citizens and police were justified in using deadly force against a person who, during the commission of a robbery, kept his hand in his pocket in such a way as to give the impression he was armed with a handgun.

In order for the perpetrator to have the means, it is not always necessary he be armed with a firearm or other dangerous weapon. In determining whether or not a perpetrator had the means, the courts may also examine other variables such as disparities in size, age, sex, strength, skills, and numbers. There are many individuals with formidable fighting skills who don't need a weapon to change your life as you know it. Women, in general, are given more latitude in using force against a stronger but unarmed man than a man would enjoy against an unarmed woman. "Personal weapons" (fists, feet, etc.) can be deadly, provided your attacker has the strength to use them in a deadly way. Multiple attackers—two or three against one—can justify your use of deadly force, even if they are unarmed, if they reasonably pose a threat of death or serious bodily harm.

Present Opportunity

Present opportunity refers to whether or not a perpetrator who has the means also has the present opportunity to use it against you. This is important because the threat you face must be **immediate.** For example, if someone threatened to stab you with a knife, but was on the other side of your security gate across your storefront and cannot reach you, he certainly has the means but momentarily does not have the present opportunity to use the knife against you. Therefore, you would not be justified in shooting him.

Present opportunity more often becomes a major issue when the robber is armed with something other than a firearm. If you shoot a knife wielding robber, and he, or the state brings a legal action against you, they may claim that the physical environment made it reasonably doubtful that he could have used the knife against you. You should be aware of a study known as the Tueller Principle. It was found that if a knife wielding felon launches an attack against someone who is carrying a holstered gun and that felon is 21 feet from the victim, the felon will cover the 21 feet in about 1.5 seconds—the same time it takes for the victim to recognize and react to the attack, draw his firearm, and fire one shot. Keep in mind the shot may miss the attacker (as some 80 percent of shots fired by police against adversaries) and even if it hits the attacker it is unlikely to incapacitate the attacker immediately. Consequently, most knife attacks within this distance are likely to be successful. It may therefore be reasonably argued that a knife or club wielding felon who is advancing within this distance does indeed have the present opportunity to use his weapon against you, barring some barrier.

Another example is one in which an individual walks into your store and says if you don't hand over your cash, he will go home, retrieve his .45 automatic, come back, and shoot you. Applying the test of present opportunity, it should be obvious you are not in immediate danger at the first encounter. The law does not allow pre-emptive strikes. Believe it or not, there are many cases on record of attempted robbery by threat of future harm.

Another factor affecting present opportunity is directly related to the obligation to retreat if that option is available and legally required. If you have the ability to retreat, you also have the ability to deny your adversary the present opportunity to harm you. For example, you have unlocked the door to your store when you observe a car screech to a halt across the street, perhaps 75 feet away. Two menacing individuals, armed with tire irons, their attention fixed upon you, exit their car and begin moving towards you. You draw your licensed handgun and open fire. Given these circumstances, the courts would have expected you to first try retreating into your store and immediately locking the door behind you. Of course, if the attackers break down the door and enter the premises, the threat they pose is far more immediate and your justification for using deadly force is far stronger.

Intent

A person who has the means and the present opportunity to cause you serious physical injury must also signal his intention to do so. For example, you challenge a construction worker or tradesman whom you've caught shoplifting, and who is carrying any number of tools which can be used as dangerous weapons such as a carpet knife, hammer, long screwdriver, etc. The individual may become verbally abusive but displays no intention of harming you with the tools he is carrying. The mere fact that he has both the means and present opportunity to harm you isn't enough. He must clearly signal an intention of causing you harm by taking the tool in his hand, attempting to use it against you, menacing you with it, or stating he intends to harm you. Likewise, any legally or illegally armed individual who enters your store has both the means and present opportunity to harm you. But this isn't enough. Intent must also be proven.

We may further refine the element of intent by referring to it as manifested intent. That is, an act which causes a third party to believe the intent is real even though the perpetrator didn't intend to actually hurt anyone. A tragic case in point occurred many years ago when a Brooklyn, New York shopkeeper decided to conduct a robbery drill for the benefit of educating his employees. He used either a toy or unloaded gun for the drill. As fate would have it, a police officer happened by. Observing what he believed to be a robbery in progress, the officer opened fire, killing the shopkeeper. A grand jury later exonerated the officer in question. The shopkeeper did not intend to rob his own store but the manifested intent, as observed by the police officer, was enough for a finding of justification. Manifested intent also becomes an issue when a robber commits a robbery with a toy or a gun he knows is unloaded or inoperable. He did not intend to shoot you as he knows he cannot do so. However, you, the victim, did not know the gun wouldn't fire, and your self defense actions were motivated by your reasonable belief based on his manifested intent. In determining whether your use of deadly force was justified, a judge or jury will look to your reasonable belief you or another innocent person was in danger of death or serious bodily harm—rather than to whether or not there was actually the ability, opportunity, and intent to cause such harm as in the toy gun example.

There are no clear cut guidelines to define what "means," "present opportunity," and "intent" mean. It's like the concept of love: we know what it is when we experience it, yet it remains awfully difficult to quantify with words. Each element is affected and modified by the variables of the situation. As a result, two juries can be presented with the same set of facts and reach different conclusions. Earlier, we mentioned that disparities in size, age, strength, skills, and numbers were factors used to determine, in part, whether your actions were justified. There are additional factors or considerations which can weigh in your favor. These would include illegal drugs in the attacker's body (if known to you), multiple assailants, statements (especially if recorded) promising death or bodily harm, and your knowledge of the attackers history or capacity for life-threatening violence.

Environmental factors may also have a bearing such as lighting, weather, or social conditions. For example, snow may impede your ability to safely retreat. Rioting and looting in your business district would also reasonably limit normally available avenues of retreat.

You may have many hypothetical questions regarding whether or not deadly force is justified in this situation or that. These are the "what if" questions. You can, in most instances, answer your own questions by applying the test of "means, present opportunity, and intent" to the situation, together with any less drastic options available to you such as retreat, calling the police, or using less than lethal force.

In summary, justification for employing deadly force depends upon the felonious actions of your adversary. In effect, he brings justification with him when he comes to rob or hurt you at your place of business. The elements of means, present opportunity, and intent must be simultaneously present. Being legally justified to take a specific action is based upon your reasonable perception of being in danger of death or serious physical injury. A phrase common to many state statutes is what the average person would "reasonably believe" to be a threat of death or serious physical injury. Following are four more frequently asked questions:

Can I legally shoot someone in the back?

Yes, but. While it may seem distasteful, the answer is, yes. Having to shoot someone in the back has a stigma attached which was probably nurtured by the western movies and TV dramas of the fifties and sixties. The true life arch coward of the Wild West is Bob Ford, who shot Jesse James in the back of the head as the latter was adjusting a wall picture. In fact, there's a line in the western folk tune which says, "that dirty rotten coward, that shot Mr. Howard (Jesse's alias), and laid poor Jesse in his grave." This stigma still finds its way into the courtroom.

You may easily find yourself in a situation where your business partner or an employee is the target of a felonious attack. You would certainly be justified in firing provided that the employee or partner isn't in the line of fire. In this instance it is a third party who is at immediate risk of death or serious physical injury and you happen to be behind the perpetrator.

Shooting someone in the back brings up the subject of fleeing felons. This is an extremely complex area of law misunderstood even by many police officers. Many states allow deadly force to be used against an armed, fleeing felon who is in immediate flight from certain specified crimes, or who continues to pose a threat to a police officer or others. However, these laws vary from state to state. In the Garner v. Tennessee decision, the U.S. Supreme Court invalidated many states' "fleeing felon" statutes, limiting the power even of the police to use deadly force in such situations. In order to avoid potentially serious legal problems, I would refrain from shooting a fleeing felon unless you can clearly demonstrate the felon continues to pose an immediate threat to you or someone else, and the action is permissible under the laws of your state. Once again, the statutes often rely on legally vague phrases such as "immediate flight" which are subject to wide interpretation. We may have a good idea of what is meant by "immediate," but at what point is flight considered to be no longer immediate? Where is the magic line where the black and white area ends and the gray area begins? For this reason, you need to avoid all the legal gray areas. "Immediate flight" is in the major league of gray areas. Another problem with immediate flight is that some juries may believe that a felon turning his back to you was a signal of his intent to disengage. Therefore, the round you fired as the felon began turning, was fired without legal justification.

Jurors, in trying to determine your guilt or innocence, will reach back into their life's experience to find a yardstick against which to measure your actions. That life experience may include literally thousands of hours of fictionalized violence. Fictional scenarios rarely, if ever, convey the extreme sense of mental anguish faced by a person fighting for his life. Consequently, your mental state, together with the decisions you made during that mental state, will not be fully appreciated by them. They will expect you or a police officer to turn off the deadly force the absolute instant it is no longer needed. One or two rounds fired after that point will appear to them to be excessive.

Just such an example of justice gone haywire occurred on August 22, 1994 when off duty police officer Peter Del-Debbio shot and wounded undercover police officer Desmond Robinson in a New York City subway car. The circumstances involved the undercover unit chasing teenagers who were armed with a loaded shotgun. The teens dropped the shotgun which discharged upon hitting the concrete platform. As you can imagine, a shotgun going off in a concrete and steel subway station sounds like a 105mm field howitzer. The errant shot wounded a bystander. Panic, bedlam, and much screaming ensued. Acting courageously within the echo of a deafening shotgun blast and a cauldron of human emotion, Officer Del-Debbio mistook Officer Robinson, whose gun was drawn, for one of the assailants and shot him four times. Officer Del-Debbio was subsequently convicted of second degree assault. While Officer Robinson has requested the courts not impose a jail sentence upon Officer Del-Debbio, Del-Debbio was found to have used excessive force because several bullets allegedly struck Robinson in the back as he instinctively turned away from the gunfire. Del-Debbio was fired from the police force and undoubtedly faced a mountain of legal fees. This case is a text-book example of a jury failing to take into consideration the extreme sense of anguish and confusion which accompany a gun battle. The Del-Debbio-Robinson incident was indeed tragic for both officers, each doing their part to make an ungrateful city a safer place to live. To have brought criminal charges against Officer Del-Debbio is further evidence that justice has been removed from the justice system.

Regardless of what your state penal laws allow you to do, it is always better to be legally conservative and cease firing when you realize the robber is attempting to flee. However, you must maintain cover and remain prepared because the robber may again turn and fire at you, or there may be a back up accomplice in the vicinity who you're not aware of. Leave your cover and it may be you with the bullet holes in the back!

Must I give a verbal warning before firing?

It depends. The range or progression of force one person may use against another person begins with mere presence and ends with deadly force. Your justification for using deadly force is enhanced if the felon ignores a command to drop his weapon and surrender, especially if your warning was witnessed or recorded. However, the law does not require you to first exhaust the entire range of force options before resorting to deadly force. You are expected to use a lesser degree of force if you can do so without putting yourself in jeopardy. As an extreme example, how much force may you use against a knife wielding robber who happens to be missing one leg and entered your store in a wheelchair? If his free hand isn't clenched around your throat, a jury may well find that any level of physical force used against this individual which results in injuring him is excessive.

Kind of warning to give.

The standardized warning given by police officers is, "police. Don't move!" Many firearms instructors are of the opinion civilians should also use this warning for a number of reasons: it is simple, direct, and easy to understand. Secondly, if a verbal warning is given in the presence of a law enforcement officer, you increase the probability of not being mistaken for a felon and possibly shot.

Technically, giving this warning may give some the impression you're impersonating a police officer. If your "impersonation" is limited to the warning, your defense is that this warning was given in the hope of not having to shoot the robber or felon and to avoid being mistaken for a felon by a law enforcement officer or a legally armed private citizen, should either or both be present.

Avoid the term "freeze." Also, racial or ethnic slurs do not belong in your vocabulary. Be especially careful never to include a slur or foul language in your warning as some may view this as provocative. Also, you're setting yourself up for a successful character assassination in any subsequent legal proceedings.

In situations where more than one store owner or worker is armed, only one person should give a warning. Commonly, a felon confronted by two or more police officers receives simultaneous and contradictory commands such as "don't move," "drop the weapon," get down on the ground," etc. This may cause the felon to pause as he doesn't know who to listen to. Confusion caused by everyone barking orders at once increases the amount of tension and stress present during the confrontation and increases the possibility shots will be fired which could have been avoided. The chapter titled "Aftermath" contains more detailed instructions regarding how to conduct yourself in a situation where a robber has surrendered to you.

In some instances, it would be advisable to first use a verbal command. For example, a robber, or even an irate customer for that matter, armed with a knife, has confronted another employee. You are not yet in immediate danger. In fact, the robber may not know you're in the store. While every situation is different, a verbal command should generally be given where the option exists to do so without unreasonably increasing the risk to yourself or other innocent persons. It would not be realistic to utilize a verbal command when you're staring down the barrel of a gun and you're hoping for an opportunity to turn the tables against your adversary, nor perhaps against a knife-armed attacker who is close enough to slash or stab you or your employee before you can reasonably expect to stop him with gunfire. A knife-armed attacker who is still on the far side of the counter may present a different tactical situation in which use of a verbal command may not only be reasonable but legally required. Consequently, the appropriateness of a verbal command depends more on the immediacy of the threat you face, than on the threat itself. If the robber complies with your verbal command, disarms himself and surrenders, you may **not** then shoot him. In this instance, a lethal threat was removed by employing a lesser amount of force. There would be no justification for escalating the amount of force being applied to someone who has surrendered. The message here is that the need to meet deadly force with deadly force is not automatic. One doesn't necessarily justify the other. A lesser degree of force must be used where, it is evident by the circumstances, you had other options besides shooting your adversary.

Any time shots are fired, a grave danger of injury or death exists to everyone in the area. If a verbal command offers a reasonable chance of avoiding the need to fire your weapon, it should first be tried before escalating to a higher level of force. The use of firearms should be reserved as an absolute last resort when there doesn't appear to be any other reasonable alternative. This is not a book about having gun battles. It is a book about avoiding gun battles and winning the ones which can't be avoided, without reasonably increasing the risk to yourself and other innocent persons.

Must I first be fired upon before I can fire?

No. "Present opportunity" means exactly that. That the felon has the means, the present opportunity, and the manifest intent to take your life or cause serious physical injury is enough to satisfy the law. You need not wait to be fired upon because he may kill you with his very first shot or knife thrust.

CHAPTER FOUR

JUDGMENT

Of all the elements necessary to win a confrontation, judgment is one of the most difficult to understand and master. Very simply, judgment is affected by the level of knowledge and intelligence of the person attempting to exercise proper judgment. The dictionary defines judgment as the power to compare and decide, understanding, and good sense. It seems logical that good judgment is based upon good knowledge.

Within the narrow science of the deadly force confrontation, the element of judgment will often decide victory or defeat. However, judgment does not exist in a vacuum. It is interdependent upon the other elements mentioned, namely, mindset, knowledge, tactics, marksmanship, and weapon. It also is affected by emotions. For example, if you elect not to challenge two robbers with your single shot derringer, you are exercising sound judgment in not making the challenge, and extremely poor judgment in relying on a derringer. If you have stepped out for a moment and, as you return, observe a robbery in progress, then run to a neighboring store to call the police rather than barging into the store with gun blazing, you are exercising sound judgment.

It should be evident that in "comparing and deciding," the more knowledge you have, and the more skilled you are with your handgun, the more options you have. Thus, your ability to exercise sound judgment will increase the more mentally and physically prepared you are for a confrontation.

Let's take a look at commercial airline pilots for a moment. Admittedly, they're a brainy lot to begin with. However, they spend much time in flight simulators where every conceivable in-flight emergency is thrown at them. In each type of emergency, the pilot may have a number of options at his disposal in order to manage the emergency. For example, in deciding whether or not to abort a takeoff, the pilot must measure the particular craft's ability to stop with the speed and loaded weight of the craft and the amount of runway he has left. You get the picture. The pilots are enhancing their ability to make the right judgment calls by practicing in-flight emergencies.

Role playing exercises and computerized, interactive simulators which duplicate felonious emergencies are used by law enforcement agencies to teach judgment and tactics. The simulators are expensive machines ordinarily not available to the general public. Even though you don't have access to simulators, there are a number of ways you can increase your ability to exercise sound judgment during a robbery.

First, imagine robberies occurring at your store. Try to think about all the logical variations. For example, one robber, or more than one robber. Gun or knife? Are there customers in the store? Do I know them or could one be a hidden back-up accomplice? Am I alone in the store? Have I been shot? Am I wearing my sidearm or is it buried somewhere in the back room? Can I activate a silent alarm? Does the robber remain on the sales floor or jump over the counter to my side? Think about all the sub-variations which might occur. In each instance try to imagine the safest, most logical method to terminate the incident. And, of course, always imagine yourself winning the confrontation, by which I mean coming out of it with yourself and other innocent persons unharmed.

Try to stay abreast of the local news. Often, a robber or robbery team hits upon a low crime area chock full of unprepared merchants. They may work the area for a period of time until they decide they've generated too much heat and it's time to move on. If a robbery team is working your area, you need

to know their techniques. Are they striking at opening or closing hours? How many are there? What kind of weapons are
they carrying? Have they injured or killed anyone?

You should not skip over news accounts of retail robberies
wherever they occur. Perhaps there is something to be learned
about how another merchant conducted himself during a
robbery. He may have employed a brilliant tactic that could be
available to you. Or, he may have badly misjudged the situation,
thus getting himself or another innocent person killed. What
was it the merchant did or didn't do that resulted in him
winning or losing the confrontation?   Often, robberies are
captured on video tape which is then shown on the news.
Watch those videos closely. What mistakes did the merchant
make? What would you have done differently? As an example,
there are many cases on record of crime victims pretending to
faint, faking a fall, or deliberately allowing themselves to fall
after being struck by a felon, in an effort to manufacture an
opportunity to draw a gun or to turn the gun side away from
the adversary so he does not see the draw. This ploy has also
been used by off duty police officers who need to get to an
ankle holster without their adversary realizing the officer is
going for a gun. Later in the book, we will manufacture many
more opportunities to defeat the robber.

As you are legally armed, try to visit a shooting range regu-
larly. There, you may meet other armed merchants with whom
you can share information and learn additional techniques for
managing a robbery you may not have thought of. There's a
wealth of knowledge available. However, don't expect it to
show up on your doorstep. You must go out and find it.

Amazingly, once you immerse yourself in the topic, you will
experience an increase in self-confidence because you will
have plans for managing various felonious emergencies which
might occur in your store. Having a plan sure beats trying to
wing a solution as the robbery unfolds. In the chapter on mindset, we stated that panic is a psychological and physiological
reaction to a sudden emergency which you are neither trained
or equipped to handle. Cramming robbery information into

your memory banks will help you avoid panic. To quote Jeff Cooper,"I knew this might happen to me and I'm prepared to deal with it."

In conclusion, judgment can indeed be acquired. More correctly, it is a mental trait than can be cultivated. Remember, we're not talking about deciding between Pepsi Cola and Coca Cola, we're talking about who might leave the store under a sheet. You need to master all of the elements, judgment being one of the most important.

CHAPTER FIVE

TACTICS

A tactic is a short term maneuver intended to accomplish a longer term goal. Tactics involves trying to anticipate what our adversary is likely to do, then skillfully reducing or structuring as many variables as possible to achieve a goal, namely, lawfully defeating our adversary. Tactical planning is an attempt to deny your adversary as many options as possible and leave nothing to chance. Tactical planning has both a proactive and reactive aspect. The proactive aspect involves steps which may be taken in anticipation of a possible armed confrontation while the reactive aspect concerns itself with how we respond or react to a threat. Tactics demand the total elimination of luck, as you understand it, as a factor in the equation for success. Tactics are derived, in part, from the study of countless gun battles to ascertain why a law enforcement officer or merchant lost to a felon and what he could have done to tilt the odds in his favor. Those of you who play chess already have an understanding of tactics.

Tactics may be divided into two general topics:

1. Personal tactics. Describes your own conduct and actions before, during and after a robbery. Personal tactics will also be discussed in the chapters titled "Confrontation" and "Aftermath."

2. Physical tactics. That is, things you can do to the interior of the store, in anticipation of a robbery, to make it more defen-

sible for you and more hostile for the robber.

To a degree, we can discuss personal and physical tactics separately. However, they are interdependent. That is, the more things you do to the interior of a store to make it more defensible, the more options and personal tactics you will have at your disposal to defeat a would-be robber.

Many merchants, and police officers for that matter, have a fatalistic outlook regarding confrontations. You will hear phrases like, "when your time is up, its up." Or, "when God wants you, he'll take you." This attitude presupposes there is nothing we can do to prolong our lives. Something I said earlier bears repeating here: Winning a confrontation is a matter of luck and skill. The more skill you have, the less luck you'll need. As a professional firearms instructor and consultant, my approach to personal survival is necessarily pragmatic: God looks after my soul, I look after my butt. I would like you to adopt the same philosophy because you are indeed responsible for your own fate.

Let's get the matter of luck out of the way. There are two kinds of luck: one is indeed called luck while the other kind of luck is called skill. For our purposes, luck is a fortuitous break from someone or something that we cannot control. An example would be a robber's gun that malfunctions and will not fire, or the patrol car that just happens to pull up at the right instant. In both instances, you got lucky through no personal intervention. The other kind of luck, namely skill, can literally be manufactured. It has none of the game of chance, roll of the dice, God smiling on me, aspects we often think of when describing someone who's lucky. The rest of this chapter will be devoted to manufacturing "luck."

The tactics we will devise are determined to a large extent by clearly identifying what's at risk, then trying to reasonably anticipate a robber's actions as he attempts to gain possession of what's at risk. In some instances, you will have to prioritize your risks in order to out think a robber, or at least have all your bases covered. For example, your business has cash registers, but also receives a cash payroll, by armored car, every Thursday at about 3 P.M. As many crooks are indeed dumb, they might show up on Wednesday for a Thursday robbery!

Before we get too deeply into tactics, it may help to take a few notes. First, what do you have that an armed robber would want? Or, what is the primary targeted risk? Obviously, most of you will respond that he's after your cash. However, for jewelers the primary risk can be jewelry as well as cash. Jewelers are more at risk than most other merchants. Valuable jewelry may be scattered in many showcases, as well as in a safe containing additional inventory.

For gunshop owners, handguns are most often the primary target rather than cash. In three recent gunshop robberies I'm aware of, the robbers went right for the guns. In one of the robberies, the robber entered the store shooting, never bothering to announce a robbery. In this case, the felon utilized particularly vicious tactics because he knew the store owner was armed and he wasn't about to take any chances. The store owner was indeed slain during this robbery.

You must assume that a potential adversary knows you have a secret location where the bulk of your cash or your most valuable merchandise is located. In some businesses, such as electrical and plumbing supply houses and building materials establishments with many commercial accounts, a robber may bypass the cash register entirely and head for the back office where he assumes he'll find a safe or a drawer bulging with cash. It doesn't matter that most commercial accounts pay by check. If robbers had brains, most would not be engaged in the business of robbery.

If your business employs a number of people and you have a cash payroll, you must assume a robber may target the payroll rather than the cash registers. Other businesses such as kiddy type amusement parks, billiard halls, bowling establishments, and fast food restaurants generate large amounts of cash. If I were a robber, I wouldn't even be thinking about the cash registers when there's a mother lode somewhere.

A business I'm aware of has eliminated the threat of payroll robberies by paying its employees by check, then arranging for an armored car service to cash the checks on the street, through a window in the armored car. The employees filter out, one at a time, to cash their paychecks. Soon, we will be discussing some new concepts which we'll develop together and which I call tactical store design and personal defense zones.

Body Armor

Some merchants in high crime areas, wear bullet "proof" vests. This is understandable as some of them have survived upwards of six or more robberies. While most everyone refers to the "bullet proof" vest, more correctly, it should be referred to as a bullet resistant vest. A well selected vest will stop most handgun rounds likely to be encountered. "Proof" is an absolute, however. Because some handgun bullets may get through the vest and most rifle rounds *will* get through the vest, we really can't call them bullet proof.

Bullet resistant vests are rated on their ability to stop or contain certain bullets fired at certain velocities. Please refer to the appendix where you will find a chart furnished by American Body Armor containing the threat level ratings of their body armor, together with the projectiles or bullets for which they are rated. Please note these projectile ratings are based upon average velocities obtained in specific barrel lengths which are also contained in the chart. These figures, while in accordance with National Institute of Justice Standard NIJ 0101.3, are applicable to products produced by American Body Armor only. Statistics for bullet resistant vests of other manufacturers may vary.

While soft bullet resistant vests have been known to stop rifle projectiles, conventional vests, including the Level IIIA, should not be counted on to stop the kind of rifle rounds likely to be used in a robbery. If a rifle is used, it will most often be a military or paramilitary semi-auto firing the .223 Remington cartridge or the 7.62 x 39mm Russian, either of which will pass through most concealable vests. Sawed off .22 rimfires and shotguns are also commonly employed, but these projectiles can usually be defeated by the Level IIA vest.

Bullet resistant vests can also be effective against edged weapons. They will defeat a slashing attack and most knife thrusts, provided the vest isn't held fast to the knife as might occur if your back were against a wall or on the floor. In either case, you cannot roll with the blow which may allow the knife blade to fully penetrate the vest. Regardless, I'd rather have a vest between me and a street ninja than just my bare skin, which cuts easily and thus is quite accommodating to edged weapons.

Deciding whether or not to wear a bullet resistant vest depends on the degree of risk you believe you face. Even the best vests tend to be uncomfortable. They're warm in summer but act as a heat sink in winter. That is, it pulls heat out of your body during the winter months. One other problem: if you're not wearing it when the robbery unfolds, don't expect the robber to wait for you to put it on. The best you can hope for is to snatch it up and hold it in front of you like a shield. Human nature being what it is, you may buy the vest and wear it for a short while after purchase. Soon, finding excuses not to wear it become easier than finding excuses not to use the dusty tread-mill or stationary bike in your rec room. Perhaps you're leaving early for a round of golf? Or, the weatherman is promising yet another blistering day in the current heatwave? Eventually, the vest is used less and less until it's forgotten altogether.

A vest does not guarantee anything. Wearing a bullet resistant vest is a tactic that tilts a few more odds and percentages in your favor. As you know, there are many cases in which police officers were fatally wounded while wearing a vest. Sometimes, a bullet will enter just above or below the vest or slip between the side flaps or may simply strike the wearer in the head or neck. On the plus side, one vest manufacturer boasts over 700 documented saves of police officers wearing the company's vest. As with seat belts, vests do indeed save lives because they greatly reduce the number of life sustaining systems exposed to gunfire.

If you use a bullet resistant vest or plan to buy one, it is extremely important that you occasionally wear it to the range while engaging in target practice. Often, vests interfere with concealment holsters and make it difficult to draw the handgun. Inside the pants holsters are especially vulnerable to interference from vests because the vest easily overrides the butt or grip of the handgun and the wearer is forced to lift the vest in order to draw. This, of course, depends on how you dress. Small of back (SOB) holsters also allow the butt of the gun to get on the wrong side of the vest each time you sit down or have to stoop for any reason. Upon returning to the upright position, the vest sometimes overrides the gun. If you must reach for a gun during a robbery and the gun managed to worm its way into your vest, you are effectively disarmed. Vests also tend to reduce flexibility and reach. As a result, shoulder holsters are especially difficult to use with vests. Yet another problem with vests is that many of the older ones were quite stiff and heavy. The National Institute of Justice has inserted its bureaucratic nose into vest manufacture with the result that many N.I.J. approved vests are more torturous to wear than the iron maiden. If you haven't figured it out, all the muscles involved in breathing must lift the vest each and every time you take in a breath. This puts considerable strain on the body and can create significant problems for people with breathing or respiratory disorders. If I'm describing you, you may want to check with a doctor before strapping on a vest. If I may digress for a moment, placing a load on muscles essential to breathing was a common form of execution in earlier times. Death was slow, protracted, and agonizing, exactly what it feels like to wear some vests for any length of time.

Strain upon the chest muscles can be mitigated somewhat by taking a deep breath and holding it while adjusting the Velcro fasteners. Adjusting the fasteners in this manner leaves room for your chest to expand and contract during normal breathing. If this is not done, not only must your chest lift the front and rear panels in order to breathe, but must also partially stretch four lengths of sturdy, two inch wide elastic straps on every breath. There are easier ways to end one's life!

If you plan to wear a bullet resistant vest on a regular basis,

I highly recommend you trade in one of your surplus handguns and use the money to buy a new vest. Vests are becoming lighter, yet offering the same level of protection as earlier models with considerably more bulk. Vests have a useful life of about five to 10 years, assuming daily use. Life varies from one manufacturer to another. Consequently, I would avoid a used vest unless you can be certain of its pedigree. Remember, bullet resistant vests are supposed to stop bullets on the way in, not on the way out.

Tactical Store Design

I'm not exactly sure how small stores get designed. I have seen some mighty convoluted and confusing retail establishments which could only have emanated from a mind clogged with other thoughts. Among all the merchandising objectives in traditional store design, whether done by professionals, or the haphazard "wherever it happens to fit" concept, we've overlooked one point: poor design just might get us killed in an armed, self defense situation. If you're not armed, store design isn't at all critical because you'll be at the robber's mercy anyway. The unarmed merchant has little choice but to accede to the robber's demands and to follow police guidelines to minimize the chances the robber may get violent.

Once we put a gun in friendly hands, everything changes. We need to manufacture some "luck." What we will now do is adapt some well established police tactical techniques and thought in such a manner that it is usable to the civilian merchant. In fact, you have a physical advantage over the police: they're constantly working in unfamiliar territory which is any place they've never seen the inside of. You, on the other hand, know where the field of battle will be. It's easier to dig the foxholes in advance than to first think about it when someone is slinging lead at you.

When you think of self defense, your mind automatically brings up the handgun you carry or have hidden somewhere. With tactical store design, the entire store becomes a weapon and participates in your self defense. Best of all, tactical store design does not require us to sacrifice established merchandising techniques. Merchandising and tactical store design are entirely compatible. As you will see, tactical store design does not necessarily require extensive renovations to your business. Merely moving the cash register from one side of the counter to the other can, at times, create a significant tactical advantage for you.

In the best of circumstances, you may have but a few seconds, if any, to gear up for a confrontation. Thus, you must use every reasonable means and tactic at your disposal to overcome any initial disadvantage.

Personal Defense Zone

"Personal defense zone," is a phrase I've coined to describe an area within the store you may surreptitiously arrange and harden in such a way so it affords you the best physical chance of defeating your adversary while simultaneously making it more difficult for him to defeat you. Consequently, if you have no choice but to exchange gunfire with robbers, you want to take whatever steps are necessary to insure you are in the personal defense zone when the confrontation occurs. The personal defense zone will:

1. Surround the primary targeted risk.
2. Afford you cover against bullets.
3. Severely limit the options available to the robber.

The nature of your business often determines where you are most likely to be in the event of a robbery. For example, hardware stores often have much of their stock hidden from view. A customer asks for a certain item which is then retrieved by the storekeeper. Stores selling durable goods generally require lots of floorwork. On the other hand, convenience stores have nearly everything in view and regular customers often know where everything is. The storekeeper generally can remain in his/her personal defense zone for greater periods of time.

In one robbery captured on surveillance video, the proprietor of a jewelry store became suspicious of a certain individual. Instead of casually moving to a covered position, the jeweler remained in the middle of the sales floor. The viewer can see the robber slowly reach under his shirt tail for a handgun hidden in his waistband on his right, front side. Things then go from bad to worse. The jeweler then produces his own semi-automatic. However, the safety is on and in the extreme stress of the situation, the jeweler cannot get his gun to fire. A one sided gun battle ensues with the jeweler wounded one or more times. The gunman flees and has never been identified or captured.

There are two lessons to be learned here. As I said elsewhere, you should remain in your personal defense zone or begin moving to it the instant someone arouses your suspicions. Secondly, it is vitally important you practice or train the way you carry the gun. Undoubtedly, the jeweler never bothered to use the safety lever at the range. Consequently, he did not condition himself to automatically disengage it during an actual confrontation.

When in the store, where do you spend the bulk of your time? For example, a pharmacist may have one or two sales clerks manning the sales floor and cash register while most of his time is spent in the area where prescriptions are filled. If you are a sole proprietor, the location of the primary target is vitally important because this is where the robber will bring you if he obtains control of you. For example, while you are stocking shelves, a robber runs in and demands cash. More than likely, he'll order you to the cash register (primary target), then make you open it. It's a wise idea to keep the cash register locked so the robber cannot readily open it without your assistance. The tactic you are using is to put the primary targeted risk in your personal defense zone or, more correctly, to arrange the personal defense zone around the targeted risk. You need to increase the likelihood you will either be at the personal defense zone when the robbery occurs or be brought there by the robber. More than likely, any confrontation with a robber is going to occur at the location of the primary targeted risk. This is important because the personal defense zone will afford you your best physical chance of defeating the robber, should you get the opportunity to resist. Once you identify the type and location of the things the robber wants, the robber's movements within the store become predictable, perhaps not with 100 percent certainty, but predictable none the less.

The "Kill" Zone

Much of law enforcement tactical planning involves identifying an adversary's kill zone, then staying the hell out of it. The kill zone is the area the felon can control with the weapon available to him. For example, a knife wielding felon may have a kill zone of seven yards or more while the kill zone of a maniac with a scope sighted rifle can extend up to one half mile or more. The kill zone of a robber armed with a firearm is an unbroken line between him and you. For example, if a robber orders you to move to a certain part of the store and, in so doing, you pass behind a large fixture, with him on the other side of it, you are momentarily out of his kill zone.

In order for a felon to quickly obtain and maintain control of you, he must keep you within his kill zone. His kill zone is highly mobile. He brings it with him whenever he moves. If the felon sticks a gun in your ribs, then marches you to the other end of the store, you are within his kill zone all the time. It is important you understand what a kill zone is because much of what we will now discuss involves shrinking and manipulating the kill zone to its smallest possible size and predicting its location with mathematical certainty.

Cover

We need to go off on a short tangent for a moment to discuss cover and concealment. Cover is described as anything that can stop the bullets being used by your adversary. Concealment, on the other hand, is something that conceals some or all of you from view but won't stop his bullets. Both cover and concealment are variable in nature. That is, something may offer cover against handgun bullets but only offer concealment against armor piercing rifle fire.

You need to think cover at all times. That is, presenting your adversary with the smallest possible target and insulating as much of your body as possible against gunfire. This will be a function of your personal defense zone. While it may have been macho and fashionable for western outlaws to duel in full view of each other, trading fire with a felon, while fully exposed, is not conducive to a long, healthy life. To the greatest degree possible, any armed response on your part should only occur from cover.

Since concealment cannot stop bullets, can it serve any purpose? Of course. Relatively speaking, cover is better than concealment and concealment is better than nothing at all. The majority of felons know absolutely nothing about ballistics and even less about cover and concealment. In many instances, a felon may attempt to shoot around concealment not knowing that he can merely shoot through it.

How might this help us? There are probably merchandise display racks near the cash register that offer only concealment. If you obtain the opportunity to seize the initiative and fire upon your adversary, there's a reasonably good chance he'll seek cover behind the nearest thing available. Unfortunately for him, you now know you can shoot through it and he will soon find out the hard way. This is just one more example of manufactured luck. You may not even have to move anything. I recently saw some actual video footage on a news show in which a robber and a store owner were ducking, reaching, and straining while trying to shoot each other over what appeared to be a rack of potato chips.

At this point you should be gaining a little appreciation of the many things you can do to tilt the odds in your favor. While you must conduct yourself in a lawful manner at all times, there is no law against being deceptive, devious, and cunning. These are terrible moral traits for an accountant, but not for a law abiding merchant who wishes to remain alive. Besides, a gun battle is not exactly an affair of honor. In all probability, your adversary is totally remorseless, is judgment proof, and will take your life at the slightest provocation. You owe him absolutely nothing while he has the means, opportunity and intent to do you harm. Once he's defeated, different rules apply which we will discuss in the chapter entitled "Aftermath."

For most merchants, the cash register will be the center of the personal defense zone because that's where the money is. Keeping the cash register locked is a tactic used to increase the odds the felon will bring you to your personal defense zone without realizing it exists. Merchants with different targeted risks must devise ways to insure that, if a robber gains control of you, he'll likely move you to the personal defense zone if you're not already there. This may be done by leaving keys necessary to access valuables in the personal defense zone. This certainly doesn't guarantee having a personal defense zone will give you an opportunity to wrest the initiative away from the robber. However, without a personal defense zone you have virtually no options at your disposal except to surrender and hope for the best or hope you're lucky (you already know how I feel about luck!). There are many robberies on record in which the merchant seized upon a sudden opportunity to arm himself and fight back. Sudden opportunities are more likely to occur with just a little tactical store planning.

The cash register plays a role here. In most retail stores I surveyed for this book, the cash register sat on the counter and was about waist high. As a result, the merchant's entire head and torso would be exposed to fire while he emptied the cash register. Also of critical importance, the personal defense zone must give you the momentary opportunity to move both your hands out of your adversary's view. This is a more significant advantage than you might imagine. Police officers have learned the hard way a felon's hands must be kept in view at all times. You should not draw a weapon when a weapon is pointed at you and the robber can see your movements. Momentarily blocking a felon's view of either you or your hands can create the opportunity for you to draw and fire. However, drawing a weapon while facing a weapon is exceedingly dangerous and will most likely precipitate a gun battle. Once again, you must weigh the dangers of resisting against the dangers of not resisting. This is a sterling example of how physical and personal tactics interrelate: in order to move your hands out of view, you must provide a "view block."

The first rule is to think higher. The cash register should be on a raised pedestal so you can see over the cash register but when you move behind it, most of your body is suddenly covered against gunfire. This is one of the key features of the personal defense zone. You will now see that one rule leads to another as the personal defense zone literally starts to design itself.

You should strongly consider purchasing what glaziers refer to as a cash enclosure. This is a custom made bullet-resistant glass structure that can be used to wrap around the front and customer's side of the cash register. These can be free standing or designed to sit on the counter. In most instances, the counter model is more practical because it involves little or no modification to the counter.

What about the area below the cash register, under the counter? This too must offer cover not readily visible from the customer's side of the counter. A stack of dry laid bricks, extending from the floor to the bottom of the cash register, inside the counter, will stop single hits from virtually any handgun. This offers you a substantial measure of protection should you have the opportunity to mount an armed defense. Better yet, you may visit a local steel mill and contract to have the entire interior face of the counter lined with 5/16 inch steel plate. The steel plate will stop most handgun rounds likely to be encountered, ordinary bird and buck shot, and lead rifled slugs normally used for big game hunting. It will also stop some rifle rounds but will not stop armor piercing rounds or full metal jacket military rounds such as the 7.62 x 39mm or the 5.56mm (.223 Remington). If both of these suggestions seem impractical, you may store any cased merchandise likely to stop a bullet such as canned goods, bundled magazines, hardware, etc. If you choose this latter approach, try not to leave any air space or pathways a bullet could sneak through. American Body Armor, besides making body armor, also has a program known as Safe Haven. This involves hardening counters and tellers' windows against gunfire. While most of their clients are banks, I'm glad to hear that about 10 percent of the business involves retailers. American Body Armor advises that the counter surface, in addition to the face, must also be hardened against gunfire. There are many instances on record in which a merchant ducked and the annoyed felon fired into the counter to try and reach him.

Hardening the inner face of the counter against handgun fire raises two new questions: what if the robber decides to jump over the counter, or decides to stand to the side of the counter?

Counter Jumpers

It isn't easy to prevent a felon from jumping over or coming to your side of the counter. I've seen video of bank robbers vaulting over tellers' windows which were nearly six feet tall. I've also seen video of robbers literally diving through a narrow counter opening as though they were leaping from a diving board. You probably couldn't conduct business over a counter that was impossible to jump over. As we're playing a game of percentages, a felon who has you well within his kill zone may not perceive a need to come to your side of the counter unless you literally invite him over.

Most store counters are too low. Counters should be at least 48 to 50 inches tall. This makes them a bit harder to vault over and also offers you an enhanced measure of cover. You will also have a much shorter distance to duck in order to get behind cover. Quite frequently, counters are no more than table height, or about 30 to 32 inches tall. You may also restrict the width of the opening, the area where customers place their merchandise while paying for it, to perhaps two or three feet. This makes it considerably more difficult to vault the counter because there is no room to swing the legs. Also, it would be a good idea not to install low shelves or food racks in front of the counter opening which a robber may use to boost himself over the counter.

There are several additional techniques which will help

deter counter jumpers. You may widen the counter by installing trays for impulse goods which are attached to the customers' side of the counter top but free standing otherwise. In order to vault the counter, the robber must reach much further in order to get his hand on something solid. This is a difficult and awkward position from which to launch a leap that will carry him over the counter because the "vaulting" arm is nearly 90 degrees to the body rather than in and tight where it needs to be.

A counter at least 50 inches high, with impulse trays which cannot support body weight, has no lower shelves to afford foot purchase, and has a work area of no more than three feet in length, is an exceedingly difficult, but not impossible counter to jump over. Best of all, the robber may not realize it until he tries it. If he stumbles and falls, take that opportunity to regain control of the situation. You'll probably not get another. In a recent jewelry store robbery in New Jersey, two individuals were buzzed into the premises where upon they held the door open for an accomplice so he could get a running start, from outside the store to gain enough momentum to vault the counter, which he did.

The entranceway to the rear of the counter must always be secured by a locked door or gate to reduce the ease with which a robber can come to your side. This gate must be at least as tall as the counter and preferably taller. It should be located as far from the cash register or primary targeted risk as possible because if a robber intends to get behind the counter via the gate, the further away the initial breach is from your personal defense zone, the more time you have to recognize the threat and possibly take action. We sometimes refer to this as the reactionary gap. That is, the further away a threat is from us when we recognize it as a threat, the more time we have to react. It wouldn't be a bad idea to install a buzzer or chime on the gate to further reduce the chances of someone walking up your back side by surprise. Many gates are nothing more than an extension of the counter with open air beneath it. Obviously, these are easy to duck under.

A second reason for moving the gate away from the personal defense zone is that the robber may not be able to keep you within his kill zone by going to the gate to gain entrance to the rear of the counter. Consequently, if the counter is difficult to vault and the robber fears losing control of you by going to the gate, he'll likely stay in the sweet spot of your personal defense zone which is exactly where we want him to stay. Any time you are outside the robber's kill zone you have an opportunity to defend yourself.

Merging Kill Zones

If you are confronted by more than one robber, or if a back-up gunman is in the store, you want to force their respective kill zones to merge or overlap as much as possible. This helps neutralize the effectiveness of a back-up gunman. If you have no choice but to engage two adversaries, it helps to have them as close together as possible. In fact, you may miss one and hit the other or one robber may then accidentally shoot the other! In order to merge the kill zones of two robbers or to limit the kill zone of one robber to one place, it will be necessary to limit the approach to the cash register to one direction only. You might call this a denied flank defense. That is, a robber or his accomplice cannot flank you (stand to your side).

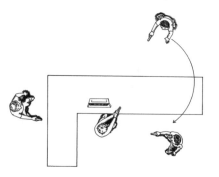

With popular, full-access, "L" shaped counter, merchant is easily caught in a crossfire because individual gunmen have separate kill zones. If a robber elects to jump over the counter, merchant has no cover available to shield him against gunfire. An armed merchant must avoid this classic trap.

You must arrange your counter so the robber does not have the option of keeping you within his kill zone by standing anywhere he damn well pleases. Thus, the vastly popular "L" shaped counters with the cash register usually located at the juncture of the two counter segments, are virtually defenseless because if the felon decides to stand to the side, rather than in front of the cash register, he has bypassed your cover. Or, if you're confronted by two robbers, one of them will almost certainly cover you from the side. We must eliminate this option and force their individual kill zones to merge or overlap as much as possible. By far, this is the single most important message of this book. This may involve nothing more than moving the entrance way to the counter and installing some merchandise racks to shut off one potential kill zone.

Modern cash registers cannot be counted upon to stop typical handgun rounds. Most likely, they'll have hard spots and soft spots just like car doors. Some cash registers are made of metal and stand upright while others have a plastic upper housing over a metal base. Many are quite flat, almost resembling adding machines. Many stores now have computerized cash registers which have a computer, a cash drawer and monitor. These offer excellent concealment if incorporated into a personal defense zone. Cash registers may provide spotty cover but I'd much rather have one between me and bullets than nothing at all. Besides, most felons will treat the cash register as cover. That is, they'll assume they can't shoot through it and will attempt to shoot over or around it.

As previously mentioned, I highly recommend the cash register be protected by an unobtrusive cash enclosure made of bullet resistant glass. It would offer you much better cover and, since you'll soon clutter it up with ads, impulse goods, and assorted documents incidental to running your business, it would barely be noticeable to customers. The top of the cash enclosure, whether free standing or counter mounted, should be at least six feet tall. The need for the cash enclosure, as well as the hardened inner surface of the counter is necessary because robbers often tend to scatter their shots.

Consequently, you may duck behind the counter only to be fatally injured by a bullet passing though it.

The Merchant Friendly Counter

Most store counters appear to have evolved or perhaps metamorphosed from most any available building materials, including junk. Some are vestiges of previous failed ventures incarnated in an effort to avoid the cost of buying or building a new one. However, the counter is an integral part of your personal defense zone and, as it will most likely stand between you and your adversary, you need to derive whatever tactical benefit you can from its presence. It must be bullet resistant, as previously stated, and must severely limit the angles at which hostile fire may reach you. An inexpensive, bullet resistant counter that meets these goals may be made as follows:

Construct the face (and side, if necessary) of the counter with two layers of 3/4" thick plywood which have been screwed to opposite sides of **metal** wall studs following construction methods used for interior walls. Do not use wood studs because some bullets, if they hit directly on a stud, can fully penetrate them. Next, fill the area between the plywood with coarse gravel. Be sure to tamp and vibrate the gravel as it is poured to insure it settles as densely as possible. As the metal studs are open on one side, they allow gravel to completely fill the voids between studs. Fill the voids to the very top. You may now add the counter surface. The face of the counter may now be finished with paneling, paint, mirrors, Formica, or wallboard. The easiest way to harden the underside of the counter surface is to line it with steel plate.

It is important to remember the lower the counter, the less protection it provides. Consequently, if you're going to rebuild your counter, be sure to make it at least 48 to 52 inches tall.

I constructed a test face as described, took it to the range and test fired it. The counter face stopped serious bullets dead in their tracks, including full metal jacket 9mm ammunition. It even defeated the awesome .44 magnum at a range of five feet. As it defeated the .44 magnum, I didn't even bother to test it with anything smaller. [Note: due to the serious danger of rico-chets and bullet splashback, do not attempt to test fire against any bullet resistant material as I did. If you must test it yourself, do it from at least 25 yards distance, stand behind bulletproof cover and insure that no spectators are present. Also, be sure to wear safety goggles and ear protection.]

If you plan to construct a new counter, you may follow the suggested arrangement as depicted in the following illustra-tions. Notice that a refuge has been provided adjacent to the cash register. This does five things:

1. More of your body is routinely behind cover, even if caught by surprise.

2. With long counters, progressively more of you would be exposed to gunfire from a second gunman positioned at the far end of the counter. The counter refuge prevents this.

3. Separate kills zones are merged. In this instance the merchant more nearly faces two robbers rather than having one off to his side.

4. Both your hands are more often out of view as the cash register is directly between you and your customers rather than to the side.

5. If a felon jumps over the counter, the refuge, provided you don't allow garbage to accumulate in it, provides effective cover while the robber is fully exposed to return fire. If you don't have a refuge, you also don't have anyplace to go to dodge his bullets. I don't recommend a refuge for merchants who have no intention of arming themselves because once the robber vaults the counter, you are trapped. A conventional counter with several means of escape does afford the oppor-tunity to flee.

Center island type counters, one in which customers may approach from all four sides, are especially difficult to defend or convert into personal defense zones because the robber has a very generous kill zone and can keep you in it no matter where he stands. In effect, you cannot manage or reduce his kill zone. If you are armed, I strongly advise you to give up the center island counter. It cannot be readily defended. The same

applies for a three sided counter jutting from a wall. The three sided counter can be hardened against a single gunman but is virtually useless against multiple gunmen.

The Sweet Spot

A vital consideration for your personal defense zone is to force the felon to take up a position that affords **you** the maximum advantage without him realizing it! So, if the felon has but one option available to keep you within his kill zone, then that's the option he will take. At the beginning of this chapter we discussed that one element of tactics was reducing or eliminating as many variables as possible. By far, the most critical variable is to reduce the robber's options regarding where he can stand in order to obtain or maintain control of you. As the robber is not a tactician, you don't want him to realize that his perceived kill zone is right on the sweet spot of your personal defense zone. The sweet spot, therefore, is the one spot where you have the best chance of defeating him. It is the place

For wall to wall counters, an offset refuge combined with a view block forces individual gunmen's kill zones to merge and also gives merchant cover against a gunman should he jump over or otherwise gain entrance to the rear of the counter. Note the gunman should have no cover available to him. Heavy lines in this and subsequent illustrations denote bullet resistant surfaces. Also, the counter surface should be hardened against bullets.

Denied access to the left of the cash register encourages one or more gunmen to remain on its right, thus offering merchant some protection against gunfire. Counter refuge at merchant's left provides cover for the merchant if gunman vaults to merchant's side of counter. There are but two avenues or lanes of attack against merchant - from outside and from inside the counter - for which the merchant must have cover. The refuge provides secondary cover in the event the merchant cannot defeat robber while he's on the opposite side of the counter.

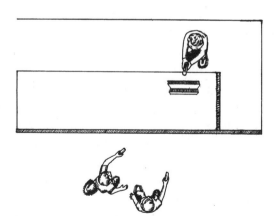

Denied flank defense: Gunman cannot flank merchant on his left side because of view block, forcing gunmen to bunch closer together, thus merging their kill zones.

where you have cover and he doesn't.

Let's take a look at additional considerations as your tactical minefield takes shape.

Many recently constructed strip malls do not have masonry walls separating the individual stores. Consequently, bullets can penetrate into the next store to cause injury or death. In fact, even hollowpoints have little difficulty penetrating several layers of wallboard. The hollow cavities fill with material and the bullet then behaves more like a bullet with a full metal jacket. The composition of the walls is something you need to take into consideration with tactical store planning. You cannot fire into a surface that will not stop your bullets. In my opinion, the only reasonably safe direction of fire, in the absence of masonry dividers, is towards the rear of the store. No matter how poorly constructed the store is, the rear wall is almost always of masonry construction, usually cement blocks.

You may recall an incident on New York's Long Island in August 1982 where a store worker attempted to install a wall shelf with a nail gun. The nail went completely through the wall, striking a worker in an adjacent fast food establishment in the head, nearly killing her. In 1997, a worker was killed by a nail fired through a wall in a virtually identical situation

The next major consideration is which way should the cash register face? To the greatest extent possible, you don't want to turn your back to the robber while complying with his demands. This means the cash register must be on the counter rather than on a shelf along the wall behind the counter. In this manner, you can keep the robber within view while complying with his demands. The cash register and pedestal, should you need one, are an integral part of the cover in your personal defense zone. Therefore, it cannot remain on the rear wall.

There are several additional reasons for the cash register to face forward: With your back to the robber, you may not see a golden opportunity to take action when, for example, the robber turns around to ascertain the source of a sudden noise or becomes momentarily distracted. Also, if the cash register is on the rear wall, you are forced to walk back from the front counter, thus fully exposing you to gunfire and all but nullifying your personal defense zone, particularly the hardened counter face and surface. Of equal importance, having to face a wall when using the cash register reduces your ability to timely observe suspicious characters entering your store and, therefore, shortens the time you have in which to react. You are more likely to turn back to the counter and into the muzzle of a gun than you would have if the cash register was on the counter. A critical tactic is to always watch the hands of anyone you deem suspicious. You cannot do this if you must turn your back to your customers in order to make change.

One of the problems you must understand is that not all robbers are experienced. Every robber must commit a first robbery and you might be his first. The timer sounding on a micro wave oven may be enough to make him jump out of his skin and pull the trigger a few times. In the New York City area, there are many news accounts of robbers becoming panicky over something, opening fire on the store owner and then fleeing empty handed. The point is, he may begin firing at any time for any reason. Whatever portions of your body you can keep covered reduces the target available to the robber.

In a recent robbery, an individual asked an employee to cash a $20 bill. As the clerk opened the cash register, the individual suddenly produced a handgun and announced a robbery. Almost immediately and without provocation, the robber fired, killing the store clerk. He then fled without taking anything and even left his $20 behind.

If you are planning a store and, at this time, have nothing more than a fresh sheet of paper, you may want to seriously consider a more thorough approach to tactical store design. This does not conflict with contemporary merchandising practices, it merely acknowledges that some store layouts are safer for their occupants than others.

Consider installing the counter perpendicular to the store front. There are two reasons for this. First, if you must open fire, you want to reduce or eliminate the possibility of stray rounds finding innocent pedestrians. Consequently, you don't want to be firing into the front windows and a possibly crowded sidewalk. In effect, you must anticipate your likely lanes of fire. If a proposed lane of fire offers a significant risk of hitting bystanders, you may not be able to return fire while the robber is free to transform you into Swiss cheese. Also, if you're standing directly between the robber and the front window, passersby may not be able to see the weapon in the robber's hand and thus realize a robbery is in progress. We mentioned earlier the New York City Police Department advises that the cash register area should be visible from the front windows to help discourage robbers from targeting you. Certainly, this advice should be followed if possible.

If the robber is forced to stand perpendicular to your front windows, it will be especially difficult for him to conceal the handgun from casual view. This increases the probability of detection and of someone calling the police. This is one of the reasons the New York City Police Department recommends that the cash register area be viewable from the street. In addition, the exposed nature of the position may deter a potential robber altogether, especially if other nearby stores are easier targets than your store. As previously mentioned, you cannot fire into the side walls if they are of wallboard construction and there's nothing substantial in your store or the neighboring store to stop bullets before they reach innocent, unsuspecting people.

Often, sales representatives for particular products will give merchants display racks free of charge. The sales representative is then allowed to place the merchandise rack within the store. The sales representative is trying to maximize sales of his or her product. If I'm describing conditions at your establishment, be sure the tactical features of your store are not compromised.

Effective Utilization of Cover

Cover will be an integral part of your personal defense zone. I have spent thousands of hours conducting qualification and tactical training for federal agents and have become quite familiar with problems related to the use of cover. For example, a right handed shooter is far more effective when shooting around the right side of cover than when shooting around the left side. He may hit the target while exposing the barest minimum of their body. Conversely, the left handed shooter is more effective on the left side of cover. Shooting around the strong side of cover seems to come naturally for most people. But, when shooting around the weak side, they often get their feet mixed up, introduce awkward bends in their wrists, expose too much of their bodies and unbalance themselves to the point of nearly toppling.

Right handed person shooting around right side of cover (his right) exposes far less of the body than would be the case when shooting around the left side. While you must be proficient with all forms of cover, you should never design a personal defense zone which requires you to shoot around the side of cover opposite your shooting hand.

Right handed person shooting around left side of cover (his left) tends to expose too much of the body to hostile fire.

Approximately 88 percent of the world's population is right handed. Consequently, we may safely say that there's an 88 percent chance the individual who attempts to rob your store will be right handed. This becomes critical because if you are right handed, you want the sweet spot of your personal defense zone to be on the **right** side of our cover. This does two things: first, you can deliver effective fire with the barest minimum of body exposed, and, the robber must move to his left, or further into the open in order to attempt to shoot around your cover! In effect, you are forcing a robber, with an 88 percent chance of being right handed, to shoot around the left side of your cover. This reduces the effectiveness of his fire while increasing the effectiveness of yours. If the cash register is located on the wrong side of the counter, it is the robber who will benefit from your cover, not you. In many actual gun battles recorded on surveillance tapes, both the robber and merchant utilized the same cover but from opposite sides. Consequently, if you are on the strong side of your cover, the robber has no choice but to be on the weak side of the same cover, giving you the advantage.

If you are right handed and planning a new retail store, your counter should be located to the right side of the entrance as you enter the store. This keeps the cash register near the windows and the sweet spot of your personal defense zone on the right side of cover. It is extremely important that you not provide an aisleway or entrance to the rear of the counter at this point because you cannot give the robber the option of taking up a position on the side of the register. Therefore, the counter must extend literally to the front window or window display. As previously mentioned, "L" shaped counters must be avoided if possible in order to utilize the denied flank defense.

If you are left handed, exactly the opposite will be true. The counter should be on the left side of the entrance because your sweet spot will be on the left side of your cover and you want to keep the cash register visible through the front windows.

Police departments advise the cash register be towards the front of the store. If you are contemplating armed self defense you may have a bit of a problem because you would like to create some distance between the entrance and the personal defense zone in order to increase the reactionary gap. I have seen cash registers within a foot of the front door. This gives you 100 percent visibility but zero percent reaction time. In stores where the entranceway is at a corner of the store, you may keep the register close to the storefront yet still have a bit of a reactionary gap.

Many stores, particularly those which are nearly square (bagel and sandwich shops come to mind) often have a counter stretching across the entire rear of the store. These are highly defensible. However, I would recommend placing the cash register and personal defense zone at one end of the counter and the entrance way to the rear at the other end. If the cash register is approximately at the center of the counter, your lane of fire will be right into the front entrance. If the store is fairly deep and the cash register is placed at the end of the counter, your lane of fire is into the side wall. This is preferable to the front windows provided the side wall is either lined with bullet resistant store fixtures or is of masonry construction. Better yet, consider extending the counter a short distance along the side wall so your personal defense zone faces the opposite wall. Be sure to block off the end of the counter with a store fixture of some sort. **You cannot allow robbers the option of standing to the side of the cash register.** As previously mentioned, your defense must be "denied flank" in nature.

You also want to make sure there is nothing within the robber's anticipated kill zone he may use for cover. Examples would include a soda or cigarette machine or some other store fixture. By now you have enough information to understand what a personal defense zone is, where the sweet spot is, and what the kill zone is. Just look around for anything the robber might use to block your return fire. If you find it, move it.

In many cases you will not be able to make significant changes to the store because you don't own it or because renovations would be too impractical or expensive. However, if you

While any cover is better than no cover at all, vertical cover shields more of the body against gunfire than horizontal cover shown in succeeding photo. In any street scenario, the vertical ends of an automobile provide better cover than shooting across the hood or trunk.

are right handed, keep your counter on the left side of the entrance, then, perhaps re-arrange the cash register and customer service area so they are on your right side. In this position, your customers stand on your right side while being served. Then, merely block off the side of the register and aisle-way to limit the robber's kill zone to the front of the counter.

In review, the following changes can be made to any store at minor expense;

1. Raise the counter height to 50 inches.

2. Harden the counter against bullets.

3. Place the customer service area at the right side of cover (left side for left handed merchants).

4. Place the cash register on a raised, bullet resistant pedestal.

5. Purchase a bullet resistant cash enclosure for the cash register.

6. Block off potential kill zones with store fixtures or modifications to the counter.

7. Locate the gate to the rear of the counter as far from the personal defense zone as possible.

8. Provide but **one** approach to the cash register and

personal defense zone for customers and robbers alike.

9. Make it more difficult for robbers to vault over the counter.

10. Provide a refuge adjacent to the cash register so you still have cover against a robber who jumps over the counter.

Compartmentalizing the store

Consider compartmentalizing your store. Instead of a curtain in the entrance to the back room, you may install a self locking, sturdy, solid wood door, or even a steel casement door. This will give you what is sometimes referred to as a "safe room." The dynamics of the robbery may be such that either you or a family member or employee can duck into the room. As a result, the robber cannot readily gain control of you. The interior wall of the safe room is a good place to store inventory or anything else which might stop bullets fired into the wall. From the safety of the safe room, call the police and remain in the room until you know they have arrived and have secured the store. The safe room should have a separate exit that's not buried in dead inventory. Obviously, the safe room must have a firearm, telephone, and a silent alarm switch. A bullet resistant window that looks into the store would also help.

Compartmentalizing the store makes it far more difficult for a robber to gain control of the premises. If he knows or suspects there are people left he cannot control, he also knows the police will be summoned. In fact, this technique can reduce the probability of a robbery occurring in your store. Compartmentalizing a store is absolutely necessary for large gunshops.

A store with two entrances, usually one to the street and a second to a parking lot or office lobby does not double, but rather triples, the options available to robbers. A pair of robbers may enter from the street, from the parking lot, or through both entrances simultaneously. Multiple entrance stores are difficult to defend, not so much because of the options available to the robbers, but because of the difficulty in trying to force their respective kill zones to merge. Also, the configuration of the store often makes it difficult to maintain a good view of both entrances.

Multiple entrance stores are easiest to defend where the counter faces one entrance and the other entrance is at your right or left shoulder. Most times, a storekeeper has one entrance at his back. This makes it difficult to identify a risk and will cost several seconds of valuable reaction time. If one entrance is indeed a blind one, robbers with even an elementary sense of tactics will use that entrance. The dangers of a blind entrance can be reduced significantly by installing a ceiling mounted convex mirror so you may observe the blind entrance from your position behind the counter. I also highly recommend the blind entrance be equipped with a chime to alert you someone is entering. The added dangers of a multiple entrance store can be mitigated somewhat by insuring no matter which entrance the robber enters, he may only approach the cash register from one direction.

Often, a merchant will expand and combine what was once two stores into one. Such a reconfigured store can have up to four entrances or more, truly a tactical nightmare. These stores usually have an archway cut through the dividing wall, with the result that one or more entrances are completely blind. If I'm describing your store, consider whether or not you need two front entrances. If not, close the one nearest to the cash register. With regard to the entrances or exits to the parking lot, you may consider leaving one and using the other as an alarm equipped emergency exit.

Having digested these options you may be thinking they are not practical or they won't work. Instead, place yourself in an unaltered store. The counter is 30 inches high, there's absolutely no cover for you and the cash register is on the back wall. You have a gun hidden under the cash register. A man walks in, pulls a gun and announces a robbery. You then notice another man standing at the end of the counter, off your left shoulder. He has a funny grin on his face. One hand is concealed from view. The robber says if he doesn't find enough cash he will kill you. What are your options?

As long as you need to have counters, doors, and cash registers, why not have them work for you rather than for the felon? It certainly can't hurt. It may be too late or expensive to consider redesigning your store. However, if you are considering renovations, relocating, or opening a store for the first time, why not follow a plan that increases your ability to defend yourself? At a minimum, merely re-arrange the counter to increase the odds of a confrontation occurring on the right side of your cover if you're right handed and on the left side for lefties.

I almost overlooked one point: the telephone. The telephone must be in your personal defense zone and you **must** be able to use it without turning your back to the sales floor. The confrontation you think is over may not be over. The need for vigilance is higher than ever. There may indeed be a second gunman nearby. Also, seeing the gunman go down from your shot, you may assume he's out of the fight as they are on television. He can resume firing at you at any time. Hollywood likes to build suspense into their movies by having the apparently defeated villain jump up from the floor for one last attack upon the good guy, whose back is conveniently turned. Bad tactic. **Don't turn your back to your adversary.**

As you can see, you have more options at your disposal than you realized. I wish I could say that foregoing the guidelines will guarantee you a win. The best you can do is create as many opportunities as possible to turn certain defeat into possible victory.

CHAPTER SIX

FIREARMS

Most merchants are casual gun users. That is, they own a gun incident to owning a business. They are not necessarily gun buffs, target shooters, or hunters. Consequently, their knowledge of guns and ballistics is limited and they can easily be persuaded into buying whatever the gun dealer wants to sell them.

In the most general of terms, a bullet stops or terminates felonious action by damaging or disrupting life sustaining organs and systems such as the central nervous system. The more damage inflicted, the more quickly the felonious activity will cease. The FBI launched one of the most exhaustive and authoritative studies ever conducted regarding wounding effectiveness of handgun bullets following the tragic Miami shootout of April, 1986, in which two FBI agents were killed and five more wounded. Independent studies were also being conducted by noted firearms authority, Evan Marshall, who assisted the FBI with their study. These studies generally show that the big bullets are more effective than small ones, fast bullets are more effective than slow ones, hollowpoint bullets are more effective than full metal jacket or solid lead bullets, and deep penetration (according to the FBI) was more effective than shallow penetration. There exist considerable differences of opinion on this latter point.

The FBI study also concluded that handguns, no matter

what caliber, cannot be counted upon to reliably stop a felon with 100 percent certainty. So, after reading the last paragraph you may conclude that, if you buy a gun that shoots big, fast, deep penetrating, hollowpoint bullets you'll have all your bases covered, something like Dirty Harry's .44 Magnum. You're partly right. The only problem is, guns that shoot big, fast bullets kick like a mad mule and sound like the hammers of hell.

Consequently, we must add another factor or qualification. We want to avoid guns which are difficult to be proficient with, or will require nearly daily practice to overcome the effects of recoil. A gun that's comfortable to fire and will not cause you to develop a sub-conscious fear of recoil (flinching) will be easier to master. A gun in a widely used police caliber that's easy to **hit** with will be more effective than a large gun that is easier to stop with but hard to hit with.

The vast majority of law enforcement and lawful self defense needs can be met with any of the following cartridges; .38 Special, 9mm., .40 S&W, .45 ACP and 357 Magnum. As of this writing, it's too soon to tell whether or not the new .357 SIG will establish a strong foothold in the police or civilian market. All of the established cartridges are currently in service with law enforcement agencies throughout the United States and are readily available at even the most remote or poorly stocked gunshops. It is always wise to avoid brand new, obscure, or unpopular cartridges because ammunition availability could become a problem. The .357 Magnum, once popular with state police and highway patrol agencies, is also giving way to the autoloader. The .44 Special is also well suited for personal defense roles although it isn't popular with law enforcement because the six shooters in this caliber require a large framed handgun. Police officers also use the .380 ACP, a marginal cartridge that's adequate for undercover use or as a back-up. It would not be my first choice in an armed confrontation.

The first rule for engaging in a gun battle is to have a gun! You would be surprised at how many merchants disconnect their brains, then take on knife and gun wielding bandits with baseball bats or broomstick handles. The second rule for engaging in a gun battle is to have the most gun you can comfortably handle. None of the aforementioned cartridges, with the exception of the .357 Magnum and flyweight .45 autos have objectionable recoil. This is easy for me to say because I've fired handguns that literally tried to take my arm out of its socket. Consequently, recoil is relative. If you're a neophyte, the muzzle flash and healthy push of the .45 automatic may seem like too much to handle. The experienced handgunner isn't even consciously aware of the .45's recoil.

A .357 Magnum revolver will safely accept and fire .38 Special ammunition. Thus, if you choose the .357, you can practice with and carry milder ammunition. Yet, you have the option of moving up to the .357 Magnum without having to buy another gun. However, do not practice with mild loads, then carry stout .357 loads. The unanticipated muzzle blast and recoil will unnerve you at a most unfortunate time. You must practice with what you carry.

Pistol or Revolver?

As you may know, most police departments have abandoned the .38 Special revolver in favor of various high capacity auto pistols. The 9mm is the most popular of these. However, the .40 S&W is coming on strong and is here to stay. In fact, some departments are cashing in their recently acquired 9mm's and moving on to the .40 S&W. At this point we must talk about marksmanship for a moment because it interrelates with gun selection.

Too many people are buying high capacity handguns for the wrong reasons. High capacity must never serve as a substitute for marksmanship and fire discipline. Consequently, high capacity handguns are ideal for people who intend to miss a lot. People who "hose the foes" are relying on luck, rather than skill, with the hope if they put out of cloud of whizzing bullets, one of them is bound to find a piece of the felon's hide.

Autoloaders are the handguns of choice for most firearms instructors. However, you must invest in your own personal skills by taking the time to become proficient and to remain proficient with the handgun. The high capacity pistol is truly a formidable piece of ordnance in the right hands. If you feel more comfortable with the autopistol then by all means buy it. But remember, hitting your target is more important than how many rounds you have available. I believe it was noted competitive shooter and gun writer, Ross Seyfried who said, "you can't miss fast enough to catch up." Think about it!

Which handgun? Gun writers often greet new handguns coming on the market for the first time as the "ultimate handgun" for self defense. The particular handgun remains the

REVOLVER

ultimate handgun until yet another handgun finds its way to the writers for testing and evaluation, usually within a month, at which time we have yet another new and ultimate handgun. It's sort of like a beauty contest. Consequently, it is, at times, difficult to select a handgun based upon magazine evaluations.

I'm not going to recommend a specific brand of handgun. All of the popular manufacturers offer quality handguns in the calibers mentioned and in somewhat different shapes and sizes. One safe method of selecting a handgun is to select the same gun being carried by your local police. Most departments subject guns to vigorous tests to insure reliability. If the police are carrying a specific model, it is a reasonable assurance it is indeed a quality, reliable handgun. So, let's discuss some of the features which make some guns more desirable than others.

First, if you indeed are a casual gun user, the simpler the gun, the easier it is to master. I generally recommend guns which can be fired double action only. This means you do not have the option of first cocking the hammer, if present, then having a light trigger pull. There are many reasons for this. During the extreme stress of a confrontation, you may not have the presence of mind to cock a gun that must be cocked, or

Front Sight   Slide   Rear Sight

Muzzle

Slide Stop and Take Down Lever

Frame

Magazine Release

Trigger Guard

Trigger

AUTOLOADER

Magazine Floor Plate

disengage its safety in order to fire such as the single action .45 automatic. If you do cock the handgun, you may experience an accidental or unintended discharge because of your inability to sense that you're applying pressure to the trigger. A double action trigger pull, usually of about 12 pounds, provides a margin of safety to help guard against an unintended discharge. A bit of a safety warning is needed here: **you should never put your finger on the trigger unless you intend to fire.** If a robber has been neutralized or has actually surrendered, your finger must be outside the trigger guard. Also, when the confrontation ends, whether or not shots were fired, you will be in such a stressful state that you may put the gun away without de-cocking it.

Some of world's foremost firearms experts are of the opinion that the ultimate defense pistol remains the .45 caliber Model 1911, or one of its many offspring, with just a bit of fine tuning to insure street reliability. Generally, this pistol is carried in Condition One, which means round in chamber, hammer cocked, and safety on. Condition One carry should be reserved for only the most proficient gun users, those who will take the time to master and maintain the shooting fundamentals and those who are willing to attend a shooting academy. Condition One carry is not recommended for marginally trained, casual, or passive gun users. Although the .45 auto was developed in the latter part of the nineteenth century, its timeless design and no nonsense cartridge are still a wise choice for the serious shooting enthusiast. Rest assured, anyone who suffers the misfortune of finding himself at the wrong end of Jeff Cooper's .45 had best have his affairs in order.

There are numerous cases on record of police officers experiencing accidental discharges while handling someone in custody. In some of these instances, the handgun, which was capable of being cocked, was indeed cocked against departmental regulations. Some of these detainees were killed as a result, usually with bullets in their backs. Just prior to the switch to auto pistols, many police departments had their revolvers retro-fitted with new hammers and triggers which did not have a provision for cocking. In fact, police departments often specify that auto pistols used for official carry have no provision for single action fire.

A second problem with a handgun capable of being cocked is attorneys sometimes will argue their client had indeed surrendered but your gun went off accidentally because it was cocked. Therefore, you owe their client a pile of money of which the attorney merely gets a third.

For all of the above reasons, the double action only, whether it be a revolver or a pistol, is the wiser choice for the casual gun user. They are just as reliable, just as accurate under defensive conditions, less likely to go off unintentionally, and they shut off one avenue of legal attack. Quite frankly, the ubiquitous Smith and Wesson Model 10 revolver, the mainstay of law enforcement until the changeover to semi-autos, is an ideal self defense handgun and would be my recommendation for anyone not willing to invest the time and money in becoming proficient with the more sophisticated semi-automatic handgun. Best of all, the used gun market is flooded with Model 10's. In some states you can probably buy one directly from a police officer for about $100.00*. If you choose the Model 10, make sure it's the heavy barrel version rather than the older "pencil barrel" model. Then, take it to a qualified gunsmith and ask him to convert it to double action only. The Model 10, which is built on Smith and Wesson's "K" frame, has metamorphosed into a number of variations. Of these, my personal favorites are the Models 13 and 65, both of which can be had with three inch barrels and round butts. They're as effective as their four inch brothers but are more concealable. Also, the round butt is a bit more comfortable for most gun users.

Aluminum and polymer frame pistols have become very popular. They are substantially lighter than their all steel brothers, making them easier to carry. However, this is accomplished at the expense of an increase in felt recoil. If you do not carry the handgun on your person, you may be better served with an all steel firearm. This will tame recoil a bit, making it easier for the occasional gun user to become proficient with his chosen firearm. The point is, there's no advantage in a light frame if the gun is not carried.

It is the collective experience of the firearms instructor profession that police tend to do on the street what they have been trained or allowed to do, or what they can get away with, on the range. The study of the effects of extreme stress on our ability to perform routine tasks is relatively new. Yet, we know under stress our ability to think and perform conscious activi-

*Police officers seeking to sell surplus duty weapons must insure that they do so in compliance with their city, state, and departmental regulations.

ties greatly diminishes and we tend to rely more heavily on our subconscious mind. Consequently, the right habits and information must be programmed into the subconscious. More than likely it's the *subconscious* mind that's going to save you.

Mental interference with survival skills was not recognized as significant until several incidents occurred in which police officers were found dead with six empty cartridges in their hand or in their pocket. Backtracking, it was discovered that during qualification shooting, police officers were invariably provided with a tin can in which to toss their empty cartridges as they fired. While on the street, police officers automatically reverted to their range habits by dumping the shells into their hand and actually looking for a place to put them, all the while taking fire! As a result, most law enforcement agencies using revolvers did away with the tin cans and tried to tailor range sessions so as not to create any artificial habits which might interfere with an officer's street performance.

Another tragic example of unintentional range conditioning occurred in 1970 when four members of the California Highway patrol died in a shootout, now referred to as the "Newhall Incident." One officer was found with empty shells in his pocket while a second officer, badly wounded, attempted to reload his revolver while a felon approached him. Although he had about four live rounds reloaded, he attempted to finish loading as he'd always done on the range. He should have closed the partially loaded cylinder and shot the felon approaching. Most police departments introduced partial revolver reloading following this incident. To the best of my recollection, speed-loaders had not yet become popular and reloading was accomplished by either the drop pouch or from cartridge belt loops.

I've saved the most incredible incident for last. A detective's pistol malfunctioned during a shootout. He stood up and raised his hand, exactly as required on the range!

I hate to admit it but I had a similar experience: my personal workshop is equipped with four florescent fixtures. I turn them on when I enter and shut them off (individually) when I leave.

In 1986, I suffered a serious hand injury with a jointer/planer in a moment of inattentiveness. I immediately sensed the onset of shock. Blood was spurting. I needed to get to the hospital. My wife was warming the car in the driveway and about to leave. Rather than run out to her, I wasted several precious seconds shutting off all the lights! Afterwards, I realized I had conditioned my subconscious mind to shut off the lights which is exactly what it made me do, despite the emergency, and despite the fact that shutting off the lights had no relevance to my need for immediate medical assistance. Shutting off the lights was a reflex action programmed into my subconscious.

The reason I've told you this is that depending on the particular type of autopistol you choose, it may be safe to carry it with the safety (if applicable) on or off, with or without a round in the chamber, cocked and locked (that is, cocked with safety engaged) etc. Of course, you should carry your autopistol only as the manufacturer or a qualified firearms instructor recommends. It is important you practice with the pistol in the same condition as you carry it. If you keep the safety lever engaged, be sure to always begin each string of practice fire with the safety lever engaged. This will program your sub-conscious mind to automatically perform the task of disengaging the safety when needed. If you disregard this advice, you may not be able to get the pistol to fire during a confrontation. Even worse, as your conscious mind has momentarily left the scene, you will not be able to figure out why the gun won't fire. It was noted football legend, Vince Lombardi, who said, "practice doesn't make perfect, perfect practice makes perfect."

The existence and interrelationship of so many tactical and safety issues mandate the beginning gun user obtain instructions from a qualified firearms instructor, an NRA certified handgun instructor or from one of the many recognized shooting schools and academies listed for your convenience in Appendix B.

Second Guns

A second, or back-up gun is extremely popular in law

enforcement for two obvious reasons, the first or primary handgun may suffer a malfunction that cannot be readily cleared and, the primary handgun may be dropped or taken away in a robbery or hostage type situation. A hidden, second gun has saved many police officers over the years. During the revolver days, it was usually faster to produce a second gun than to attempt reloading the primary arm. With practice, autoloaders can be reloaded so quickly there's no benefit to carrying a second gun primarily to avoid reloading the first one.

If you elect to have a second gun handy, it should be functionally similar, if not identical to your primary handgun. During an actual confrontation, your mind will be bombarded with so much stimuli it will not be able to differentiate between two different handgun systems. Having mechanically similar handguns eliminates one potential cause for failure. You must also take elaborate precautions to insure that if a reload is necessary, you do not get the magazines mixed up.

An ideal combination of handguns would be, for example, the flat and compact Smith and Wesson Model 3913, an excellent handgun for comfortable carry to and from your business, (if permitted by the laws in your area,) and to wear concealed while in the store. The second gun would be a Smith and Wesson Model 59 series which is of higher ammunition capacity but mechanically Identical to the Model 3913. A Walther PPK or PPK/S may also be carried in conjunction with a larger Smith and Wesson pistol. If you are a Glock fan, I would strongly consider the Kahr 9mm handgun or the miniaturized Glock 26 or 27. As the Kahr is an exceptionally slim handgun, those of you who prefer inside the waistband holsters should take a long, hard look at this superb little handgun.

Concealed or Stored

The most common problem faced by the armed merchant is what to do with the handgun. In my opinion, the handgun should be **worn** concealed at all times. This guarantees that wherever you happen to be within the store, including the bathroom, it will be nearby in the event of a robbery. I know you may find this recommendation unattractive because it requires you wear a shirt with long tails or a sport jacket. Consequently, you're going to disregard my advice and throw it in a drawer anyway.

DeSantis Style 67 "Small of Back" holster is an ideal choice for a merchant who is constantly on his feet. Regardless of holster selected, the handgun must be concealed from view with an appropriate garment such as a jacket or long-tailed shirt.

One of the author's favorite rigs consists of a 9mm Glock 26 and a Desantis Style 86 mini-scabbard made of durable synthetic Millennium. Magazine extension adds finger purchase but has been internally blocked so as not to violate magazine ban.

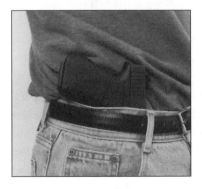

"Mexican carry," that is, carrying a handgun tucked into the waist-band without a holster (recommended by some gun writers) should be avoided. Besides possibly losing the handgun in an initial physical confrontation with an adversary, one cannot obtain a consistent grip because handgun is free to change angles or shift position. Author recommends holsters be utilized.

If you are not wearing the gun when the robbery unfolds, odds are you will not be able to retrieve it. In many cases I'm aware of, merchants were not able to get to a handgun stored somewhere in the store until the robbery was essentially consummated and the robber was in the act of fleeing. As explained earlier in the book, this is not the time to initiate a gun battle because shooting at fleeing felons places you in an extremely fragile legal position. Also, it is rather obvious your actions are motivated more by anger and revenge than a need to save your life.

If you elect not to wear the gun anyway, even though I've implored you to do so, then it should be stored, thoroughly hidden but readily accessible, in your personal defense zone. If you have two personal defense zones, you should definitely have a second gun, one for each zone. Remember, the personal defense zone is where you will most likely be when a robbery occurs, or, where the robber will most likely bring you if he obtains control of you. Therefore, do not store the gun somewhere in left field where there's virtually no chance of getting to it.

As of this writing, 17 states have passed legislation prescribing the manner in which unused guns may be stored. Current and proposed legislation, including proposed federal legislation, generally require unused guns be stored unloaded in a locked container or with a trigger-guard lock of some kind. If this is so in your state, you may not have the option of secreting a readily accessible, loaded gun somewhere in the store. Of course, your state legislation may limit the law to residences and exempt guns in business establishments during working hours. After closing, the unloaded firearm would have to be stored in a theft resistant container such as a safe. For these reasons you need to be familiar with all laws which impact upon your lawful use and ownership of firearms. Anti-Second Amendment politicians are seeking to pass legislation holding the gun owner civilly liable for injuries and deaths caused by felons with stolen guns where it is found the guns were improperly secured or stored by the lawful owner.

Common sense, and, in some cases, your local or state laws may require the handgun not be readily accessible to your employees. First, the gun may get stolen and second, an employee may elect to use it when deadly force is clearly not justified, or, even if justified, an employee with little or no training will almost certainly use it improperly, possibly with tragic consequences. As explained below, if you are going to permit your employees to have access to your handgun, you must ensure they are thoroughly trained in its use and such action is permitted under your local or state firearms laws.

A personal friend, now deceased, operated a highly popular gun and jewelry business from a converted ground floor apartment of his home in Queens, New York. This individual was virtually paralyzed, head to foot, with arthritis. As a result, he kept several handguns secreted behind the counter at strategic points as he could not draw from a holster. One evening, his four year old grandchild was playing behind the counter and happened to find one of the handguns. She pulled the trigger. The bullet went through the showcase and struck a customer in the leg. Considerable legal difficulties and a civil action followed. In New York City, it is quite difficult to obtain a pistol permit and quite easy to lose one. It is not uncommon to see children behind store counters. If you keep a handgun there, be sure that it is not accessible to them.

While discussing handguns, the question comes up whether or not your employees should know you have a gun. This is indeed a delicate matter and highly persuasive arguments can be made for either position. I'm of the opinion that the more unknowns a felon must manage, the more difficult it will be for him to succeed. Producing a handgun with tactical perfection is perhaps the ultimate surprise you can spring on a would-be robber, short of a SWAT team that just happens to be on a coffee break in your back room. Felons who are willing to take on an armed adversary are more inclined to strike in a pre-emptive manner. That is, they hit harder, faster and with more violence. If a dishonest, present or former employee fingers you for a robbery, he will disclose the fact you're armed and where you keep the handgun.

The problem of not disclosing the presence of a gun to employees makes it more difficult for you to train them to respond in such a manner as not to interfere with your ability to defend them as well as yourself. You must weigh the pros and cons and arrive at a decision that's correct for you and your business. However, if you have a second or back-up gun, the knowledge of this gun should be withheld from everyone. This is your ace in the hole. Leave it that way.

While on the subject of guns and employees, the question comes up as to whether or not to permit employees to carry guns. Generally, some types of businesses have used armed employees for years such as gunshops, cash handling businesses, and corporations large enough for their principals to be potential terrorist or kidnap targets. Franchise type retail businesses rarely permit employees to carry guns. There are several cases on record in which employees successfully used guns against robbers only to be fired for their efforts. The corporate position is understandable. If an employee is shot by a robber, it is often difficult to fix responsibility on the owners. If an employee wrongfully shoots someone or uses the gun against another employee, the corporation faces significant legal problems and bad press. Consequently, from a legal and public relations point of view, having an employee shot by a robber presents fewer problems than having employees shooting at robbers.

If you have armed employees, you are strongly encouraged to send them to a recognized firearms training school or academy to insure they are adequately trained. As previously stated, you too must attend such a school. Also, I'd check with the insurance company to make sure your coverage extends to these employees. Records documenting the training received by these employees should be maintained. From a legal point of view, if it isn't documented, it didn't happen. While you remain civilly responsible for wrongful or accidental acts committed by employees, it does reduce one legal area that can be used against you. It is known as negligent assignment or negligent training. An attorney trying to prove negligent assignment must show that employee in question was not qualified or trained for the position he held.

If the armed employee in question was hired for security purposes, he or she may be classified as a security guard in your state. You should be aware several states, with more to follow, now have a security guard certification program with a mandated block of instruction on firearms and use of force issues. Consequently, it is necessary employers be in compliance with any state laws governing the use and training of armed employees. Even if your state has no laws regulating armed security guards, you are under a legal obligation to use reasonable care in assuring they are properly selected, trained, equipped, and supervised. Otherwise, you may lose a civil suit brought by someone they wrongfully injure.

As a robbery can go in any direction, you may find yourself ordered out from behind the counter. The robber goes back there to clean out the cash register and search for the extra cigar box of currency which he believes may be nearby. While his search will be quick and haphazard, you cannot leave a handgun in such a manner it may easily be discovered even in the most cursory searches.

You need to exercise some cleverness, cunning, and common sense here. If you have followed my advice and are going to raise the cash register high enough so it is still usable but now offers a measurable degree of cover, you have also gained some extra storage space which you didn't have previously. You may hire a carpenter of known reputation, explain your needs to him and ask him to design and build a cash register pedestal with a disguised access within which you may conceal a handgun. The front and customer's side of the pedestal must be lined with a bullet resistant material.

A bit of additional deceptiveness is helpful here. You may place a plausibly realistic toy gun exposed below the cash register. If the robber finds the toy gun, he may think you intended to use it as a decoy and may therefore assume you do not have a real gun. As a result, he may lower his guard slightly and you have manufactured yet another opportunity to gain the upper hand.

While stashing things for the robber's convenience, I would also keep a small petty change box filled with rolled pennies, worthless stock certificates, some foreign currency, a fistful of $1 bills and a $20 bill on top. This does two things: first, he did find a cashbox with things of pseudo-value and which may placate him enough to not want to shoot you and second, you are cluttering up his hands and making it more difficult for him to manage his firearm. I would also remove the wire carry handle from this box so that the robber must tuck it under his arm or wrap his fist around it. Keeping one arm busy leaves but one hand to hold the handgun.

Ammunition

Prevailing practice is to use factory-loaded ammunition for occasional target practice, to function check and carry in the handgun. "Service equivalent" commercially reloaded ammunition can be used for the bulk of your practice to help cut costs, provided the ammunition is of good quality. Service equivalent means there's no detectable difference in noise, recoil, or point of impact between factory fresh ammunition and similar but reloaded ammunition. An alternative to reloaded ammunition is to use budget priced ammunition such as CCI Blazer, Olin White Box, UMC, etc. Using a 115 grain, 9mm bullet as an example, you should not be able to tell whether you are firing a factory round or reloaded round. Self-defense ammunition should be hollow point* because it is generally more effective and also reduces the possibility of passing completely through your lawful target to strike an unseen innocent person or passing through store fixtures and merchandise.

On occasion, a quality handgun and quality ammunition just don't seem to function well together. If a certain brand or specific loading of ammunition is not reliable in your handgun, and you are certain there is nothing wrong with your gun, you should switch to a different brand. It has been my experience some loadings of the 147 grain sub-sonic, 9mm cartridges do

---

*Prohibited in some states.

not have sufficient recoil impulse or energy to cycle some handguns with 100 percent certainty. When used in Glock pistols, the 147 grain subsonic round was extremely unforgiving of even the slightest limp-wristing, or not holding the handgun firmly enough, allowing your wrist and elbow to flex too much during recoil. During an intensive handgun testing program conducted in my division, I noticed that female agents had considerably more stoppages than males when using the Glock pistol and the first generation, 147 grain subsonic. This is not a criticism of the Glock. I own two of them and they're my primary defensive handguns. However, I feed them 124 grain +P ammunition.

If your handgun malfunctions at the range, try to eliminate other causes of malfunctions such as not cleaning the gun, and lubricating it properly, or not gripping the handgun firmly enough. When testing the reliability of ammunition, you need to first eliminate as many other potential causes of problems as possible. A brand new gun must be cleaned and lubricated, then fired at least 100 rounds before using it for defensive purposes. In fact, some manufacturers specify a 200 round break-in period. Never judge the reliability of a handgun, especially a new one that needs to be broken in, with hand-loaded or re-manufactured ammunition.

Although factory ammunition is loaded to the highest standards, defective rounds do make it past the inspectors. The most frequently encountered defects are the case mouth rolled partially inward, creating a bulge on one side of the cartridge, bullets loaded upside down and reversed, or non-existent primers. Defective revolver ammunition is often discovered at loading. However, defective pistol ammunition often escapes detection while being inserted into magazines and is not discovered until the handgun malfunctions. For this reason, carry ammunition must be inspected before it is loaded into magazines. After all, if your handgun malfunctions during a confrontation, it is the robber who is lucky.

Shotguns

In my opinion, the best way to introduce a shotgun into your defense plans is to entrust it to whoever is not likely to be the first person confronted by a robber. This will be discussed a bit later in the book.

You may be tempted to keep a shotgun in the store instead of a handgun. You have seen Hollywood villains lifted off their feet by shotgun blasts and hurled through plate glass windows. Wow, you thought, just what I need. While Hollywood exaggerates the effectiveness of shotguns, it is always wise to avoid the business end of one of them. A common phrase in law enforcement circles is only an idiot shows up for a gun battle with a handgun. There's an element of truth to this that needs explaining. In law enforcement, the handgun is used primarily for sudden, unforeseen emergencies. Any time police officers have a reasonable expectation of armed resistance, they always bring shoulder weapons, relegating their handguns to back-up roles.

While the shotgun is more effective than a handgun in trained hands, it is also unwieldy in close quarters and considerably slower to maneuver into firing position. It is also easier for the robber to attempt to disarm you. For these reasons, the Emergency Services Unit of the New York City Police Department, which has as much experience dealing with felony crime as any other such unit on earth, no longer uses shotguns for hostile entries. Instead, they are used primarily for perimeter security. From a safety point of view, I'm not comfortable leaving a loaded shotgun, even with the chamber empty, in a place where it is accessible to untrained employees. While you are out of the store, the teenage clerk you recently hired may be tempted to show it to a friend with tragic results. Sounds ridiculous? The majority of accidental shootings occur when a firearm is found in a store or residence by chance.

The shotgun selected should be 12 gauge with a barrel no longer than 20 inches. With regard to ammunition, I would recommend #4 buckshot, rather than "00" buckshot. Number 4 buckshot has approximately 27 pellets, each of .22 caliber.

This was the standard load of the U.S. Secret Service because it is highly effective against a human target yet the individual pellets are more easily contained by household and office fixtures and walls, posing less of a threat to unseen persons than larger shot sizes such as "00" buckshot. A standard 12 gauge load of "00" buckshot consists of nine pellets, each of .33 caliber. Incidentally, Number 4 buckshot should not be confused with Number 4 birdshot, a load used in turkey and goose hunting. Generally, there is little or no need for a store owner to use rifled slugs. Slugs pose a significant hazard to innocent people and can be lethal at distances greater than five hundred yards.

An inexpensive, double barrel shotgun with 20 inch barrels, or if necessary, professionally shortened to that length, would be my first recommendation to a storekeeper who insists on having a shotgun but has no special interest in firearms. The store keeper must also have a handgun as a primary firearm. This shotgun is quickly loaded, there's nothing to jam, and is quite maneuverable in close quarters. An elastic shell holder around the stock can provide a readily available source of ammunition. In the event you fire both rounds during a confrontation, I would then revert to my handgun rather than reloading the shotgun. Of course, reload and continue using the shotgun if the circumstances are such that you can do so without putting yourself at additional risk.

I do not recommend pump action or autoloading shotguns for the following reasons: Regarding the pump action, I have witnessed a very high rate of user caused malfunctions. Most often, the user "short cycles" the action with the result that the fired shell is not ejected or a fresh shell not fed into the chamber. Short cycling is a virtual certainty for a casual gun user gripped by extreme stress. Merchants reading this book will range from individuals who have never fired a shotgun to individuals who know their way around a shotgun better than they know their spouse. Consequently, my recommendations apply to the casual or inexperienced gun user rather than the individual who fires 10,000 rounds yearly in trap or skeet events.

Amazingly, old, narrow minded police administrators, truly conservative, crew cut, white boxer shorts types, maintained a nearly religious phobia against autoloaders of any kind. They relied mostly on mechanically operated firearms because they were theoretically more reliable than the autoloader. Perhaps they acquired their negative attitudes about autoloaders in the military? However, they failed to view the interaction of gun and user together as a functioning unit. In my own agency (IRS:CID), range malfunctions virtually disappeared when we traded in our pump-action Remington 870's for Remington 11-87 autoloaders.

Some experts offer a plausible argument the sudden switch to semi-automatic pistols was aided, in part, by the wholesale retirements of World War II vintage police brass during the late 1970's, thus clearing the way for more contemporary and progressive thinking. To give a sterling example of obsolete police thinking, when I joined the U.S. Treasury Department in 1966, one could still find police administrators advocating that an empty chamber be kept under a revolver's hammer for "safety." This was a valid safety practice with single action revolvers and early double action revolvers which lacked an internal hammer block.

The comments made regarding the use of cover apply with even greater urgency when using shoulder weapons. Shoulder weapons are especially awkward to use around the side of cover opposite your shooting side. That is, a right handed shooter firing a shotgun around the left side of an object. Consequently, if a shotgun is available in your personal defense zone, you must ensure "strong side" cover is available. For this reason, anyone who is serious about using shoulder weapons for law enforcement or self defense, should learn to become ambidextrous with them. If you must fire around the left side of cover, shoot the shoulder weapon left handed.

Other Weapons for Gunshop Owners

While most knowledgeable people automatically select the shotgun as a defensive firearm, gunshop personnel not manning the sales floor are probably better armed if they are equipped with a short barreled, magazine fed carbine, chambered for a handgun cartridge, such as the Marlin Camp Carbine or Ruger's new Police Carbine fitted with either a ghost ring sight or a scope no more powerful than 1.5X and used with hollowpoint ammunition. Another carbine which comes to mind is the good old M-1 carbine provided commercial hollowpoint or soft point ammunition is used rather than full metal jacket military issue stuff. In the hands of a trained marksman, the carbine can be used against adversaries in close proximity to store personnel. In effect, you may take shots with the carbine which may not be taken with the shotgun. Also, the carbine's longer length sometimes results in a substantial increase in velocity over the same cartridge fired in a handgun. Thus, its ability to stop a felon is increased. In most instances, carbines chambered for the .223 Remington or 7.62 x 39mm would not be appropriate for use in retail shops due to the risk of over-penetration. Likewise, carbines chambered for traditional deer hunting cartridges such as the .30-30, .30-06 or .308 would not be a wise choice for self defense within the point-blank confines of a retail shop for the same reason.

In comparing the shotgun with a carbine, you must recognize one is not necessarily better than the other. Rather, each has its own tactical advantages and disadvantages which must be weighed in order to select the shoulder weapon right for your needs. The shotgun hits hard without significant over-penetration when buckshot loads are used. However, recoil is uncomfortable for casual gun users, particularly smaller statured individuals. Also, shotguns often have a psychological effect on the individual it is pointed at. Often, resistance ceases when the shotgun is displayed, reducing the need to actually have to fire a gun to eliminate a deadly threat. The carbines are light and handy, carry a generous supply of ammunition, and are more quickly reloaded. When comparing carbines to handguns, the advantage for the carbine is not that it might deliver its round to the target with a bit more energy but that the shoulder fired weapon is far more accurate than the handgun during felonious encounters, particularly as the range or distance gets much beyond seven to 10 yards. As previously stated, shoulder fired weapons are almost always better choices for individuals who are not likely to be the first person confronted by an armed robber.

CHAPTER SEVEN

MARKSMANSHIP TRAINING

Firing a handgun is a learned skill, just like learning to play a musical instrument or being good at any particular sport. Generally, the more one practices, the better one gets provided you don't practice improper shooting techniques. Also, many shooting techniques taught as recently as the 1960's are no longer used. At the time, firearms instructors often adapted or blindly applied basic target shooting fundamentals to combat shooting. For the most part, it didn't work. Also, instructors of that era were much less forgiving of variations in human anatomy because they didn't have to be. Prior to the civil rights movement, a candidate for the New York City Police Department had to be 5'8" in stocking feet, 5'10" for state troopers. Minimum height requirements were common throughout law enforcement. As a result, instructors didn't have to deal with major variations in size and physical strength and ability. Consequently, it has now become necessary to be more flexible in how students are permitted to handle firearms. Before we start punching holes in paper, let's talk about some shooting fundamentals.

Grip

When fired, a gun behaves somewhat like a wily squirrel. That is, it senses the weakest part of your grip and tries to escape in that direction. If you don't believe me, try this. If you are right handed, fire one round unsupported in a conventional bullseye target stance and notice the handgun moves towards your left or where the fingers can't quite wrap around the butt. Next, invert your hand and fire one round up side down. The handgun will now move to the right! Next, turn your hand palm up and fire with the handgun on its right side. The gun will now recoil upwards. Lastly, turn your palm facing downwards and the handgun will also recoil downwards. In order to grip the handgun properly, the less exposed butt surface you have, the easier it is to control the handgun.

Try this, hold an imaginary handgun in your shooting hand. Your fingertips should be about one inch from the palm. Next, take the heel of the non-shooting hand and fill the space between the fingertips and palm of the shooting hand, this grip fully encircles the butt and is especially effective with autoloaders. Use all ten fingers to shoot the handgun. I've witnessed shooters dangling their pinkies in mid-air as though they were drinking a cup of tea. The handgun should be gripped firmly but not with a white knuckled death grip. The amount of gripping force needed to keep your pesky three year old child from running off is just about right for the handgun.

Books devoted entirely to shooting techniques provide much more in-depth coverage of shooting fundamentals. Unfortunately, all too many authors discuss this or that grip, then pronounce it as best for everyone. We need to be a bit more flexible. Most of you will have hands of average proportions, be they small, medium, large, or X-large. Some, however, have very long fingers and short palms while in others, the opposite is true. Then there are individuals with thick, thick, really thick hands, often accompanied by short, stumpy fingers. These are usually the individuals who were forced, as children, to take piano lessons! Yet others have hands resembling Alaskan king crabs. Unfortunately, one grip does not fit all.

Grip is critically important because this is where body and the gun come together. In order to obtain the right grip, you must start with a gun that fits you. Aftermarket grips may be purchased as an aid to better gun/user fit. Also, it is better to have a lower capacity handgun that fits your hand than a high capacity gun that doesn't. There are so many handgun models available most anyone can find a grip that suits him or her. For example, if you have short hands, a Glock Model 17 or 19 will almost always fit better than a SIG-226 because the reach to the trigger is shorter. Conversely, individuals with hands resembling catchers' mitts would be wise to avoid the Smith and Wesson Model 3913. Instead, they might take a look at the Heckler and Koch Model USP.

Proper two-handed grip on auto pistol. Note no portion of the pistol's grip is visible and support hand is slightly forward of the shooting hand.

While it is common to cross the thumbs behind the hammer when gripping the revolver, author prefers this grip which allows for greater control of the revolver. Note the S&W "K" frame revolver looks like a miniature because of model's very large hands.

This occasionally encountered shooting grip does little in controlling recoil and should be avoided.

"Cup and Saucer" grip. While still taught in some NRA shooting schools, this grip should be avoided because support hand does not assist with recoil recovery.

This bizarre Hollywood shooting style was used in one scene of the "Godfather." Never take tactical lessons from television or the movies.

Ideally, the handgun will act as a linear extension of the shooting arm when gripped properly. For a time, it was fashionable to hook the index finger of the non shooting hand around the front of the trigger guard. However, this technique has fallen into disuse. With autoloaders, it is important to remember not to cross the thumbs behind the slide, a holdover from revolver days that refuses to die. Not only can this result in a painful injury as the slide rips through your thumb, you may also induce a malfunction during a real life confrontation. With a revolver, placing the thumb behind the hammer is a bad idea as under stress you may interfere with the hammer and prevent the gun from firing.

Stance

Over the years, many stances have come and gone such as the FBI crouch and various hip shooting techniques. A proper stance enhances our ability to control the handgun, to hit the target, to traverse and engage multiple targets if necessary, and possibly to absorb a bullet or other blow without getting knocked off our feet.

There are several major stances in use. The two most popular are the Isosceles stance and the Weaver stance. There are several variations of these stances.

The Isosceles Stance

The Isosceles stance is named for the fact that the arms

With the isosceles stance, recoil is controlled by a triangle formed by the shooting arms. Recoil energy is centered between both arms.

Body should be upright or leaning slightly into the handgun. Weight is evenly distributed over both feet.

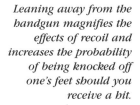

Leaning away from the handgun magnifies the effects of recoil and increases the probability of being knocked off one's feet should you receive a hit.

form an isosceles triangle with the body. The shooter pretty much faces the target head on. Its chief advantage is that it is probably the most natural stance to assume as it requires little or no thought. In fact, if you were to hand a gun to a totally untrained civilian and ask him to engage a silhouette target with two hands, he would automatically fall into a perfect or nearly perfect Isosceles stance. Incidentally, the triangle is the strongest geometric shape. You will notice it is used for tripods, weight support, and structural crossbracing. The stance also allows for excellent traversing, and most shooters can cover a 180 degree arc without moving their feet.

The Weaver Stance

The Weaver stance requires a bit more practice to learn. This stance dates to at least the 1930's and was re-discovered and used successfully in competition by Jack Weaver during the late 1950's. A person assuming the Weaver stance places his body and feet as though he was boxing. Thus, the strong foot

Blading away from the adversary makes you a smaller target and directs the recoil of your handgun directly into the shooting arm. Of course, one-hand unsupported shooting should only be done when absolutely necessary.

is back and the weak foot is forward while the body is slightly bladed or turned away from the adversary. For police officers, the stance offers somewhat better protection against a sudden kick to the groin or a jab to the solar plexus in situations which don't quite require a handgun. But, if it becomes necessary, the officer need not do a foot shuffle to get into a proper shooter's stance. The disadvantage for police officers is that return fire may slip between the front and back panels of a bullet resistant vest. For both civilians and police officers, traversing to the side opposite the shooting hand is a bit more difficult with the Weaver stance.

The Weaver stance, with its unique push/pull tension exerted upon the handgun, coupled with the fact the stance allows better absorption of recoil, often results in higher range scores. Affirmative action programs removed sex/height requirements with the result that large numbers of females and smaller males were becoming law enforcement officers. All things being equal, larger people, with more sheer muscle mass, are usually stronger than smaller people and are less affected by the effects of recoil. But, as more and more females joined the ranks, firearms instructors found the Weaver stance allowed smaller individuals to better manage the handgun during recoil and recoil recovery. This often allowed a marginal shooter to shoot a qualifying score. The chief advantage of the Weaver stance is also its chief fault: the stance sometimes fails because it requires the shooter to push with his shooting hand while pulling rearward with the non-shooting hand. As a result, every appendage requires its own set of contradictory instructions which can get mighty confusing when the lead is incoming.

One other serious problem with the Weaver stance is that in sudden, dire emergencies, police officers often instinctively revert to the Isosceles stance because of it utter naturalness. During my years with IRS:CID, the Weaver stance was introduced and taught as an option. However, during highly stressful tactical exercises, particularly the trips through the New York City Police Department's "fun house," agents trained in the Weaver stance invariably reverted to the Isosceles stance when it became necessary to engage a "felon."

Perhaps I've mellowed a bit but I have become more concerned with what I refer to as a total body presentation rather than with the execution of this stance or that with technical perfection. Not everyone fits in the same exact mold. You will note in the martial arts, as well as boxing, participants display varying stances yet maintain proper balance and go on to win. Consequently, I did not force individuals to use a stance that didn't feel natural for them. As a result, some agents used the Isosceles stance, others used the Weaver stance, while many more adopted a hybrid stance that combined the best features of each.

As federal agents often retire at an older age than uniformed police officers, I found it necessary to make allowances for the physical restrictions imposed by middle age such as an arthritic back, bad knees, and assorted old sports injuries from previous lives. Likewise, readers of this book will cover all age groups. A 21-year old will naturally be more flexible than a 68-year old.

One of the greatest advantages of the Weaver stance, and one often overlooked by gun writers, is that the Weaver stance is the only stance that allows you to get the greatest amount of

Author prefers straight arm variation of the Weaver stance. Recoil is directed up the arm and into the body for maximum control and a quick recovery for follow-up shots, if needed.

your body behind cover while still being able to fire effectively. Even advocates of the Isosceles stance fall into the Weaver stance, or some variation thereof, when shooting from cover.

For enhanced control of handgun and quicker recoil recovery, force of recoil should travel directly into the arm with unsupported shooting or the Weaver Stance. Here, shooter has bent his wrist and is not sufficiently bladed away from the target. Recoil recovery will compromise speed and effectiveness of subsequent shots.

The Isosceles stance may be considered to be the last and best refinement of a long line of stances in which the shooter faces his target square shouldered and head-on. Thus, it was in wide use before firearms instructors began placing increasing emphasis on shooting from cover. A shooter who instinctively reverts to the Isosceles stance at cover will expose from one half to two thirds of his body to hostile fire.

I prefer to use the "Chapman" variation of the Weaver stance. With this variation, the shooting arm is kept straight rather than bent. I like it because it works great with cover and the arm serves as a giant pointer to guide the shooting eye to the target. This variation is actually simpler than the original, bent arm stance because the shooting arm is punched straight out and as the non-shooting hand is slightly ahead of the shooting hand, rearward tension applied to the handgun by the non shooting hand is automatic. No thought required.

Breath Control

This was a biggie during the bullseye era and is still critically important in gallery type competition. It is my opinion breath control can be pretty much ignored as a combat shooting element. You may have to return effective fire after being chased down the block, into your back room, after being punched or shot in the gut, kicked in the testicles, or when you have a mouth full of pepperoni pizza. Also, it is extremely difficult to breathe normally after your body becomes thoroughly adrenalized anyway. The body controls breathing with the subconscious mind. Leave the function where it is. Your conscious mind will be pre-occupied with more important things and there's no point in doing for your body what your body can do for itself.

Sight Alignment

It's very simple: the bullet goes where you point or aim the gun. Point shooting is one method of aligning the gun with the target that's effective at close range. Point shooting requires less time to return fire than formal aiming. Also, full use of the sights requires adequate lighting and assumes you can use the sights with your eyes as is. Point shooting, as you may have guessed, is aiming your entire body at your target with the gun serving as a natural extension of the shooting arm. The gun is either at, or just below eye level.

A more effective method of shooting involves bringing the gun up to approximate eye level and acquiring what is most often described as a "flash sight picture." A technique I've used with great success is to tape over the rear sight of my student's handgun. They are then instructed to merely center the front sight in the middle of the gun frame and to align the front sight where they want to hit. However, they are not looking through the front sight but slightly above it. Therefore, the gun is slightly lower than their line of sight to their intended target. In effect, they are both pointing and aiming, much like a shotgun is fired. This is highly effective in reduced light and at short range(up to about 15 feet). This technique is especially useful for shooters who wear glasses and who cannot quite obtain a usable sight picture with or without the glasses. During an actual confrontation, if you have time to change your glasses, you're probably not in mortal danger.

A number of years ago I was a student/instructor for a

course at the SIG Academy in Exeter, New Hampshire. I convinced those in charge to completely remove the rear sight from one pistol, which I then used. Much to my amazement, my scores didn't suffer one bit although I will admit that my shots at 25 yards were a bit more scattered. It was only necessary to put the front sight on target and get about the same amount of slide showing on either side of the front sight, exactly as a traditional shotgun (without rear sight) is used. However, I sincerely believe I shaved a quarter second from the time interval between gun in holster and hole in target.

While on the subject of sights, some sights are better than others. I prefer a coarse sight picture with lots of daylight around the front sight. Frankly, I've already proven to myself I don't even need a rear sight. Fine sights are okay for target shooting but useless for defensive shooting. If you have difficulty using the sights on your handgun except in bright light, you may explore changing the sights. Novak sights are becoming quite popular on both new guns and for retro-fitting. You may also have a gunsmith widen the existing rear sight notch of your handgun a bit.

A new sighting system which I have used and which I highly recommend is the Ashley Express Sight by Ashley Research and Engineering (P.O. Box 330806, Ft. Worth, TX 76163). The express sight consists of a prominent front sight and a shallow "V" rear sight. They're very fast to align, usable in reduced light, and very forgiving of age related declines in eyesight. In fact, my carry gun, a Glock 26, is equipped with express sights.

A serious student of defensive handgunning should master point shooting as well as aimed shooting because, as the distance stretches to 15 feet or more, point shooting becomes less effective and the handgun must be aimed at what we wish to hit. While felony confrontations generally occur at close range, the robber's backup gunman may be more than 50 feet away when he starts firing at you. Through practice you may determine the maximum distance at which you are effective with anything less than aimed fire. There are many experts, most of whom are more heavily credentialed than me, who feel point shooting is an obsolete discipline likely to get you killed. However, if you limit yourself to aimed fire, and are unable to define the sights in poor light conditions during an actual confrontation, you will not have a plan B.

Regarding laser sights, I recommend they be avoided. Lasers require batteries and tiny electrical contacts, both of which are likely to fail if not maintained. Also, the few models I've used were difficult to sight in and even more difficult to keep properly sighted. I have observed numerous shooters using lasers. If the little red dot didn't materialize, they began looking for the dot rather than fire with the factory sights. There's no future in this. Some of the more respected names in defensive shooting include guys like Cooper, Ayoob, Pride, Chapman, Jordan, Shaw, etc. To the best of my knowledge, none are using laser equipped handguns.

Laser sights may have a narrow band of tactical merit in a home defense situation where you're aware of an intruder and you are waiting patiently in ambush. I could also envision them being used by tactical police units in certain isolated instances. However, people tend to rely on all sorts of electronic wizardry to compensate for missing skills. They use them as a crutch in order to avoid truly learning how to shoot the handgun, or so they think. If the fundamentals of shooting are not mastered, the handgun may be pulled off the target while firing, resulting in a miss or superficial wound, with or without lasers. Therefore, lasers will not compensate for poor marksmanship and failure to master the shooting fundamentals, while those who are good marksmen and have mastered the fundamentals will derive virtually no benefit from lasers. Another potential hazard with lasers is, under stress, the user may become preoc-cupied with the laser dot and fail to properly identify the target as a lawful one. Under stress, we tend to see only what's directly in front of our eyes. Peripheral vision suffers. This is often called tunnel vision. Under stress, we may see the laser dot but not see it is located on the chest of a loved one.

Trigger Control

If the grip is where the gun and shooter come together, the trigger is where the gun and mind come together. This is the transfer point where psycho-motor instructions are converted into mechanical energy, namely, making the gun go bang. Of all the shooting fundamentals, lack of trigger control is the single greatest detriment to accuracy.

Far too many experts pre-occupy themselves with the rearward travel of the trigger when discussing trigger control. In his book, *Fast and Fancy Revolver Shooting*, Ed McGivern stated a trigger must travel forward at exactly the same speed as it traveled rearward. In an effort to test and possibly contradict him, I deliberately "jerked" the trigger rearward, then tried jerking it forward. That is, I tried to race the trigger forward. Much to my amazement, the rush forward had a much more pronounced jerking effect than jerking rearward. My entire shooting arm jumped. McGivern was absolutely right. I credit my own ability to master the double action trigger pull to McGivern's advice, which, incidentally, was contained merely in a line or two somewhere in the middle of the book, totally without emphasis.

As with any endeavor, practice is needed. Of course, the gun must fit. For some reason or other, I could never quite acclimate myself to the trigger pulls on most Smith and Wesson pistols. It seemed the sear released in the wrong place and my trigger finger was starting to curl to the right (I'm right handed) and was running out of travel space before the sear released. Much to my amazement, a 1/8" inch pad at the front of the trigger caused the sear to release in exactly the right place for me.

Try this, place your trigger finger on an imaginary trigger, then start moving that finger rearward. If you're right handed, you will notice that the finger tip first moves slightly left, then straight back, then, at the end of the trigger stroke, it begins moving to the right. The trigger finger is moving in an arc. Ideally, the sear should release to fire the gun just at the point where the trigger finger is at or near the end of its direct rear-

ward travel and before curling back on itself to the right. If the
gun you've chosen or are considering, does not fire at the point
I've described, the gun is probably too small for you. SIG
owners have the option to adjust the trigger through the addition of a factory optional "short" trigger. The trigger really isn't
short, but rather, is thinner. If more distance is needed between
the trigger and backstrap of the handgun, aftermarket grips
may prove helpful.

During my years with IRS:CID, we went through three
complete firearms changeovers. In the late 1960's, we received
enough Smith and Wesson Chief's Specials and Colt Detective
Specials to outfit the entire division. In the early 1980's, we
switched to K-frame Smith and Wesson Models 10 and 15
revolvers. Finally, in the late 1980's, we adopted the SIG Sauer
Model 228 pistol. I function tested each and every handgun
that passed through the Manhattan District. I noted considerable variations in trigger quality, even with guns bearing
consecutive serial numbers. Some were silky smooth while
others felt as though they'd been lubricated with sand.

Most double action trigger pulls will average 12 pounds
right from the factory. I never found a factory 12 pound pull to
adversely affect accuracy for anyone with average hands and
strength. What destroys accuracy is gritty, uneven trigger pulls,
or a trigger that "stacks." That is, it suddenly becomes very
heavy just as the sear is about to release.

Guns intended for personal defense must fire every time you
pull the trigger. Consequently, any gunsmithing performed on a
combat handgun should be directed to smoothing and polishing
metal parts rather than lightening the trigger pull, hammer fall, or
cutting coils from springs. My feeling is if the factory wanted this
or that spring one or two coils shorter, they would have made it
that way. Needless to say, not all gunsmiths are really gunsmiths.
Gunsmiths must be chosen with the same care one might use to
select a surgeon. Most gunsmiths are truly competent but a few
don't know their backside from the proverbial hole in the
ground. Remember, a light, target trigger job is not a substitute
for mastering the fundamentals of shooting.

For safety reasons, a light, target trigger pull also has no place on a defensive handgun which will be used in physically strenuous, high stress confrontations. Further, Massad Ayoob, an internationally recognized firearms expert, stated in a recent article, any trigger that releases with less than four pounds pressure would be described as a "hair trigger" in a court of law. A so-called "hair trigger" makes it easier for opposing attorneys to impeach your character or to suggest you fired your handgun accidentally.

Perhaps the greatest "trigger abuse" I have witnessed is a shooter backing off on the strain screw contained in the forward edge of the grip on Smith and Wesson revolvers. If you remove the grip panels from your S&W, you'll notice the strain screw provides tension to the mainspring that powers the hammer. You will also notice the screw does not have a separate lock screw to hold it in place. In other words, this screw is non-adjustable. If you loosen it, it will continue to unscrew on its own. At some point, the revolver will no longer fire. This screw must be kept tight at all times. It is not an action adjustment screw as many believe. If the double action pull on your S&W feels heavier than 12 pounds, the gun requires the attention of a competent gunsmith rather than your screwdriver.

In order to develop proper trigger control, the trigger finger and trigger must make contact somewhere before the first joint. For most people, the optimum contact point will occur at the middle of the first finger segment or slightly inward towards the first joint. If you must insert your finger beyond the first joint, chances are you have very long fingers or large hands and the gun is a bit too small for you. Once again, aftermarket grips may be needed to adjust the fit. Do not go beyond the first finger joint.

An excellent exercise for strengthening the trigger finger and developing a smooth trigger stroke is to do the following: making sure (double check) the gun is completely unloaded (magazine removed, chambers empty) point the gun in a safe direction* and work the trigger in cadence with ordinary dance music. Each click of the trigger, both at the trigger return and

---

A "safe direction" is one in which any accidentally fired bullet would be safely stopped and contained, with no human injury caused.

hammer fall, must fall on the beat. All you are doing is substituting the trigger for the hand and foot tapping that most people sub-consciously do with upbeat music. At first you'll miss the beat, but very quickly you'll be able to get the trigger to click exactly on the beat. Occasional practice thereafter will keep your trigger finger conditioned.

An amateurish trigger manipulation technique I've witnessed many times was trigger "staging." Staging is a technique in which the trigger is pulled in double action mode to the point where the hammer is nearly ready to fall. Then, the trigger pull is interrupted and re-commenced so as to fire the gun as though it had been fired single action. In effect, the gun is being fired pseudo-single action but the trigger is being used to cock the hammer, rather than the thumb and hammer spur. It is far easier to stage a Smith and Wesson trigger than a Colt trigger. For this reason, many unknowing people thought that S&W's were better guns than Colts because the Colt wasn't conducive to staging. Likewise, the reputations of gunsmiths sometimes teetered on how easily their action jobs could be staged.

Trigger staging serves no practical or tactical purpose and should not be practiced. Nor should the quality or suitability of a handgun be decided upon a technique that's irrelevant to realistic combat shooting. Staging, even under calm range conditions, is a hit or miss proposition. It won't work during an actual confrontation because your mind will be pre-occupied with staging the trigger for a single action-like let-off rather than trying to hit your adversary. Secondly, staging introduces at least a one second delay to each round of your return fire. That's an awful lot of time to waste in a gun battle.

The only way to become accustomed to the double/single action trigger pull of most autopistols is to practice at the range. You will need to fire two round strings, first round double action, second round single action, hundreds of times in order to develop muscle memory. Regrettably, some people use the first double action pull as a throwaway round merely to cock the handgun, at which time serious shooting begins. This is nonsense.

With regard to mastering the single action trigger pull, there are two schools of thought. Some experts advise releasing the trigger just far enough to re-set the sear, while others advocate a complete release of the trigger to insure the trigger is not short stroked and to insure the sear is re-set. Those of you who own a bathtub full of handguns are more likely to have problems here than the person who limits himself to one pistol. Glocks and S&W's have a rather quick trigger recovery while SIGs and Berettas require a bit more forward trigger travel to re-set the sear. If you own a bunch of guns, I recommend full or nearly full release of the trigger to ensure your body isn't shooting a SIG while your mind is in Glock mode. This will help guard against a shooter induced stoppage. In either case, it is advisable to condition your finger to go a bit beyond the sear re-set point to insure against short stroking the trigger.

One last thing about triggers, never install trigger shoes on a handgun intended for self defense shooting. They have a tendency to loosen, then jam against the trigger guard with the result the gun will not fire. Frequently, trigger shoes are wider than the trigger guard with the result you risk an accidental discharge when holstering the pistol, should the shoe catch on the lip of the holster.

CHAPTER 8

DEFENSIVE
SHOOTING TECHNIQUES

"Fast is fine but accuracy is final."

—Wyatt Earp

I've had countless opportunities to observe civilians as they practiced with their handguns. Those who make a feeble attempt to practice combat style shooting often imitate what they see on television. At best, they have but an approximate idea of what they should be doing. This is understandable because the average citizen seeking information on how to become a better combat marksman will find himself bombarded with conflicting techniques and points of view. Consequently, before we discuss shooting techniques, we need to discuss the mechanics of how information on shooting techniques is disseminated.

Regarding shooting techniques, we might say there is a "circle of information" which describes how information passes from one user to another. As a result, gunwriters are in a position to greatly influence contemporary techniques. Also, many people believe if it appears in print, it must be true. Many police firearms instructors are also gun enthusiasts and subscribe to popular gun magazines. Consequently, a new shooting technique first reported in the gun press finds its way to the police shooting range where it is tested and perhaps modified into yet another variation. If the new technique or variation works better than the existing one, chances are it may be adopted. Perhaps there is no better example than the "Weaver stance," which we will examine shortly. This stance was first used in competition shooting, then taught in the private shooting academies and reported upon in gun magazines. It was subsequently tested and adopted or taught by hundreds of law enforcement agencies, including the FBI. Conversely, some improvements in the art and science of defensive shooting had to be learned the hard way by taking casualties in actual live fire situations. This is exemplified by changes in training techniques resulting from the tragic Newhall incident, also discussed in this book, in which four California highway patrolmen lost their lives in a single gun battle.

Gunwriters specializing in handgun topics seem to draw their expertise from two endeavors: some made their bones on the competition circuit and established national reputations for their skill with a handgun. Others, bring to the pen, years of hard law enforcement experience in truly dangerous conditions. Often, these men are gunfight veterans and write from personal experience. Jim Cirillo, a former member of the short lived New York City Police Department's stakeout squad, was involved in a dozen gun battles. When Jim Cirillo has something to say, I listen carefully, very, very carefully! In between is a third class of gunwriter with credentials in both law enforcement and competition. Unfortunately, there is also the occasional gunwriter whom I suspect has "shot" all his felons with a typewriter. Yet others have parlayed a single minor brush with someone having a bad day into a writing career as an "experienced" gunwriter. As you can see, just because a shooting or combat technique is endorsed by a particular writer or shooting academy doesn't necessarily mean it's right, wrong, or correct for you.

Some shooting techniques producing higher competition scores are also valid for self defense. Others are not. As you immerse in the science of self defense shooting, you must either accept or reject this or that technique. Following are some suggestions to assist you.

1. The simpler the technique, the easier it is to program it into muscle memory and the less practice required to maintain an acceptable level of skill. Also, the simpler the technique, the more likely it is to work under conditions of extreme stress such as being shot at.

2. Conversely, more complex techniques require more practice to maintain acceptable skill levels and are more likely to fail under stress.

3. The technique you select for yourself must be entirely compatible with your physiology. For example, while the kneeling position reduces the amount of your body exposed to gunfire, individuals who cannot quickly assume the kneeling position because of arthritis or an old football injury should not use it.

4. Techniques which rely on gross motor skills work better under stress than techniques requiring fine motor skills. Gross motor skills utilize the major muscle groups while fine motor skills use the smaller muscles of the fingers, require varying degrees of eye/hand coordination, and often require a degree of tactile sensitivity. Often, these suffer the most during stress. Consequently, a shooter should not rely on a fine motor skill to perform a task that can be done with a gross motor skill.

The type of practice you engage in must reasonably simulate defensive shooting techniques which can save your life. Bullseye shooting will no more prepare you for armed confrontations than driving a Hyundai will prepare you for the Indianapolis 500. With bullseye shooting, the shooter soon becomes pre-occupied with shooting groups in the center of the black, especially if people are watching. He'll try both single and double action fire. Soon, he realizes he can group a bit better shooting single action, and the double action mode is forgotten altogether.

However, before we discuss marksmanship training, we must first be able to see the target. You must know whether or not you shoot better with or without glasses, if you wear them. I once had a disconcerting experience when a storekeeper retained me to teach him defensive shooting techniques. He'd owned a gun for several years. We put up a target at about seven yards. Upon drawing his revolver, he began tilting his head up and back trying to find the sights first with the upper half of the bifocals, then the lower half. Imagine these antics during a gunfight! I've seen the problem before with federal agents going into middle age with the result that their eyesight changed so suddenly they didn't immediately recognize the link between eye sight and a sudden drop in scores.

To set the record straight, hands-on training with an ordinary instructor is infinitely superior than trying to learn from a book written by a well known instructor. The best I can do is to whet your appetite. Appendix B contains a partial listing of schools and academies, all of which offer competent instruction at reasonable cost.

Setting Realistic Training Goals

First, a little war story. A number of year ago I attended an advanced pistol school in Austin, Texas, with representatives of Glock, SIG Sauer, and Smith & Wesson. On a particular afternoon I had my back to the range when I heard the unmistakable staccato burst of a sub-machine gun, or so I thought. I turned and saw Tom Campbell of Team Smith & Wesson, and one of the world's top shooters, firing 10 round bursts from a stock Smith and Wesson handgun in about one second! That's a cyclic rate of 600 rounds per minute! Even more impressive was the target. The center was gone. No misses.

During the early part of this century lived a portly man named Ed McGivern (who I mentioned earlier), a trick and exhibition shooter. Mr. McGivern could fire five rounds into a playing card with a revolver, in slightly under one half second. Thus, his cyclic rate was comparable to that of Tom Campbell, but with a revolver of all things!

I've given you this information so you can appreciate what a handgun is capable of in professional hands. Also, you need a relative yardstick against which to measure the reasonable and realistic performance standards I want you to strive for. None of the following exercises I have tailored for you will ever require you to fire faster than one round per half second, or three rounds in one second. In effect, I'm going to give you the keys to a car capable of 180 miles per hour, but require you to go no faster than sixty miles per hour.

Try this: Look at the second hand or digit on your wristwatch, then, tap your finger or a pencil at your desk. Tap once per second plus another tap that falls exactly between the second marks. Your cyclic rate will be one round per half second. In a space of one second, you will tap three times: once at the beginning and end of the second and once in the middle. Practice tapping until the cadence becomes fixed in your mind. Reinforce the cadence with daily practice. Then, start the cadence from memory and apply time to it to see how close you are to remembering the cadence. Adjust your speed accordingly.

Targets

Avoid bullseye targets. You also don't need conventional silhouette targets just yet. An excellent training target for civilian purposes is either the FBI "Q" target or the NRA international rapid fire pistol target if you disregard the scoring rings. These are readily available at well stocked gunshops. The "Q" target is suitable for your needs because the emphasis is on hits rather than groups.

The target I most recommend to civilians who are just beginning to master the art of defensive shooting is one you can easily make yourself. The next time you have occasion to visit a well stocked lumber yard or building supply house, purchase a roll of paper underlayment (not tar paper). In some stores, this may be purchased by the foot. Underlayment is a coarse, fibrous paper generally used under linoleum flooring. Or, an even easier source of raw materials is used file folders. Next, borrow the oval serving tray, the one used for Sunday dinners. Lay it upside down on the paper or file folder. Using it as a template, draw a line around it. Cut a bunch of ovals with a scissors. These will be your targets. Besides underlayment and folders, you may use any coarse paper available, including heavy duty wrapping paper or old wall paper if you can get it to relax.

Training ovals are convenient to use because the target carriers at most ranges have but a single clip intended for a

Discarded file folders can make excellent training targets. All that is needed is a serving dish used as a template, a pencil, and a pair of scissors.

Target made from file folder, using a serving dish as a template, yields a target that approximates the vital area of an adult male. (Incidently, the model in this photo stands 6'2").

bullseye target. The training ovals we've made can be used with standard target clips without falling off or curling inward. Also, if you hold the oval over your chest you will notice it approximately covers the vital area between the notch at the top of your rib cage to your navel and from nipple to nipple. The desired point of impact is center of mass, approximately between the nipples. I might add this is not as generous a target as it appears to be up close. When fired at seven yards under realistic time limits as explained below, it will prove challenging to even experienced gun users.

The object will be to hit any of these targets anywhere but every time. Remember this goal: **anywhere but every time.** A hit at the edge counts the same as a hit in the middle. It will apply to every exercise we do. Do not pencil or mark in an aiming point of any kind. Felons are not so obliging. A blank target is a bit more realistic. This has been one of my pet complaints with most silhouette targets: law enforcement officers use aiming points in training when no such crutch is likely to be available on the street. The Speedwell "B-21" "PC" Modified Target, a target I designed for my former agency, is completely devoid of aiming points and is sized to simulate a human of about 165 pounds rather than a 400 pound behemoth justifying the use of light artillery.

It should be noted many of the training academies listed Appendix B would consider the training oval to be too generous a target. They rightly point out that in order to stop a felon from doing whatever it was that prompted you to shoot, you must deliver an adequate bullet to the central nervous system. This is a rather narrow target, perhaps four inches wide, that extends from the hairline to the waist. It's rather easy to get theory and reality confused. Considering that young law enforcement officers, receiving regular firearms training from professional, full time firearms instructors, can only manage an average 20 percent hit rate, anywhere on a felon's hide, I stand by my opinion the training oval represents a **practical** target for the average citizen who may not get to practice as much as he should.

Distance

Initially, all firing will be at approximately 10 feet. You don't have to bring a tape measure with you. It's not that important. The vast majority of armed encounters occur within seven feet and virtually all of them occur within seven yards. Robberies are not done by telegram. It's a personal, in your face event. So, not only are we practicing at realistic distances but at that distance, it is easier to attain your marksmanship goals within the prescribed time limits.

Following are some range safety tips, then you're ready to go.

To the greatest extent possible, you will practice with a holstered pistol if permitted by the range personnel. Do not practice with the pistol on the table or bench. When drawing and holstering, keep your finger **off** the trigger and outside the trigger guard. The trigger finger does not enter the trigger guard until you are on target and intend to fire. It is removed when the handgun starts back for the holster. Pistols with exposed hammers which remain cocked after the first round **must be de-cocked** before holstering, while the pistol is still facing downrange. If you don't follow this advice, you will eventually shoot yourself. In each instance, you will first go through the motions of the exercise before applying any time limits.

Cross draw and shoulder holsters, which are both sexy and popular with the celluloid commandos, should not be used. Both types make it easy to over-swing the target and are quite dangerous to your non shooting arm as well as those standing next to or behind you. For these reasons, I recommend all of the following exercises be done while wearing the handgun on the same side as your shooting hand. I recommend that whatever holster you select, the trigger guard must be covered. Holsters which permit you to insert your finger into the trigger guard while fully holstered are conducive to accidental discharges. Incidentally, most law enforcement agencies do not permit crossdraw firing on the range and holsters which expose the trigger guard are not permitted.

If your pistol is capable of both single and double action fire, begin each string in double action. The bulk of your shooting should be with two hands. The gun is easier to hit with and control when held by two hands.

Before doing anything, check with the range staff to insure they do not have a prohibition against defensive type shooting. Some ranges do not permit firing faster than one round per second. Other ranges may not permit the use of silhouette targets of any kind. If an alternate range is not readily available, simply hang a conventional bullseye target backwards and use that. Also, if they do not permit drawing from the holster, you may begin each exercise from a ready position. In the ready position, the gun is pointed downrange, never at your feet or at the floor just in front of you. That is, the gun is in your hands, anywhere between shoulder and waist level and your finger is outside the trigger guard. To fire, merely raise the gun the distance required to achieve sight alignment or to point shoot, place your finger on the trigger and fire.

You will attempt to achieve your marksmanship goals in six stages. Before firing, please refer to the additional range safety tips contained in the Appendix A. I also recommend you practice these exercises with a friend with whom you may alternate serving as coach. The coach's job will be to remind you to keep your finger out of the trigger guard and also to time you. An inexpensive stop watch is convenient but not necessary.

How long will it take you to achieve these goals? Quite frankly, there's no rush. Try to thoroughly master each of the following stages before proceeding to the next stage. You are not locked into a fixed schedule. But first, you must avoid a nasty habit I see during firearms training which is pausing after each and every round and craning the neck to see where the bullet impacted. Shoot and peek. Shoot and peek. Do that during a gun battle and it's shoot and be shot. Sure, you can see bullet holes in paper but seldom on a real life adversary. More importantly, you will do on the street or in your store what you have conditioned or allowed yourself to do in training, good or bad.

About Trying to Train Yourself

Before going to the range, you must practice drawing and holstering in a safe place with a completely unloaded (double check) pistol or revolver until you are positively keeping your finger out of the trigger guard and off the trigger before ever trying to draw a loaded gun.

If you have purchased a new or used handgun, be sure to read the instructions which came with the handgun and to abide by the manufacturer's suggestions for using their product. If your recently purchased used gun came without instructions, write or call the manufacturer to obtain instructions before using the handgun.

When working with a holster for the first time or testing or breaking in a new holster, have your coach or firearms instructor confirm you are practicing safely. You may also videotape yourself and watch slow motion.

I highly recommend you obtain lessons from a qualified firearms instructor or from a shooting school or academy rather than trying to teach yourself. The following exercises are intended for experienced gun users rather than someone handling firearms for the first time.

Any time firearms are used, a danger of death or serious physical injury exists as a result of your own gun handling or a gun being used by someone else. If you are a new or inexperienced gun user, do not use these exercises without the supervision of a qualified firearms instructor.

Stage One

1. With a holstered pistol, draw, grip the pistol with two hands, and fire one round in three seconds. **Don't cheat.** You must hit the oval. Repeat over and over again until you are comfortable with your performance.

2. Once you can do step one with boring regularity, fire two rounds in three seconds. If you subtract the time it takes to draw and acquire approximate sight alignment, your cyclic rate will work out to approximately one round per half second. Once again, practice this drill until you are bored to tears.

3. Beginning with the pistol in a two handed stance and below shoulder level, bring the pistol to shoulder level and fire one round in two seconds. Once you can do this with regularity and with every round in the oval, fire two rounds in two seconds. You cyclic rate will again be about one round per half second.

The cyclic rate we have established will be fast enough. Most of you will not have the time, the money, the patience, or the inclination to **maintain**, rather than merely achieve, a higher cyclic rate. Tom Campbell maintains his incredible speed by firing over two thousand rounds per week. Besides, you don't need to fire faster. Your goal is to see how fast you can fire **accurately**. Hits win gun battles, not speed.

Stage Two

Once you have achieved the goals in stage one, you may proceed to stage two. Using the cyclic rate of one round per half second, start firing some three and four round strings, then a few five round strings. Adjust the time limit by adding one half second for each additional round fired. Consequently, using two rounds in three seconds from the holster as a base line, a three round string would require three and one-half seconds while a four round string requires four seconds. Do not establish a habit of always firing the same number of rounds. Fire some one round strings, a lot of two and three round strings, some four round strings, and an occasional five round string.

Stage Three

Move your target to seven yards or about half way down a fifty foot indoor range and repeat all of the above exercises necessary to insure 100 percent hits at that distance. If you cannot achieve reliable hits firing two rounds in three seconds, then fire one round in three seconds or two rounds in four seconds and work your way down to three seconds.

Stage Four

About 80 to 90 percent of your practice will be at seven yards but you do need to be competent at greater distances. Run your target out to 50 feet. From the holster, draw and fire two rounds in five seconds. When you are satisfied with your performance you may increase to three rounds in five seconds, then three rounds in four seconds.

Stage Five

Multiple adversary drill

Store owners run a very real chance of have to defend

themselves against more than one adversary. Many merchants are successful at this with nothing more than blind luck. A key to winning against multiple adversaries, even three or four of them, is to merge their respective kill zones as we have discussed earlier.

Note: Do not fire these multiple adversary drills if doing so will cause your bullets to impact into the sidewalls of the range rather than the backstop. Bullet impacts into the side walls causes damage to the range and increases the possibility of injury to you or to others using the range. Outdoor ranges are usually better suited for multiple adversary drills.

Place one target at five to seven feet and another at seven yards. You may have to rent two range points to do this. Draw and fire two rounds at the closer target and one round at the more distant target. Begin with a five second time limit. Then go to a four second time limit and finally a three second time limit.

Next, keep one target at seven to 10 feet and the second target at fifty feet. Fire two rounds at each target starting with the closer target. Begin with a six second time limit and work down to five seconds. At your discretion, you may try to do this exercise in four seconds.

Going back to the first multiple adversary drill, fire two rounds at the closer target, one round at the distant target and return to fire your fourth round at the closer target. A realistic time limit with 100 percent hit certainty is four seconds.

Stage Six

Having achieved your marksmanship/time goals in the preceding five stages, it is time to try concentrating your hits closer to the center of the training oval. At seven yards or less, simply count anything within two inches of the edge of the paper as a miss. At distances greater than seven yards, count anything within one inch of the edge as a miss. Repeat all of the exercises practiced, always trying for 100 percent hit certainty. It is not necessary to go to a smaller target. As previously stated, the oval approximately covers the vital organs of an adult male. If you can honestly hit the training oval, anywhere but every time, your level of marksmanship will be equal to or better than that of the average police officer.

You may now practice on genuine silhouette targets. As these are substantially larger than training ovals or the FBI Q target, do not let the more generously sized target cause your shooting skills to deteriorate. In fact, the silhouette target will be used primarily to acquire a feel, and to condition the mind to shoot at a manlike target. Most commercial ranges have target carriers available for use with silhouette targets. If your point is not so equipped, ask the range officer to change the target carrier for you.

Following are some additional exercises you may practice to increase your overall competence. With competence comes confidence and resourcefulness.

1. Practice some strong hand only shooting. The circumstances may be such that you only have one hand available to fire your handgun. It is important you eliminate any bends at the wrist so recoil energy is transferred straight up the shooting arm as illustrated. When recoil energy is directed away from the shooting arm, recoil is more pronounced and it takes longer to recover from the effects of recoil in order to fire more rounds.

2. Practice weak hand, unsupported shooting. Conceivably, you may be wounded and must then resort to shooting with your left hand or not at all. This must be unsupported shooting because if your strong hand is available to support the weak hand, it's available to shoot the gun. This differs a bit from police training methods which sometimes allow supported weak hand shooting in their qualification courses.

3. Practice reduced light shooting. If you are a member of a gun club, you may have the option of reducing the lighting. Also, if you are using a commercial range and know the owner, he may oblige you by turning down the lights. The lighting should be reduced to a point where you cannot define your sights. If it's too dark to identify the threat, you don't have justification to fire. As a civilian, you are rarely in total blackness. If you cannot control the lighting, you may wear dark sunglasses

on indoor ranges or DeSantis Low Light Simulator Goggles outdoors. The objective is to obscure the sights, not to create total blackness. Police needs are a bit different than yours. Under no circumstances will you be probing blackened rooms for hidden, barricaded gunmen. That's a job for the police.

4. Learn how and when to reload. Reloading is not merely replenishing the ammunition supply. When performed correctly, it is a technique that can save your life. Better yet, ascertain where you may take courses offered by professional instructors and sign up. In most instances tuition will be less than the cost of a handgun. In the back of this book you will find an appendix listing some of the more well known shooting schools and academies. The techniques you learn will much better prepare you for a deadly force confrontation. Needless to say, you must have extra ammunition available in your personal defense zone. This ammunition must be in extra magazines if you are armed with a pistol or a reloading device of your choice if you have a revolver. Attempting to reload "from the box" or from an envelope or coffee can containing loose rounds constitutes a major tactical error during a hostile confrontation. Spare ammunition, along with firearms, must be carried or maintained with the thought it may someday be needed.

It is also wise to use combat reloading techniques while practicing. This helps program the necessary reloading techniques into your sub-conscious mind where they need to be. Pistol and revolver reloading will be covered in the next chapter.

With regard to storing spare ammunition in your personal defense zone, revolver shooters may consider tacking a few DeSantis 2X2 pouches to the underside of the counter. A speedloader pouch may also be affixed in this manner. If you do this, you will always have spare ammunition in your personal defense zone stored in such a manner that it will be readily available if needed and which should not get lost in the pile of junk which frequently accumulates under a counter.

Autoloader pistol shooters should order at least four extra magazines for their handgun. One or two may be affixed to the underside of the counter using a magazine pouch dedicated for the purpose. These will not be the same magazines you carry on your person if you carry the handgun. Extra magazines are needed in order to rotate magazines a few times a year so the magazine spring doesn't eventually take a set and weaken.

Shooting the Shotgun

Shotguns require additional safety considerations. Whenever you are using firearms of any kind, always wear ear and eye protection. If you are inexperienced with shotguns, you must practice under the supervision of a certified firearms instructor. The shotgun should be held firmly to the shoulder as this lessens the effects of recoil. When using an autoloading shotgun, be sure to keep all five fingers of your support hand on the fore-end and away from the operating handle. Also, keep your fingers out of the action of an autoloader. If you inadvertently release the bolt on your finger, a painful injury, with broken bones, may occur. Also, proficiency should be obtained by first practicing with milder skeet and low velocity (sometimes called "low base") field loads before attempting to fire buckshot.

Anyone wearing a Pacemaker should never fire a shoulder weapon of any kind without first getting permission from his or her cardiologist or doctor. Generally, shooters requiring Pacemakers arrange with their doctors to install the Pacemaker on the side of their body opposite their shooting side.

Many indoor ranges will permit you to fire shotguns provided you use fine birdshot such as number 6 or 7-1/2. A range in my area permits rifled slugs only: no bird or buckshot of any kind. Consequently, be sure to check with the range staff before using a shotgun.

You only need to know two methods of shooting the shotgun;

1. Firing from the shoulder while pointing it at your adversary

2. Firing from a modified hip position. If you place the butt of the shotgun at your hip, as seen frequently in fictional crime dramas, you will most likely shoot over the target, even at ranges as close as seven yards. Instead, bring the butt of the shotgun all the way up to the armpit. This levels the gun and

largely eliminates overshooting.

Contrary to what you see on television, it is quite easy to miss with a shotgun. The shotgun must be pointed directly at the adversary when firing. Merely pointing in the robber's general vicinity isn't enough. With regard to cover and concealment, handgun bullets generally penetrate more deeply than individual buckshot pellets. Consequently, items which may be shot through with a handgun may stop individual shotgun pellets. As buckshot leaves the shotgun barrel, it begins to spread into a pattern. The amount of spread is controlled by the amount of constriction at the muzzle which is called a choke. A barrel which has been shortened generally does not have any choke with the result that the buckshot pellets will spread more quickly. You must keep this in mind when considering a shotgun for defensive purposes. As the buckshot pattern continues to spread as it moves further away from the muzzle of the shotgun, the danger to innocent bystanders is increased. You should not discharge any firearm whenever there are innocent people in your line of fire or beyond a lawful target. A single buckshot pellet is fully capable of inflicting a fatal wound. There are other, rather sophisticated shotgun techniques in use by law enforcement which, in my opinion, might only tend to confuse you. It is better to know a few things very well than a whole bunch of things superficially.

One other point on shotguns: Shotguns are available with, or can be modified to accept, a pistol grip, thus eliminating the butt stock. These "pistol grip only" stocks should be avoided because they hold little advantage within the limited tactical framework we have previously established for the shotgun and they are far more difficult to shoot accurately.

Practice shooting from cover. Many indoor ranges are equipped with movable panels which may be rotated into position to simulate cover. Obtain permission to use them. Practice from both right and left cover. You will immediately notice it is much easier to shoot around the right side of an object if you're right handed and the left side for lefties. Think about this as you establish your personal defense zone at your place of busi ness. When practicing with cover, make an honest effort to get the bulk of your body behind cover. All of the exercises previously described can and should be fired from cover. If your range is not equipped with movable cover panels, you may use

An ordinary windshield sun shield may be used to practice shooting from cover at any range with a table across the shooting points. It's portable and sets up in two seconds.

one of those fold-up cardboard sun screens intended for the windshield of your automobile. These are light, convenient, set up in an instant on the table or bench at the firing point, and they serve the purpose.

Practice proper shooting technique from cover. Both hands remain on the gun. Do not rest the gun against cover. This could interfere with slide travel and left handed shooters may cause an ejected shell casing to become lodged in the ejection port. Also, do not lean against cover. Keep your weight balanced over your feet. You will not be able to commit any of these sins with the cardboard sun shield.

When using cover, it is not necessary that the handgun be perfectly vertical. For some people, canting or tilting the handgun a bit allows them to get a bit more of their body behind cover. Within typical combat distances, any deviation from point of aim caused by canting the handgun will be too slight to worry about.

There are many old marksmanship manuals around in which you may see an obsolete cover shooting technique where the weak hand is placed flat against the cover and the strong hand is rested in the web between the thumb and index finger of the weak hand. Do not use this technique. Also, the "cup and saucer" hold in which the support hand cups the bottom of the shooting hand is completely ineffective. The support hand is not used to hold the gun up, but rather, to help to aid recoil recovery.

CHAPTER NINE

RELOADING TECHNIQUES:

Reloading the Revolver

The only methods of reloading a revolver which should be considered are the speedloader, made either by HKS or Safariland, or the DeSantis "2X2" pouch.

When it is necessary to reload, a right handed shooter transfers the handgun to his weak hand. The right thumb is used to activate the cylinder release. Then, the cylinder is swung open with the middle and ring fingers of the left hand. This is the point where reloading techniques tend to vary, depending on which firearms expert you're consulting. The technique I prefer to use is to invert the weapon so that the muzzle is pointed upwards to allow gravity to work for you. Then, the extractor rod is slapped smartly rearward by the shooting hand. As the shooting hand is already there when you opened the cylinder, you might as well put it to use. The extractor must be long enough to insure complete removal of the empties and you must accomplish this in one stroke. Indecisive, multiple strokes on the extractor rod sometimes allows a shell casing to get under the extractor, a malfunction that would be virtually impossible to clear while being fired upon.

Next, turn the handgun muzzle downwards so as to allow gravity to assist in reloading. The speedloader is gripped with the strong hand and brought to the cylinder. I strongly recommend, regardless of the kind of ammunition you keep in the revolver, spare ammunition, whether in a speedloader or 2X2 pouch, should be jacketed hollowpoint rather than any form of semi-wadcutter design. Semi-wadcutters tend to hang up on the chamber mouths and make reloading, under stressful conditions, far more difficult.

Left Handed Revolver Reloading
Unfortunately, I don't think anyone has ever made a "left handed" revolver. Revolvers are ergonomically designed for right handed people. One simple technique for reloading the revolver by a left handed shooter is the following:

1. With the right hand, come over the gun and the left hand so the right thumb can activate the cylinder release and the right index and middle fingers can push the cylinder open (cylinders always open to the left side of the frame).

2. With the right hand momentarily supporting the gun, release your shooting grip and grasp the handgun exactly in the manner described for a right handed person. From this point on, left and right handed individuals will eject fired casings and reload the revolver in the same manner by using the right hand to put fresh cartridges in the chambers.

3. Close the cylinder by pushing it shut with the left thumb.

4. Using the right hand to assist, return the handgun to your left hand shooting grip.

With practice, it is entirely possible to perform step one with the left hand only. However, you would have to juggle the revolver to do so. This requires a fine motor skill which renders the technique susceptible to failure under stress.

One of the largest causes of failure with speedloaders is caused by the user. Once you release the cartridges, allow gravity to do its job. Holding onto the speedloader, particularly with the HKS loader, often creates a binding action between the speedloader and chambers with the result that the rounds do not chamber. Even shaking doesn't help. Once the rounds are released, allow the speedloader to fall to the ground. Do not retrieve it or attempt to put it in your pocket. Once used,

Author recommends you use (left to right) either the DeSantis 2x2 pouch, Safariland speedloader, or the HKS speedloader to reload revolvers.

A jacketed hollowpoint cartridge (left) is easier to load into a revolver chamber with any type of reloading device than a semi-wadcutter design (right). The setback or step designed into the semi-wadcutter bullet tends to catch the chamber wall, thus slowing down the reloading process, particularly when you are under stress. If you prefer semi-wadcutters, carry them in the revolver but have streamlined cartridges available for reloading.

afford it all the respect due a used condom. Remember what I told you about police officers preoccupied with shell casings during gun battles. The cylinder is then closed by the fingers of the weak hand. The handgun is then transferred back to the shooting hand. As the speedloader is accessed by the right hand by both left and right handed shooters, speedloaders should be worn on the right side of the body or stored in such a manner as to be conducive for a right handed retrieval. Needless to say, clean revolvers are easier to reload than dirty ones.

If you are using the 2X2 pouch, reloading techniques are essentially the same to the point where it becomes necessary to

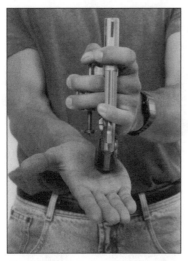 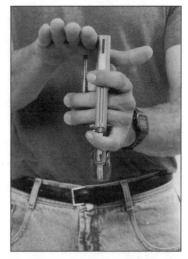

If the thumb of the support hand is used to activate extractor, the butt of the revolver should be firmly rapped into the palm of the shooting hand to ensure all empty cases fall clear of the revolver. This is especially important with revolvers with short extractor rods such as the S&W "J" frame revolvers.

There are several acceptable methods of clearing empties from a revolver. Revolver is held vertically so gravity may assist. Extractor rod may be smartly rapped with palm of shooting hand.

When reloading revolver from belt loops or DeSantis 2x2 pouch, load chambers furthest away from the frame. Rotate cylinder with fingers of support hand so chambers to be loaded are always in this position.

introduce fresh ammunition to the cylinder. A 2X2 pouch holds cartridges in pairs. They should be reloaded in pairs. Use the fingers of the weak hand to rotate the cylinder so the two chambers being reloaded are always furthest from the gun frame. All too many shooters keep the cylinder rigid, then attempt to charge the chambers near the frame. This is difficult to do under range conditions and probably impossible in combat.

As previously stated, when practicing reloading on the range, always try to reload using combat reloading techniques so the moves may be programmed into muscle memory. Also, try to reload by feel. That is, try to reload without taking your eyes off the target. This requires practice but is not necessarily difficult to accomplish. A gunsmithing technique that can smooth reloading is to have the chamber mouths slightly chamfered. This breaks the sharp edge of the chamber mouth and will not affect reliability unless the gunsmith is a bit heavy handed. Remember to tell him that the revolver is to be used for self defense, not target shooting.

One thing to remember about reloading: It is not likely you will know how many rounds you fired during an actual confrontation. At your first safe opportunity, your handgun must be fully reloaded. In the case of revolvers, it is probably better to dump the whole cylinder and reload rather than to gingerly use the extractor rod to lift the fired cases up for individual removal. Generally, fired cases remain elevated while live rounds re-chamber when the extractor rod is released. However, add nervous and shaky fingers to the equation and there is a great danger of getting a round under the extractor star, in which case your gun becomes a high tech paper weight.

It is also wise to practice partial revolver reloading. That is, the six empty cases are ejected, two or three rounds are reloaded and the target is re-engaged. If you condition yourself to always fully reload the revolver, this is what you're likely to do regardless of the felonious emergency you face. As previously mentioned, at least one of the four officers killed in the Newhall incident might be alive today had he brought his partially reloaded revolver to bear against an advancing adversary.

Reloading the Autoloading Pistol

There are three generally accepted conditions under which you must reload the autoloading pistol. Selecting the proper reloading technique is dictated by the number of rounds left in the magazine, if any, together with the remaining degree of emergency you face at the instant you decide to reload. Consequently, becoming proficient at pistol reloading requires continual practice and is best learned under the direct supervision of a firearms instructor.

However, before we can discuss pistol reloading, we must first talk about operating the slide as virtually anything you do with or to a pistol involves slide manipulation. Along the left side of the pistol you will find the slide stop or slide stop lever, as it is also known. Some also call it the slide release. The slide stop performs two functions: it holds the slide open after firing the last shot, and it may be used to release the slide after reload-

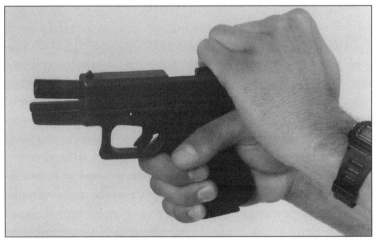

Reaching over the top of slide with support hand is widely taught and is a perfectly acceptable method of retracting or releasing the slide. Note pinky must remain clear of ejection port.

ing. Slide stops vary in efficiency with various gun models. Sometimes the thumb of the shooting hand cannot quite reach the slide stop. A second problem with slide stops is some require a herculean thumb to release the slide.

During my years as a firearms instructor, I found the

absolute quickest way to return a slide to battery following a reload, particularly with SIGs and Glocks, was to utilize the slide stop. But there are two potential problems with using the slide stop during an actual confrontation: first, it requires a fine motor skill, second, it requires an acute sense of timing to really be quick with the slide stop. This is important because your thumb will be poised over the slide stop waiting for the magazine to lock so the slide may be released. As this sense of timing, together with fine motor skills in general, will suffer under stress, you may get the cart before the horse and release the slide a nanosecond too soon, resulting in an empty chamber. An alternative to the slide stop is to pull the slide rearward with the non shooting hand. This releases pressure on the slide stop which allows it to drop out of the way by spring tension. The slide is then released and should return to battery provided there is at least one round left in the magazine. There are several methods of manually releasing the slide. One variation is known as the slingshot method. As its name implies, the slide is gripped with the thumb and index finger of the non shooting hand, pulled rearward and released, much like a slingshot. The second major variation involves bringing the four fingers of the non shooting hand across the top of the slide, first making sure that the pinky, the finger closest to the ejection port, is indeed clear of the port and not blocking it. This latter method places greater emphasis on arm strength while the former, sling shot method utilizes the major muscles of the shoulders, chest, and back. For most individuals, females in particular, the slide is more easily drawn to the rear by the slingshot method provided the shooting arm is kept reasonably straight. If the gun is drawn closer to the body, the non shooting arm will acquire more kinks than a dog's hind leg, and this will greatly reduce the amount of leverage that may be exerted upon the slide. A little trick you may utilize with either slide manipulation method is to push forward with the shooting hand while simultaneously pulling rearward with the non shooting hand. This doubles the amount of muscle mass being used.

    As we shall soon see, there are several instances when it

may be necessary to manipulate the slide during a confrontation: reloading with the slide locked in the open position, reloading with the slide closed which may occur if the slide failed to remain open, or when the magazine wasn't properly seated and the slide allowed to close on an empty chamber. I have seen many instances in training where the shooter inadvertently locked one of his thumbs over the slide stop while shooting, thus preventing it from raising to catch the slide. Last but not least, it will be necessary to manipulate the slide in order to clear a malfunction. Following the need to keep it simple, it is better to learn and practice one technique appropriate for all circumstances than to try to remember a bunch of different techniques to perform one function but under different circumstances.

As speed may be achieved by moving faster, economy of motion, or both simultaneously, economy of motion usually pays the greatest dividend in terms of achieving a given level of quickness because raw speed is practice sensitive while economy of motion, once learned, is easily remembered and doesn't deteriorate with lack of practice.

Based upon my years of experience, I have found it is quicker to bring the slide to the hand than to bring the hand to the slide. Consequently, once the magazine is seated, the non shooting hand is poised in position to release the slide. This is done by turning the gun counter clockwise (right handed shooters) so as to put the top of the slide within the grip of the non shooting hand. The slide may now be gripped utilizing the thumb and three strongest fingers of the hand, namely, the index, middle, and ring fingers. By inverting the handgun, both arms are kept reasonably straight for increased leverage and the shooter may bring his larger back and shoulder muscles to bear. Learning to rotate the gun counter clockwise is important in clearing malfunctions because it helps to look into the ejection port to see what's going on in there. This cannot be done if the gun is held vertical at all times. We will have a pretty thorough discussion about malfunctions later in the book.

While on the subject of slides, it is important to note the

newest trend in autoloaders, and revolvers for that matter, is to make them ever more compact and light. Generally, as the slide is lightened by shortening it, it is necessary to use much heavier rebound springs to compensate for lack of slide weight, otherwise, the gun will pound itself into scrap metal. Some of these rebound springs are so tough and ornery than men of above average strength cannot draw the slide rearward using either the slingshot or over the top method. The only slide manipulation technique that works is the one I just described provided you remember to use the push-pull technique. Now then, on with reloading.

The most commonly accepted names for the different types of reloading possible with the autoloading pistol are: emergency reload, tactical reload, and tactical magazine exchange.

Emergency Reload

As its name implies, an emergency reload is required when the pistol has been fired completely dry. Most often, the slide will be locked to the rear. Some experts will qualify this situation by requiring that a dire felonious emergency still exist. I feel any exchange of gunfire resulting in a bone dry weapon constitutes an emergency requiring immediate attention, regardless of whether or not the gun battle is over.

Tactical reload

A tactical reload is used when an undetermined number of rounds remain in the pistol but the user elects to take advantage of his covered position and/or a lull in the action to bring his pistol back up to full capacity. Generally, the original magazine is discarded whether or not it contains rounds.

Tactical Magazine Exchange

Once again, it is always tactically wise to take advantage of any break in the action to bring the pistol back to full capacity. Here, you have reason to believe hostilities may be at an end or at least the immediate threat you faced has been considerably mitigated and you wish to get the pistol back to full capacity without discarding existing rounds in the gun. Consequently, the first magazine is caught in the palm of the non-shooting hand while a fresh magazine is inserted into the pistol. The discarded magazine is placed in a pocket for possible future use. With both the tactical reload and tactical magazine exchange, you must always be sure to have a fresh magazine available for reloading before removing any live rounds from the gun. Remember, it is better to have a few rounds in the gun than just one chambered round and a magazine full of fresh ammunition inadvertently forgotten atop the dresser in your bedroom.

The subject of overall gun capacity comes up whenever reloading options are discussed. The chief advantage of the high capacity pistol is it postpones or eliminates the need to reload. The ability to unleash clouds of angry, whizzing bullets serves no tactical purpose whatsoever. Another major advantage of the high capacity pistol is its magazine tapers to a single column at the magazine lips. Consequently, these magazines

Proper reloading technique. Note shooter is not attempting to reload in left field. The elbow of his shooting arm has been brought back to the side, pistol is tilted about 45 degrees so magazine well is visible, and index finger of support hand is extended along front edge of magazine. This greatly enhances eye/hand coordination as coordination tends to suffer the further one's hand is from the focus of the eyes.

Magazine is locked by one continuous and fluid motion of shooting hand. That is, support hand is in constant contact with magazine from its retrieval from the magazine pouch to its locked position within the handgun. Avoid reloading Hollywood Style. In other words, partially inserting the magazine, then going into a windup to ram it home.

Gripping the magazine in this manner reduces eye/hand coordination and increases the probability of misaligning magazine with magazine well, thus slowing down the reload.

are far easier to insert into the magazine well than a single column magazine as typified by the .45 auto or SIG Model P-225. You cannot have too much ammunition in a gun battle. Consequently, always carry at least one, and preferably two spare magazines, regardless of your pistol's capacity.

A seldom mentioned need for carrying spare magazines is it may be necessary to discard a nearly full magazine to clear a malfunction. We'll discuss malfunctions in a moment. Techniques necessary to reload the pistol are different than those utilized for the revolver. Spare ammunition is carried on the weak side while the pistol remains in the strong hand. Magazines should be carried upside down with bullet facing forward. I often see people carrying two magazines facing in opposite directions. I can't imagine what they're thinking about.

To reload, first make sure you have a fresh magazine with which to reload. Then, shift the gun slightly in the shooting hand to activate the magazine release. With most guns, this will cause the magazine to fall free of the pistol. With Glocks and the earlier magazines that did not fall free, the preferred technique is to release the magazine, then rip the magazine clear of the pistol with the support hand as it begins its travel to the spare magazine. The fresh magazine is gripped in such a manner that the index finger is extended up the front edge of the magazine. This assists in inserting the magazine into the magazine well as eye/hand coordination tends to suffer the further the hand is from the focus point of the eyes. Next, and most important, the magazine is inserted and locked with one stroke. The hand is rolled somewhat so that the palm can ram the magazine home. Some people partially insert the magazine, then go into a pitcher's windup, locking the magazine in place with a separate motion. Two problems: the magazine may fall out while you imitate something you saw on television and, it takes longer. Speed of reloading is best accomplished by economy of motion rather than trying to move like a lightning bolt.

While on the subject of magazines, many experts advise loading magazines one round short of full capacity as this materially reduces stress on the magazine spring, resulting in longer life. I prefer to fully load, then rotate my magazines if they are of the single column variety and load a round short with high capacity magazines. If you short change your magazines by one round, you should have some way of documenting this, perhaps by engraving a "-1" on the floorplate. After a shooting, investigators will try to account for all rounds fired. If you fired two rounds but three rounds are missing from the gun, you may have a problem. If your two rounds found the robber, who was responsible for the round in the innocent bystander? The magazine marked "-1", together with this paragraph, should satisfy investigators the round missing from your gun was never there.

CHAPTER 10

MALFUNCTIONS

Unfortunately, even the best handguns can malfunction on occasion. A handgun, being a mechanical device can, at times, fail to function properly despite the use of the finest raw materials and the greatest possible care in its design and manufacture. As this firearm may be used in lawful self defense, it is incumbent upon the user to understand overall reliability is based upon the interaction of five factors: handgun, magazine (clip), ammunition, the user's physical skills, and his state of mental preparedness. Let us take a closer look at how we may reduce the likelihood of a stoppage. Also, it is necessary to practice clearing malfunctions or stoppages on the range should it ever become necessary to do it during a confrontation.

Great pains must be taken to avoid malfunctions. There are at least 14 things you can do to minimize malfunctions:

1. Select a new, high quality handgun enjoying widespread popularity with the law enforcement community.

2. Allow for a break-in period. The gun should be fired at least 100 rounds with factory loads before deploying it for self defense needs. Some manufacturers recommend a 200 round break-in period before using the gun for defensive purposes.

3. Always keep the handgun clean and properly lubricated.

4. Restrict yourself to first quality, factory loaded ammunition.

5. Inspect each and every round before loading into a magazine or speedloader. Look for crushed or rolled case

mouths, or inverted or missing primers.

6. With pistols, always carry the gun in the same condition. Do not carry with safety on one week, safety off the following week, round in chamber today, empty chamber tomorrow.

7. After several trips through the magazine lips, into the chamber and out again, the soft brass casings tend to get buggered up and this may lead to a failure to extract. If you're constantly loading and unloading, remember to rotate your ammunition. Ammunition bearing scratches and extractor marks should be set aside for practice and not carried.

8. Magazines must be periodically disassembled and cleaned, making sure they are properly re-assembled. Damaged magazines must be replaced, not repaired. Always inspect the magazine lips for damage if dropped on a hard surface. Also, avoid purchasing bargain basement magazines of unknown quality. When a partially loaded magazine is dropped, and happens to land on its base, the momentary absence of tension applied to the rounds often causes them to stand on end or completely reverse themselves in the magazine! If you drop a magazine while loading it, remove all the rounds loaded and start over again.

9. Don't be afraid to hurt the gun. Far too many shooters ride the slide forward so as to close the slide as gently as possible. Often, this causes the slide to remain out of battery with the result the gun will not fire when needed. The gun is designed to slam-bang. Therefore, allow the slide to travel forward under its own power.

10. Remember to place your strong side thumb behind the slide when holstering. Sometimes, a new, tight holster will pull the slide out of battery with the same result as in "9" above. When holstering, push the gun into the holster with both the grip and slide, not the grip alone.

11. Always grip the handgun firmly. Do not limp-wrist it.

12. Make sure the magazine is properly seated by listening to it "click" into position, then tugging on the magazine to insure it is locked in place.

13. Do not load and fire single rounds through the cham-

ber, without a magazine. The gun is designed in such a manner that rounds being fed from the magazine slip under the extractor. When you manually chamber a round, the extractor must snap over the case rim, thus applying greater stress to the extractor. Of course, should you ever find yourself in an emergency with loose rounds and no magazine, disregard this advice and shoot the gun by whatever means necessary in order to survive.

14. Avoid customizing the handgun unless absolutely necessary. Most handguns enjoying favor with the police community are okay right out of the box. They are also accurate enough as is. I have seen more guns ruined by "accuracy" and "reliability" jobs than anything else. While some guns can be made more reliable through some judicious polishing, the outcome depends mostly on the skill of the gunsmith.

It should be noted the New York City Police Department, together with most other departments with extensive gun battle experience, carry their authorized guns as is. They will only permit approved, aftermarket grips to be added to the handgun. Several well known federal agencies, known for occasional bouts of elitism, have a habit of demanding tedious custom specifications on their firearms, sometimes with disastrous results. I'm aware of one batch of 1,500 revolvers ordered with such tight tolerances the guns proved unreliable. Likewise, another federal agency's transition to autoloading pistols was plagued by gun failures caused by changes demanded by the agency.

Clearing Malfunctions

While revolvers are inherently more reliable than autoloading pistols, they are almost always impossible to clear and return to duty within the permissible time span of a heart beat or two. If a cartridge fails to fire, merely pull the trigger a second time to bring a fresh round under the hammer. The most common malfunction I experienced with my troops was unburned powder granules becoming trapped under the extractor star. When this happens, you cannot close the cylinder. Nor can you clear it under fire. Quite often, the shooter attributes the malfunction to the gun becoming "hot."

Powder residue is difficult to spot and remove. It even resists multiple passes with a toothbrush. When cleaning your revolver, it may be necessary to scrape away powder flakes or granules using the tip of a screwdriver. When doing so, be sure to clean both the cylinder recess, together with the back side of the extractor star. This problem can be minimized by not lubricating the underside of the extractor star, or its cylinder recess, and by using the previously described revolver reloading techniques.

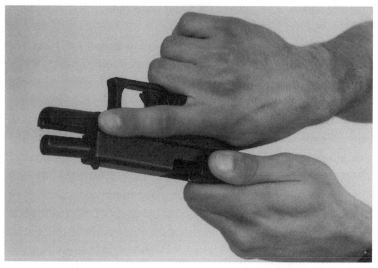

Author has found inverting the pistol so as to bring the slide to the support hand is perhaps the quickest way of releasing the slide or clearing a malfunction while under stress.

For a while, there was a bizarre shell ejection technique in vogue in which the extractor star was activated with the thumb of the weak hand while simultaneously hurling the shells rearward, in a horizontal manner, under the left arm. A variation of this method used the shooting hand to slap the extractor rearward. The theory was to keep ejected shell casings from accumulating underfoot. The horizontal position of the handgun during ejection often caused unburned powder flakes to become trapped under the extractor and sometimes resulted in the extractor star catching a shell casing. As previously mentioned, if you manage to get a round under the extractor, go for a second gun if one is available. The best way to become proficient at clearing pistol malfunctions is to practice. Dummy ammunition can often be found at gunshows or, you can arrange with a reloader to load some ammunition without powder or primers. I would take the extra safety precaution of soaking the dummy rounds in cold gun blue (available at most gunshops) so the homemade dummies more closely resemble factory made dummy rounds and are not as easily confused with live rounds. Merely assembling dummy rounds without making them easily distinguishable from live ammunition can result in carrying a handgun with one or more dummy rounds in the gun or mixing a live round in with your dummies. Either way, the result can be disastrous.

Visit the range with a friend. Hand him your magazine and some dummy and live rounds, asking him to load them in whatever order he pleases. Next, insert the magazine into the pistol and commence firing. When the pistol "malfunctions" you will do three things: First, "tap" smartly on the base of the magazine to insure it is properly seated. "Rack" the slide once rearward to clear the ejection port and to chamber a fresh round. The ejection port should be turned downward to allow gravity to assist. Come back to the ready position and fire again if required. The sequence is: tap, rack, ready, bang.

Failure to work the slide with authority may create a malfunction known as a double feed. In each and every double feed I witnessed on the range, the condition was caused by the shooter rather than the gun. Double feeds are not easy to clear and I would go for a second gun if one is available. To clear one, it is usually necessary to lock the slide to the rear, rip the existing magazine out of the handgun, work the slide to clear the ejection port and chamber, then insert a fresh magazine and chamber a round. Often, ripping out the magazine will cause the topmost round to jam vertically in the magazine lips. Hence, a fresh magazine is needed.

A common but avoidable malfunction with auto pistols is the "smoke stack" or "stove pipe" jam, a condition where the slide catches a fired casing in the ejection port. This malfunction is classified as a failure to eject, and is most often caused by limp-wristing, handloads, a dirty, dry gun, weak extractor spring, a worn extractor or any combination of the aforementioned. For a time, the remedy for the smoke stack jam was to wipe the slide with the non shooting hand. The problem here is the shooter does not know whether or not the slide traveled rearward far enough to pick up a fresh cartridge. If so, this round may be hanging loose in the ejection port or may have partially chambered as a result of the slide's forward, if incomplete, travel. If the slide is worked, you may then induce the double feed whereby a cartridge is in the chamber and another is lodged firmly against it. Most of the double feeds I witnessed were induced by the shooter attempting to clear a less serious stoppage.

In order to clear a smoke stack jam without inducing a double feed, you may pick the stuck shell out of the ejection port, allow the slide to fully close, then work the slide once rearward, even if it means ejecting a live round. If the fired casing is wedged essentially parallel to the gun and cannot readily be picked free, look into the ejection port. If a live round has been partially dislodged from the magazine, pull and hold the slide to the rear while shaking the shell casing free of the gun. Then release the slide to chamber the round. If a live round has been pulled free of the magazine and is partially chambered, you may again hold the slide rearward and shake both the shell casing and the live round out of the gun. Once the ejection port is clear, release the slide to chamber a round.

A malfunction similar to a double feed can occur with a failure to extract. Here, the extractor did not remove the fired casing from the chamber and a live round is now wedged against it. It is necessary to rip the magazine out of the pistol, and hope the extractor can gain sufficient purchase on the fired casing to extract it. If successful, re-insert a fresh magazine and chamber a round. A fresh magazine is necessary as the top round in the magazine removed may have been dislodged or upended when pulled from the handgun. Besides insuring sufficient ammunition in the event of a emergency, extra magazines are needed to replace a magazine that will not feed as a result of the need to clear a malfunction. Any failure to extract, assuming a reasonably clean handgun and fresh, first quality factory ammunition, requires the immediate attention of a gunsmith. If it failed to extract once, it will fail a second time.

Left handed shooters and right handed shooters shooting around the left side of cover must be especially careful not to hold the handgun directly against cover, as this may block the ejection port and prevent a shell casing from ejecting. Most times, a fresh cartridge will have been stripped from the magazine. Utilizing the tap-rack-ready-bang drill will often result in a double feed.

After the malfunction is cleared, you then return to the "ready" position, ready to fire if necessary.

I know this all sounds a bit tedious, but malfunction drills are an essential part of any comprehensive program of firearms instruction geared to prepare the student for a deadly force encounter. Earlier in the book we mentioned "knowledge" is an essential element in winning an armed confrontation. Part of the knowledge needed to win is knowing how to keep your gun free of malfunctions (proactive) and how to clear a malfunction (reactive).

CHAPTER 11

CONFRONTATION

The elements necessary to win a confrontation, namely, mindset, knowledge, judgment, tactics, marksmanship, and firearm have now been discussed at length. Hopefully, you may now appreciate why they are so interdependent and interrelated. In writing this type of book, it is really easy to get the cart before the horse. We almost need to discuss everything simultaneously.

Some experts may argue knowledge is a function of mindset but I elected to break it out for ease of explanation. Consider the six elements to be a team. What would happen to a baseball team that's a player short? They can indeed still win a game if they are exceptionally strong players. I guess they'd eliminate the right fielder, except for left handed batters, and hope for the best. What if the team is two players short? Eliminate right field and second base and hope that the shortstop and center fielder can fill the gaps. Victory is still possible but not likely. Three players short? Perhaps it's better to forfeit the game.

The merchant who has a gun and nothing else is the same as a baseball team that's **five** players short! Think about it. The six elements are ranked in order of importance. A well prepared citizen with a .38 Special is more effective than his unprepared counterpart with a truck load of guns and ammunition.

You need to know what's going on in the felon's mind and where his mindset comes from. The robber or felon comes from an environment where the gun is far more than an instrument for obtaining valuables by felonious means. The gun can also represent power, respect, authority. For criminals, it is the judge, jury, and executioner, and, if you believe society's liberal elements, also has some sort of subliminal ability to enhance sexual prowess.

Unfortunately, the robber has the initial mental advantage. He knows he's entering a hot situation and you don't. Also, he has no regard for the emotional or legal consequences, except for his own skin. Most likely, he is classified as a sociopath, one without conscience or feelings. In addition, the sum total of his life's experience, which probably includes some harsh jail time, have all contributed to give him the mindset of a carnivore

Okay, the robber has a gun and the initial mental advantage over you but his "team" is many players short. You can win the confrontation. The robber makes a mostly correct assumption the merchants are mere lambs waiting to be fleeced. If that's his mindset upon entering your store, he has made your job easier. He thinks you're a lamb, you know you're a wolf. He doesn't expect resistance. He expects compliance because armed resistance is the exception rather than the norm. Sadly, the only obvious effect of gun controls is to disarm people like you, not the criminal. Remember that next election day.

And speaking of lambs and wolves, one other tactic that can save your life is secrecy. While most of my readers can probably be classified as casual or incidental gun users, some of you are indeed experienced pistoleros. You may have attended a shooting academy and studied under world renowned experts such as Jeff Cooper. Unfortunately, there's a tendency for some people to flaunt their unique skills. If a felon learns of your skills, perhaps from a disgruntled former employee who has fingered you for a robbery, he will change his tactics to compensate for your skills by striking in a preemptive manner. That is, you will be shot suddenly, often and frequently, before you realize you're in a gun battle.

Let's paint a little scenario. Imagine a neighborhood bully who relishes the opportunity to humiliate the neighborhood wimp, virtually on a daily basis. One day, the wimp decides he's had enough and hires the biggest and meanest bodyguard imaginable to protect him. The bully's mindset is adjusted for a no resistance, can't lose situation but when the monstrous bodyguard jumps out of the shadows, the starch flows right out of the bully and his first thought is, "Oh shit!"

How about this. You see a friendly looking dog, tethered to a five foot leash. You walk over and decide to pet the "friendly" dog. The dog seems of good spirit and allows you to kneel right beside him. But when the dog suddenly bares his long, white fangs and the growl begins deep within him, you realize you've made a big mistake. Now, you're no longer concerned with petting the dog but in hoping you can run six feet faster than he can run five feet.

These examples should make my point. You need to change the robber's thought process and make him realize, very quickly, he's made a terrible mistake. In effect, you need to regear his mindset and cause him to think defeat instead of easy victory. We want to provoke the emotions of fear and panic in the robber. An armed confrontation is essentially a battle for control of people and premises. Effective return fire keeps the robbers from gaining control of you. It should be remembered if the robber gains control of you, you are at his mercy.

The robber is not particularly resourceful. He has no plan B, no reserves. He didn't think he needed any because he has the gun. Once he realizes you too are armed, he becomes the bully confronted by the bodyguard. You have neutralized his advantage provided you have rehearsed robberies in your mind to the point you can minimize lag time. Lag time is the time it takes for you to identify a threat and respond to it.

What felons fear most is an armed citizenry. Countless jail house interviews and studies point to the same thing: robbers rarely knowingly take on armed people unless the potential reward is too much to resist as in an armored car robbery. You may recall the recent rash of muggings and killings of foreign, mostly German tourists in Florida. The perpetrators caught were asked why they targeted foreigners. The uniform reply was because the foreigners didn't carry guns.

As I've said over and over again, confrontations are won in the mind. Faced with an imminent confrontation, your body automatically prepares you for fight or flight. Flight may occur in the literal sense or by staying put and surrendering. Within the confines of your business, fleeing may not be an option unless you think you can outrun bullets. By turning to run you have disobeyed the robber's orders. You were disobedient, disrespectful. You ignored the authority granted by his gun. This will enrage him and in many cases, he'll start shooting at you because you've pissed him off. Realistically, you have two options during a robbery when you are caught in the kill zone: full and immediate compliance or full and immediate resistance when and if the opportunity presents itself. Sorry, no half measures allowed here. Of course, compliance may also serve to give you the opportunity to resist more effectively. This is especially so when the robber is ordering you to your personal defense zone. There's no point in disobeying the robber and running for a gun, risking getting shot in the back, when the robber is going to bring you there anyway. It should be remembered, from a purely tactical point of view, most shooting experts will agree it is better to offer immediate and effective resistance, and thus prevent a felon from obtaining control of you, than to have him obtain control, disarming you in the process, then hope you can regain control of the situation. It is better to maintain the initiative than to lose it, then hope to regain it.

Resistance isn't always practical. Generally, you need several seconds of warning to alert you to the fact a robbery is about to occur. If you look up from the newspaper into the barrel of a gun, you cannot immediately resist, if at all. This is where the element of judgment can save you. It helps to casually eyeball each and every person who enters your store. I would also strongly advise you to install one of those electric eye devices or pressure sensitive mats that chime whenever someone crosses the threshold. This advises you some one has entered the store and will cause you to notice him seconds earlier. When you have the capability of armed defense, paying attention to customers is no longer an option, it is now mandatory. Have you ever walked into a store during a very slow period and the merchant did not look up from his newspaper or periodical until you were right in front of him? In this instance, put an imaginary gun in your hand and pretend you were a robber. What options did the merchant have once you were before him and he hasn't even bothered to look up?

Remember, trying to outdraw a gun already drawn and pointed at you is almost guaranteed to be a losing proposition, unless you can take advantage of some momentary distraction of the robber to dive behind cover as you draw. Keep in mind offering any resistance to an armed criminal may get you or others killed or seriously injured—but then again, so may complying without resistance. No one but you can make the decision of which course of action will more likely bring you and others through the robbery unharmed. The purpose of this book is not to tell you that you must resist but to increase your knowledge, skill, and judgement so you may do so more effectively when and if you feel resistance is appropriate.

Watch the Hands and Eyes

You're in your store when someone enters. Something about this individual troubles you. Perhaps he's a stranger. He looks very nervous. His eyes are darting about. One hand is concealed from view. It is a smart tactic to always observe a questionable person's hands. If both are visible, remain relaxed but at heightened alert (Condition Orange). If one or both hands are not visible, you need to remain in Condition Orange until his intentions become known.

Felons often carry their guns tucked into the front of their trousers with the butt covered by a shirt tail. A second common carry for felons is also in the waist band but at the small of the back. During winter months they will also utilize coat pockets. Felons rarely use holsters. In the former position, a right handed felon will raise the shirt tail with his left hand and draw with his right. It's a quick and fluid movement. They often practice the draw in advance.

A recent phenomenon is the increasing use of bullet resistant vests by felons. Enough of them have been stolen that they now show up on the backs of felons with predictable regularity. Learn how to recognize whether or not someone is wearing a vest. The best way to do this is to observe uniformed police officers. You will notice their shirts appear a bit tight, the thickness of the upper body is disproportionate to the rest of the body, there is a swell just above the belt and their shoulders are just a bit more rounded. On female officers, the vest tends to flatten their breasts, giving them a male-like appearance. Also, when seen from the rear, it appears as though they have an ironing board up their shirt.

In order for the felon to conceal the vest, he may be overdressed for the season. If you detect a bullet resistant vest on someone not in uniform, it doesn't automatically mean he's a robber. Vests are also worn by plainclothes cops, undercover officers, anti-crime units, federal agents, etc. Remember, you may not resort to force until the intentions of the person are clear: either a weapon is produced and /or an announcement of a robbery is made.

You need to know about bullet resistant vests because it is an occasional adversarial tactic that may be used to try to defeat you. Police officers are advised to shoot to the center of mass which is the middle of the chest, right between the nipples. If the felon shows no indication of being hit, police are then instructed to shoot for the head or the area below the vest which is the pelvic area. The pelvic area offers a larger and more stable target, and would be my preference as an alternate aiming point, especially for the casual shooter. James Cirillo, a police combat veteran of the 1960's was assigned to a unit that experienced 238 separate gun battles. Mr. Cirillo writes that felons often toppled when struck in the pelvic area, even with such ineffective rounds as the .38 Special 158 grain, round nose lead bullet.

What should you do? If you draw a gun at the earliest suspicion, you will surely lose your authority to have it. Also, the "victim" who hadn't quite communicated any desire to rob you, has now hired an attorney because, as a result of you displaying a gun, he is now incontinent and impotent, can't hold a job, suffers insomnia, deep mental anguish, constipation, migraine headaches, and loss of respect within his community. Therefore, you owe him a barrel full of money, upon receipt of which he will make a full and remarkably speedy recovery.

When you become suspicious, casually but purposefully walk to your personal defense zone if you're not already there. Don't show any suspicion. Once at your personal defense zone, move your hands out of view. Prepare to draw your firearm. Act pre-occupied, unconcerned. If it is a robbery, one of your best chances to defend yourself will occur almost immediately. Use these precious few seconds to shorten your lag time so your reaction to the felonious emergency is unhesitating and decisive. If you have to think about it, you'll probably lose.

We talk and pull triggers with different portions of our brain. Try talking and dry firing simultaneously and your brain begins to become confused. Generally, you'll continue pulling the trigger but your words will fall in cadence with the trigger. It's trying to tell you, please talk or shoot but not both. Consequently, most people stop talking when they shoot and stop shooting when they talk.

The mind doesn't switch between functions that quickly. It's like being rudely interrupted while talking. Your mind has to change its train of thought from what you're saying to the fact it's being interrupted. The only analogy I can think of is playing guitar, something I do. It's relatively easy to sing and strum chords but nearly impossible to sing and pick a melody line simultaneously. Apparently, the same rules apply for words and triggers.

Say the robber displays a gun and begins to announce a robbery, something like, "put all the damned money in a bag or

I'll blow your stupid head off, move! move! move, dammit!" If you were alerted to a potential robbery, moved your hands out of view and can now draw unnoticed, you can make an armed response before he finishes making the robbery announcement. Since he was talking, his mind wasn't geared for shooting. This is one of the best opportunities you will have to seize the initiative. But remember, it presupposes all six elements of survival are with you, you have a personal defense zone, you're in it, and you can draw unnoticed. I used a stop watch to time how long it took me to quickly enunciate the robbery announcement in the first sentence. It averaged four and one half seconds. Consequently, if these were the actual words used to announce a robbery, you would have had ample time to draw and fire while he was talking and you were already in a heightened state of awareness.

This is the time for lightning quick, unhesitating, reflexive action, based upon extensive preparation, knowledge of the laws of your state, and a commitment to personal survival. This is not the time for moralizing or procrastination. You have mentally and physically prepared yourself for this moment.

One aspect of self defense is misunderstood by law enforcement as well as the law abiding public. If you were to poll a graduating class of police cadets or federal agents on what, in their opinion, was meant by self defense, the respondents would invariably couch their answers in the measured, legalistic phrases of their class instructors. As a result, self defense has become a legal concept rather than a survival concept. In reality, self defense is a survival concept that now exists within a legal framework. This may seem like a lot of legal babble but I'm driving towards a critical adjustment in your thought process and, therefore, your mindset.

When placed in mortal jeopardy, we must respond to the felon's actions in a lawfully correct manner. Our response is reflexive, measured, not excessive, legally correct, and so on. If he does this, we can do that, but if he does that, I guess we should do this. In each case, particularly in the classroom exercises received by law enforcement trainees as well as academy classes for private citizens, the felon is allowed to possess the initiative to which we respond or "self defend." As a result, students leave the academies with that thought in mind. That is, it is the felon who maintains the initiative.

If a good friend of yours is a law enforcement officer and you ask him for guidance in this area, undoubtedly, he will infect you too! What's lost is the fact that once we are placed in jeopardy, we do not have to remain on the defensive. We can indeed go on the offensive, we can wrest the initiative away from the felon, we can overwhelm our adversary with brilliant tactics, fire superiority, accurate fire, a defensible position. We can force him to "circle his wagons," retreat, confuse him, trick him, induce a state of near panic, make him cry, soil his pants, plead for his life, flee in blind panic. Best of all, we can do all that **without** using excessive force. Self defense can indeed be defined in many ways but first and foremost, it is an attitude--I'm going to win, he's going to lose. A strong mental commitment to win can never be excessive.

Multiple Adversaries

In real life, multiple adversaries are more difficult to successfully engage whenever they have completely separate kill zones as we have discussed. Tactical store planning will force their kill zones to overlap and help bring your adversaries into approximate alignment. During an actual confrontation, the one closest to you should be engaged first because he poses a greater threat. If one robber is armed with a handgun and the other with a knife, engage the more deadly threat first which, in this case, is the felon with the gun, unless the knife wielder is within arm's length and the gunman is distant.

If you face an approximately equal threat in both weapon and distance, first engage the one who is doing the talking. He'll probably be the leader. Criminal conspiracies have a strange pecking order. The gang leader remains in control because everyone assumes he has the most brains and also because they fear his power and temper. Thus, we have leaders and followers. Taking out the leader forthwith has a tremendous psychological affect on the accomplice who, for all intents and purposes, is nothing more than a human robot. He draws his strength from the leader. This is the essence of gang psychology. If he was leadership material, he'd have his own gang. There's no one to tell him what to do, even if he knows his assigned roll. Also, if he sees his leader defeated or neutralized he will feel especially vulnerable because the guy with the "brains" was neutralized. What you have done is to bring him a lot closer to a panicky state where he can use the deadly force available to him with the least effect. There are literally thousands of cases on record of accomplices breaking off the attack and fleeing the instant their leader was taken out.

Search and Destroy?

Assume for the moment that as you open your store, you realize it has been burglarized. Worse, you suspect the intruder is still in the store or warehouse somewhere. On occasion, a felon will attempt to secret himself in a store to await its closing, after which he hopes to crack a safe or remove everything of value. Also, an escaping felon may run into a storage area or back room seeking a way out. Under no circumstances should you search or conduct a sweep for a hidden or barricaded felon. This is among the most dangerous tasks faced by police officers. Exit the premises immediately and call the police. Remind yourself you are a private citizen, not a SWAT team commander. The police have specialized equipment and training to deal with hidden felons. Don't attempt to do their job for them. It could get you killed.

I can recall scores of stories regarding intruders who apparently thought they were Santa Claus and became stuck or wedged in exhaust systems, chimneys, air shafts, security bars, crawl spaces, etc., all while trying to gain access to a closed establishment. Sometimes the intruder died of asphyxiation or exposure. Should you discover an intruder is indeed trapped in your place of business, do not attempt to free him. Instead, immediately call the police and let them manage the situation. Resist the temptation to ignore the intruder's plight so as to "punish" him. If not, you may be held accountable for his injuries. Call for help immediately.

Warning Shots

Warning shots were popular in old western movies and 50's vintage detective thrillers. I'm not sure if Hollywood borrowed the technique from the police or if the police borrowed it from Hollywood. At any rate, most police departments and federal agencies no longer permit warning shots, and for good reason. First, any firearms discharge poses a risk to both the adversary and innocent parties. Second, firing a warning shot in a non threatening situation is reckless and highly questionable. Any attempt to use lethal force in a non lethal manner can subject you to serious legal problems. If you are justified in using deadly force, you should not be wasting ammunition by firing into the ceiling or floor. If you fire two warning shots from a five or six shot revolver, you will have but three or four shots left with which to defend yourself. Often, it isn't enough. If you fire warning shots to try to stop a felon from fleeing, he may return the fire and a gun battle will ensue that could have been avoided. Of course, you are now at an additional disadvantage because you have wasted some precious rounds. Consequently, my advice to you is to refrain from firing warning shots.

Multiple Good Guys

Quite often, more than one merchant within a store is armed. Business partners are often both armed and multiple armed people may also be found in gun stores, check cashing establishments, etc.

Perhaps the greatest danger they face is a failure to communicate. Yeah, everybody is armed but nobody wants to initiate a conversation about who will do what, with which, to whom, in the event of a robbery. As a result, these individuals run a very real risk of shooting each other. Armed partners or co-workers must avoid having two personal defense zones directly facing each other. Otherwise, the partners may be shooting at each other during a robbery.

Ideally, the second personal defense zone will be at the robber's right or left shoulder. In this manner, friendly fire from armed partners will intersect at approximately 90 degrees. Friendly fire is mutually safer when it intersects at an angle smaller than 90 degrees and becomes increasingly hazardous as the angle increases above 90 degrees. At 180 degrees, business partners would be firing directly at each other.

Often, one partner is manning the cash register or sales floor while the second partner is in a back room. If you are the person in the back room and a robbery occurs, avoid the temptation to rush right in with gun in hand. Instead, sound an alarm and remain in your personal defense zone. The entrance to the back room will provide the cover from which you can shoot. Your tactical position is strongest if you remain behind cover and if you avoid putting yourself in the same kill zone as your partner. Just as you want to merge multiple robbers' kill zones to reduce their effectiveness, you need to keep your personal defense zones separate to increase your effectiveness. If two robbers enter your store and know someone is in the back room, one robber will gain control of the cash register person while the second robber will try to obtain control of you. This is why I strongly recommend back rooms and offices off the sales floor be locked at all times. If a robber runs right in and sticks a gun up your nostril, it's all over. They win.

Some stores, particularly sporting goods emporiums, often have a "seat of the pants" approach to self defense. Since the store can have any number of armed personnel, the attitude is the store cannot be successfully robbed because the robbers can't get everyone. Therefore, the defensive plan is essentially strength of numbers augmented by macho attitude. If this is your defense position, it means you are willing to accept casualties. You may someday find yourself in a re-enactment of the Gunfight at the OK Corral. The robbers may indeed be defeated but you will never know it from under the sheet.

Gunshops often have loaded shotguns readily available to counter personnel. Gunshop owners are not expected to be tacticians, otherwise, they would recognize just how difficult it would be to deploy a shotgun while facing a firearm. A shotgun is more practical if concealed in a back room or a personal defense zone that is not used to service customers. If a store employee or business partner, rather than you, will likely be the first person confronted by a robber, you have a reasonable chance of effectively deploying the shotgun.

With gunshops, the person with the shotgun should be whoever is not directly involved with servicing customers and who is not likely to be behind the counter if a robbery occurs. Gunshops must keep all separate offices locked at all times. Back offices should also have closed circuit TV surveillance of the counter area. Gunshop owners must recognize that robbers willing to take on a gunshop are either very fearless or very stupid. Either way, you must take every possible and reasonable precaution to make it extremely difficult for them to obtain control of the premises. This is done by compartmentalizing.

I would also strongly suggest gunshop counter personnel have a discreet method of alerting others in the store that suspicious persons have entered. This can be nothing more than buzzers placed at strategic locations which will sound a soft warning or alarm in back offices or gunsmithing areas to give personnel in those areas notice that counter personnel have become suspicious of someone. The more advance warning you can give these people, the more effective they can be in defeating one or more robbers. This tactic will alert personnel who can make the most effective use of shoulder weapons without alerting the suspicious person(s) a warning has been sounded.

A recent gunshop robbery is worth mentioning. A police officer, on duty and in uniform, stopped at a local gunshop to purchase an item of police equipment. Despite a marked cruiser outside the store, a robber tried to rob the store anyway! To the best of my knowledge, the police officer was wounded in the shootout that followed and the robber was himself killed by the shopkeeper.

It is incumbent upon gunshop owners in particular to have both proactive and reactive defensive plans in place long before a robbery occurs. All predictable variations of a possible robbery must be discussed and defense plans developed.

A robber may take one partner by surprise, then attempt to force the other partner to give up his gun, himself, or both. Nothing good can possibly happen by giving up the gun. These are some of the things armed partners must talk about. This topic will be discussed under hostage situations.

Innocent Bystanders

Without training, most bystanders will respond to a sudden call to duck, get out of the way, or take cover by first confirming the potential danger for themselves. If they cannot readily identify a threat, they will stand there and look at you as though you've lost your mind. Consequently, don't expect instant cooperation from innocents. They're not trained.

A number of years ago, the owner of a jewelry store became suspicious of someone after buzzing him into the store. As the jeweler waited on a customer who was accompanied by a child of perhaps 10 or 12 years old, the jeweler noticed a gun butt in the man's waistband. The jeweler then whispered to the customer to leave the store immediately because the strange man had a gun and a robbery appeared imminent. The customer laughed off the jeweler's warning and refused to leave the store. She told the jeweler the stranger was most likely an off duty cop. Moments later, gunfire erupted. To my knowledge, no one was hit and the would-be robber fled.

You must remember two things about innocent bystanders: first, don't expect them to display any tactical brilliance during a felony. Second, your decision whether or not to resist must consider the potential danger to innocent parties. At a minimum, avoid shooting in their direction as they may become frozen with fear and remain exposed to gunfire. Keep in mind you may also be held legally liable for bullets fired by the robbers which hit innocent bystanders, whether customers or your own employees, on the theory there never would have been shots fired if you hadn't resisted.

Also remember shots fired inside your store by either you or the robbers can ricochet in unpredictable directions, endangering bystanders who were not even in the direct line of fire.

If You Cannot Resist

I have studied many surveillance video tapes of robberies in progress. It seems there are three main types of entries. Some robbers stroll in cool and casual, walk up to the cash register, then announce a robbery. Other robbers will enter the store and browse, waiting for a customer to leave. Then, they make their move. The last and perhaps most difficult to defend against are the robbers who rush the store at full speed. They have you under control before you realize a robbery is in progress. In one instance, the robber literally dove across the counter to gain access to the cash register area.

Despite planning, you may not get an opportunity to resist. In this case, crime prevention units of major police departments advise you to:

• Calmly obey the robber's demands.

• Do not draw a weapon when you're facing a weapon.

• Do not make any sudden moves. If you must obtain a key or move to a different part of the store, ask the robber's permission before doing anything. Explain why it is necessary to do something before doing it.

• Any verbal resistance to the robber must be avoided.

• Do not attempt to bargain with him.

• Do not patronize the robber.

• Do exactly as you're told.

• Activate hold up alarm buttons only if it can be done without being seen. Buttons should be located at several points throughout the store as well as store rooms and bathrooms. A foot switch is especially practical near the cash register.

• Do not encourage him to shoot you by telling him that you got a good look at him and you're going to call the police. Many people say and do amazingly stupid things under stress.

There are several other things you can do to lessen the

degree of the emergency you may find yourself involved in.

Do not leave packing cord, rope, or rolls of strong tape in plain view. The robber may not have planned to tie you up but he may get the idea if you leave a ball of twine around for his convenience.

Be resourceful. By anticipating likely threats, you may develop plans for dealing with them. Keep a window scraper on the floor below the lowest shelf at the register and in your back room so you may increase the possibility of freeing yourself if tied up. Immediately start trying to free yourself if left alone. The robber may be planning to set the store on fire or to shoot you at the conclusion of the robbery. A scraper may also be used to cut through telephone and electrical cord as well as duct tape.

Based upon my recollection of newspaper accounts of robberies, the victims most often bound by robbers are residents in their homes, jewelers, and restaurant owners. Often, the robbers need time to attempt to break into a safe, thoroughly ransack a house, or to carefully select the items they want from among hundreds of less valuable items. Binding also occurs in robberies which become hostage situations.

If you have no choice but to submit to binding, first offer your hands in front on the slight chance the robbers thought process is sufficiently stressed that he'll bind your hands in front without thinking. Whether your hands are bound in the front or rear, perhaps the best position which will allow you to cut the binding (assuming you have planned in advance to gain access to a knife or razor) is to cross your wrists with the top of the weak wrist in contact with the bottom of the strong one. Your wrists will cross at about 90 degrees. Never offer your hands with the bottom of your wrists touching (palms facing each other) or with the top of your wrists in contact. In the latter two positions, it is exceptionally difficult, if not impossible, to maneuver a knife or window scraper against the bindings. It should be noted that police are usually taught to handcuff detainees with the top of the wrists facing each other. Even if the detainee has a handcuff key, it is virtually impossible for him to use it to free himself.

Also, remember the corners of most masonry surfaces have sufficient coarseness to abrade through most binding materials. Broken glass of any kind also works well. Sharp edges may sometimes be found on the inner edges of sheet metal office cabinets or any other stamped metal such as radiator covers. You should inspect your place of business, including the back room, to locate, in advance, surfaces which may be used to cut through bindings in the event you cannot reach a cutting instrument. For example, if I were bound in a bathroom, I wouldn't hesitate to smash the top of the toilet tank in order to obtain a shard of ceramic that may be used to cut or abrade through a binding. Loose floor or wall tiles, especially if glazed, are razor sharp when broken. Exposed threads on plumbing or electrical conduit may be used to abrade bindings if nothing else is available.

You may be chuckling to yourself after reading the last two paragraphs. However, hundreds of robbery victims are bound, trussed, or hogtied each year. Consequently, the risk of binding is not quite as remote as you might think. The resourceful merchant, knowing this, will plan in advance for the possibility. Besides, it is much easier to identify cutting and abrasive surfaces in advance than to first think about it when you've been bound and your mind is so frazzled it ceases to function.

Assume for the moment you were marched into the back room and tied up. If you free yourself and there's a back exit, get out of the store and call police. If there's no rear entrance and you have a weapon, arm yourself and wait to see if the felon comes back to you. If he does, his guard may be down because he thinks you are immobilized. This may be your only and best chance at survival. The tactical advantage rests with the person who lies in wait. Go after the felon and you reduce your odds of surviving.

Be aware there are many lawfully armed police officers and federal agents on the streets, as well as legally armed civilians in states which issue concealed carry permits. In the event of a robbery, the second person to draw a gun could be an off duty police officer rather than an accomplice. Also, you must realize you cannot simply jump to the conclusion that anyone in your store in plainclothes with a gun under his jacket is a criminal.

Throughout the robbery, its aftermath, and during hostage situations, you are at serious risk of being mistaken for a felon and fired upon by police. As soon as you can safely do so, put your gun away to reduce this possibility, and greet arriving police officers with your hands in plain view. If the police order you to drop your gun, do so immediately and without turning in their direction.

Other Felonious Emergencies

According to studies published in *Security Management Magazine*, murder, rather than industrial accidents, is the leading cause of death in the workplace. While a significant percentage of these murders are incident to a robbery, many murders are committed by disgruntled employees or as a result of domestic violence that spills over into the workplace. However, it is beyond the scope of this book to provide a detailed treatise on identifying and managing disgruntled workers or their fractured love lives.

There are some steps you may take, not so much to avoid violence but rather, not to invite it. When terminating an employee, be as tactful as possible. Do it in private. Do not use the occasion to vent your anger or to tell him or her exactly what you and everyone else thinks of them. For some, loss of a job may be the last straw. It may cause them to become violent or suicidal. Unfortunately, suicidal people often want company for the trip to the hereafter. Any threats by disgruntled or terminated workers must be taken seriously. Often, they **do** go home, get a gun, and return with tragic results. Make sure you know your work force. If one of your managers is a tyrannical taskmaster and seems to enjoy making other people miserable, remember the bullets intended for him can also find you.

All threats should be reported to the police and you should ask them for guidance in managing the problem. Often, they will advise you there's nothing they can do unless the threat was documented or until such time as the threat is carried out. However, notification to the proper authorities places you on stronger legal ground because it demonstrates you did try to arrive at a non-violent solution by working within the framework of the legal process. If a confrontation then materializes, a grand jury would be more inclined to believe your tale of unavoidability based upon your prior efforts to avoid the very confrontation that did indeed occur.

If an individual tells you he'll be back with a weapon and you report this to the police, they will probably send a cruiser to stand by at your business for a reasonable length of time. It all depends on whether the threat was direct and immediate or one of those vague, "you'll live to regret this day," type of threats. You also have the option of hiring an armed, licensed security officer for whatever period of time you think is necessary. I'm not talking about the minimum wage, square badge types. Instead, find a private contractor who specializes in executive protection, perhaps a former Secret Service agent, who has the expertise to build a security envelope around you.

Domestic violence that spills into the workplace has become such a significant problem that many of the larger corporations have instituted guidelines and procedures through their security departments to identify workers who are at risk and to take steps to insure the worker and those around them are safe.

You have read about the situation many times: a jilted lover or spouse (most often a male) ignores an order of protection, shows up at his girlfriend's or wife's place of work, kills her plus those around her, then turns the gun on himself. Several years ago, approximately eight women on Long Island, New York were murdered under these circumstances, some at their place of work, within one year. This was an especially significant event because most of them had obtained orders of protection in the local courts.

If your retail operation is large enough to warrant an internal security force, the chief of security must be notified of any domestic or employment related situation that may turn violent. Security personnel have numerous proactive tools at their disposal to prevent violence. In the case where a female employee is being harassed or stalked by a former husband or boyfriend, your security chief may arrange for special parking privileges for the affected employee, and also provide an escort to and from the parking lot.

The small business owner must be reasonably alert for problems within the workforce which could affect him, even if his workforce is but one part time cashier earning the minimum wage. Be alert for signs of domestic violence. Perhaps a particular female shows up with a black eye or bruises, she gets upsetting phone calls, is frequently forced to punch out early, etc.

Although orders of protection are of questionable value in preventing violence, as an employer you should know if one is in effect. Also, if you have an abused employee, encourage them to obtain an order of protection or restraining order as they are also called. If obeyed, it can reduce the possibility of violence occurring in your establishment. As previously mentioned, you must avail yourself of the legal tools available to you whether or not you believe they may work. If you have no alternative but to use deadly force against a homicidal, vengeful individual, you are on firmer legal ground if that individual has violated an order of protection.

If your business generates a significant amount of cash, you must also be alert to the possibility an employee may set you up for a robbery. We often refer to these as "inside jobs."

On Palm Sunday, 1993, a popular florist in Middle Village, Queens, New York, was shot and killed as he closed his florist shop. His wife sat in the car with the day's receipts of $3,400.00 when three armed men approached. Joseph DeSantis, armed with nothing more than good intentions, was shot dead going to his wife's aid. The robbery was masterminded by a 21-year old former employee who had been fired several weeks earlier after being caught stealing a nominal amount of cash. He has since been convicted of murder.

If you have a compulsive gambler on your payroll, their need for cash can become so great that they will sometimes set you up for a robbery, even if you are a family member. Gamblers are not difficult to identify. Often, they ask for salary advances, frequently ask to borrow nominal amounts of money which they don't repay, from co-workers for lunch or gas, and they brag to co-workers if they happen to win. The most obvious sign of all is when bill collectors come knocking on your door. Likewise, individuals with drinking or drug problems, or who are seriously in debt, can pose a security problem for you and your business.

You will recall the premise of this book is to **avoid** gun battles and to win the ones you cannot avoid. One of our key survival elements is knowledge. You must know what's going on around you and recognize other people's problems may become **your** problems. You are especially at risk from the potential adversaries we have just discussed because, frequently, you know them, at least by sight, and don't recognize them as felonious threats until it is too late.

There are elements in society who will tell you that in the vast majority of robberies, nobody gets injured if the robber's wishes are complied with. Therefore, armed resistance is neither wise nor necessary. They're partially right. I'm sure violence occurs in but a small fraction of robberies. Unfortunately, many robberies are intertwined with murder sprees. As a result, you have no way of knowing which robber is going to order you to lie face down, then shoot you in the back of the head in order to not leave witnesses. Another robber may, shoot you, then flee empty handed.

The confrontation is no sporting event. If you don't move fast enough, if you move too quickly, if you wear a hearing aid and didn't quite understand what he commanded, if you don't have enough money, or if the robber has had a bad day, you may indeed be shot. The reasons why robbers shoot storekeepers are too numerous to mention. Again, only you can make the decision whether the risk of resisting is outweighed by the risk of complying. I urge you to take the course of action your judgement tells you is most likely to result in your coming through the situation with yourself and other innocent people alive and unharmed.

CHAPTER 12

AFTERMATH

Your conduct in the seconds immediately following a robbery is critical for a number of reasons. First, the confrontation is not over even though the robber has fled. What you do now can cost you your life or the life of an innocent bystander. Earlier in the book we mentioned there are four parts to a confrontation. The immediate aftermath of a robbery begins when the robber has been defeated or has just fled out the door. It ends with the arrival of the first police officer. Without getting bogged down in semantics, the immediate aftermath of a robbery may also be considered a part of the confrontation. However, the chief difference between the two is that different tactics are needed to manage each and you will also be gripped by different emotions.

Robberies can end in any number of ways. Most frequently, the robber gets the cash register contents, then flees. Less frequently, the robber is shot, the store owner is shot, both are shot, or police arrive while the robber is still in the store. Then, he may exchange fire with the police or barricade himself, holding you or a store worker hostage. Let's explore some likely scenarios and the things you can do to ensure the confrontation is ultimately resolved in your favor.

Never chase after a robber.

In the chapter titled "Mindset" we discussed the need to anticipate and control certain emotions such as rage, anger or revenge. Accept the fact the robber has fled and hope your insurance company will cover the loss. Do not let the desire for revenge control you. Remember, deadly force should only be used to save lives, not to recover a handful of cash, even a big handful.

Quite often, a storekeeper will arm himself as the robber is fleeing, then chase down the street after him, firing, and screaming wildly. Invariably, innocent people are killed or wounded. Sometimes a robber will turn around and start firing at his pursuer, often hitting the storekeeper or a bystander.

Discipline and judgment require we not initiate a gun battle in a situation where our lives are no longer at immediate risk, where a gun battle could have been avoided or where the robbery is over. There's no point in provoking a second confrontation. Under these circumstances, not only are you responsible for injuries and death caused by your gunfire but you may also be held accountable for death or injury caused by the robber's gunfire.

Following are several more good reasons not to chase after fleeing felons;

1. While running, you can easily be mistaken for an armed felon, especially if the police have been summoned. You are then at risk of being shot by a police officer. Perhaps it is the robber who may get lucky as the police may see you with a gun and not the robber. Also, chasing after the robber brings you under the complex laws dealing with fleeing felons. Avoid the situation entirely.

2. By chasing after a gunman, you are no longer acting in self defense but are now attempting a citizen's arrest. Citizen's arrest may be permitted in your state of residence. However, it is fraught with legal risk. You are acting on your own. You do not have a municipality to assume liability for injuries you cause in good faith or for making a wrongful arrest. Good samaritan laws do not apply here. Most lawyers will advise you under no circumstances should you attempt a citizen's arrest no matter how morally or legally correct you think you are and no matter what the penal code says.

3. You have just lived through one of life's most traumatic experiences. If you are middle aged, a bit out of shape, have a heart condition or hypertension, the added stress of a foot chase may be enough to bring on a heart attack or stroke.

4. The robber may have an armed accomplice waiting in a car or just outside your business, serving as a lookout. If you chase after him you may find yourself in a crossfire or shot in the back by someone you didn't know was there. Also, the accomplice, if present, may be inside the store, posing as an ordinary customer. This is a clever tactic often used by robbers, especially bank robbers. By appearing to be a customer, depositor, or shopper, the accomplice's sole purpose is to provide back-up security for the robber you're aware of. It is their job to deal with the chance encounters with armed plainclothes officers or a store owner who elects to resist and all but tunes out everyone and everything but the obvious robber and his gun. The first time you become aware an accomplice is present is when he starts shooting at you. For this reason, deciding whether or not to resist a robber depends, in part, on who else is in the store, their location, and whether or not they are known to you or are complete strangers, in which case one could be a back-up accomplice. If there is a back-up accomplice present, odds are good he'll be of the same race as the robbers you're aware of, one or both of his hands may be concealed from view and he'll probably not display any fear or concern for his personal safety.

5. Assuming you succeed in overtaking the robber, what will you do next? You don't have handcuffs and even if you did, I would not advise you to use them because the art of handcuffing a felon while simultaneously denying him the opportunity to attack you can easily be the subject of a second book. As previously stated, you are not a trained police officer. Therefore, you must stay out of his kill zone.

6. In some neighborhoods and situations, you may find yourself surrounded by an increasingly hostile crowd of onlookers who may go to the robber's aid. They may attack you!

As you can see, chasing after felons can be exceedingly

dangerous. It's the equivalent of walking across a minefield in snowshoes. It's just not worth it.

Following are some smart tactics which can prevent a bad situation from becoming even worse;

1. Immediately arm yourself if you are not already armed, then lock the door. Of course, if you're five feet from the door and 50 feet from your gun, lock the door first. The robber may run 50 feet, then decide it wasn't such a good idea to leave witnesses and may want to return to finish what he started. Anticipate this. Locking the door will also help preserve any evidence left at the scene. Try to remember what the robbers touched. This will make the police department's job easier in trying to obtain fingerprints.

2. Call the police. Try to give them as many details as you can recall, especially if you observed a getaway car.

3. Try to calm yourself. Breathe deeply. Drink some water. Your mouth is probably as dry as a cotton ball. Tell yourself it is over and that you're going to be okay. Have yourself taken to the nearest hospital emergency room as quickly as possible after the police arrive. There, doctors can examine you and, if necessary, give you mild sedatives to reduce the dangerous degree of stress you are experiencing. Prompt medical attention can help avoid a stroke or heart attack during the hours following a robbery.

4. Ask any witnesses present to give you their names and addresses. Expect most people, especially in high crime areas, do not want to get involved. Do not forcibly detain any witnesses.

5. Your local anti-crime unit may be able to provide you with a criminal description worksheet. It would be a wise idea to keep some handy. If you have one, try to write down as many details as possible. This will aid the police in identifying and apprehending the robber. If you don't have such a worksheet, jot down as many details as you can remember on anything available.

6. Be observant. Let your eyes and ears be your weapons. If more than one robber, remember if they called each other by

name. Observe race, skin coloring, age, height, weight, clothing, identifying marks such as scars and tattoos, accents, and the color or type of handgun or other weapon used. Try to observe the direction in which the robbers leave. If you observe a getaway car, note as many details as possible such as make, model, color, body damage, license number, additional occupants, etc.

7. The police should be on their way. Under no circumstances should you greet them with a gun in your hand. They may not know who you are. They are responding to a robbery in progress and expect to find an armed felon. You'll do nicely. In your agitated state you may forget you are holding a gun.

8. Quite often, a robber will strike a particular establishment a second time, usually within a month. If the first robbery went smoothly (for him) he may indeed strike again. If you are the victim of a robbery, it is necessary you remain at an increased level of awareness as there's a better than average chance you will suffer a second robbery in the near future.

Hostage Situations

Some robberies degenerate into hostage crises. This is especially so if a silent alarm was sounded and police, who happen to be in the area, arrive as the robbery is still in progress. Hostage situations may be discussed as either part of the confrontation or part of the aftermath. I have elected to discuss it as part of the aftermath because, in the vast majority of instances, the robber didn't intend to take hostages but instinctively does so when faced by police or armed merchants. Consequently, a hostage situation is a second phase of the confrontation.

If taken hostage, remain calm. Comply with the hostage taker's demands.   Ask permission before moving.   Police departments now rely on highly trained and skilled hostage negotiators and your chances of surviving a hostage incident are nearly 100 percent. Do not reach for a hidden weapon unless you are 100 percent certain you can do it without being detected and you are also 100 percent certain of hitting the robber with your first round. You should be aware that of all the broad categories of hostage situations, that is, incident to a robbery, terrorist act, disgruntled employee, psychotic, etc., the hostage crisis incident to a robbery is among the quickest to be resolved.

In some hostage situations, the hostage taker may be so careless you may easily escape through a back door or window. If you escape, remember the police may have your location surrounded and you could be mistaken for the felon. When fleeing, get both hands into the air and do exactly what the police tell you to do. Make sure both hands are empty. Any object, even your wallet, can be mistaken for a weapon in poor light. Do not reach for your wallet or any other identification. Keep your hands away from pockets and your waist. If the police do not know you, you may initially be treated as a bad guy. They may pounce on you and handcuff you. Remain calm. It is normal procedure. Felons sometimes pretend they're victims in order to escape and the police have learned not to take any chances. Police policy is to detain everyone, secure the premises, then sort out the good guys from the bad guys. You'll get an opportunity to identify yourself. Do not fight or resist the police. They are already at a heightened state of alertness and any resistance on your part could result in serious injuries to you.

If you or an employee are being held hostage when the police arrive, your instructions may be to tell the cops it was a false alarm to get them to leave. You may want to work with your local civic groups and the police to devise some sort of secret signal to alert police you are not acting under your own free will. One such signal I might suggest is, with both hands resting on the counter, calmly and slowly grip one thumb with the other hand. This signals that you or someone else is being held. Of course, the police must know the signal if its going to work. Not only can such a signal save your life but it can save the lives of police officers as well.

In the absence of a pre-arranged signal, try to make it known a hostage crisis is in progress. Perhaps a discreetly pointed finger or a stare can alert responding officers that something is amiss. This is also a very good time to act nervous and to stutter even if you don't have a speech impediment. Your body language must contradict your words.

If the robbery goes bad, from the robber's point of view, he may take a human shield. You've seen this scene hundreds of times on virtually every crime drama that's ever been on television. Invariably, the good guy is ordered to drop his gun which he promptly does. Never take tactical lessons from television. Under no circumstances should you surrender your gun. The robber's gun may be a fake or a toy. I realize this may be extremely difficult for you to understand, especially if that human shield is your son or daughter. Once he has your gun, he is free to shoot you if he pleases. If the robber is armed with a knife, he cannot readily hurt you nor can he readily hurt the human shield because he or she is his life insurance. If the robber fires upon you while holding a human shield, remain behind cover and do not return fire.

More than likely, a human shield will be used to back out of the store to prevent you from firing. There's little you can do in this situation. Hold your fire and hold your cover. You are not a trained police officer or SWAT team commander. You are not expected to solve the hostage crisis, in all probability, intervening in these situations will almost always make things worse. Some of you may, in fact, possess the skill and resolve necessary to shoot a felon who's behind a human shield. The problem is you cannot guarantee the felon won't squeeze off a shot, sometimes referred to as a reflex shot, as he's dying. This situation requires the brain be destroyed. When a felon or robber is facing you, the "window of opportunity" is only from the tip of the nose to about an inch below the hairline and from eye socket to eye socket. The target is not the entire head. Consequently, let me officially go on record by stating, you should not attempt to shoot a hostage taker hiding behind a human shield.

If shots are exchanged between the police and the robber(s), make every effort not to become involved. Stay behind cover. During the 1994 Christmas shopping season, two police officers entered a Brooklyn, New York bicycle shop with guns drawn in response to a robbery in progress alarm. A man posing as a store worker behind the counter calmly told them it was a false alarm. As the officers lowered their guns, a gunman jumped up from behind the counter and opened fire, killing one police officer with two shots to the head. More police responded and fired over 50 rounds into the store in order to suppress the robber's fire while extracting the mortally wounded police officer. The owner of the bicycle shop cringed on the floor of a back room as bullets whizzed all around him. The store owner would have certainly been shot if he had attempted to produce a gun during this wild shootout. Incidentally, one robber was killed and two more captured during this robbery.

Don't show up for a gun battle with a baseball bat. There are more bats behind cash registers than at ball fields. Bats are too heavy for light work and too light for heavy work. In addition, depending on how they are used, they may legally constitute a deadly or prohibited weapon in your state of residence. There is a very narrow band of permissibility attached to bats and other blunt instruments, especially if you're justified in using deadly force and a bat is all you have. A bat is not my first choice in a self defense situation. Also, if a robber or an irate customer gets behind the counter, he may use your own bat against you.

It is my opinion blows to the head or neck from any blunt object are not justified unless deadly force is justified. Hopefully, the criminal laws in this country will be changed to the effect that blows to the head or neck with a blunt object constitute presumptive evidence the attacker was trying to kill his victim.

Wounded Felons

Let's change the scenario. You have exchanged gunfire with a robber and he falls wounded or apparently wounded. What should you do?

1. Maintain cover. There may be an accomplice in the store (perhaps posing as a customer as previously discussed) or the robber may be faking a wound and is trying to lure you into the open. Also, an accomplice outside the store, such as the getaway driver, may have heard the shots and can run into the store at any time.

2. Call 911 immediately. Earlier, I advised you a telephone must be in your personal defense zone and you must not turn your back on your adversary while calling.

3. Do not lay down the gun. De-cock it if necessary and remove your finger from the trigger. Keep the gun on your person.

4. Do not attempt to tie up, handcuff, or otherwise restrain the robber. **Stay out of his kill zone.** He will definitely give you a one way ticket to the promised land if given half an opportunity. If the robber had one weapon visible, assume he has a second weapon somewhere.

5. If the robber suddenly bolts up from the floor and flees, let him go. Do not chase him and do not shoot him. Do not station yourself between the robber and the exit. Our primary objective is to terminate deadly force confrontations, not prolong them.

6. If you are holding a robber at gunpoint and he appears cooperative, do the following: order him to drop his gun and, if necessary, kick it away from himself. Order him to lay face down on the floor and tell him to turn his face away from you. Maintain a safe distance. Keep the counter between you and him. Stay behind cover. Move a few feet from where the robber last saw you. He may bolt up and try to attack you at any time. The robber may be feigning cooperation with the hope you will make one little mistake.

7. You are legally responsible to ensure no further harm comes to the robber. Once you have custody of an individual, you are responsible for his safety, no matter how heinous the crime he has committed. You cannot allow your customers or employees to use the defeated robber as a soccer ball.

8. Failure to promptly summon medical assistance for a

robber you have justifiably shot can subject you to a variety of charges, especially if you are not injured, and a phone is readily available. It can transform a justifiable shooting into a legal nightmare. When calling 911, be sure to tell them a robber has been shot and in immediate need of medical assistance. In fact, ask the 911 operator to send "police and an ambulance" whether you think anyone needs medical assistance or not. Even if no one has been injured, they may be by the time the ambulance arrives. If it isn't needed, no harm was done. The 911 tapes of your call are available to all parties concerned and they will certainly be examined. These tapes can help solidify your legal position and shut off yet another avenue of legal attack against you.

What if you are shot? If you know you've been shot, there's an overwhelming chance you will survive your wound. Do not give up. Don't assume because you were shot the confrontation is over. Often, police officers give up or stop fighting when shot. This is where mindset comes into play. You must continue to resist. If you stop resisting, the robber may use this opportunity to finish you off.

If the robber has fled and you are shot, call for help. Running or extensive walking will further increase your heart rate and thus increase the rate at which you are bleeding. In fact, running any distance may spell the difference between whether or not you survive your injuries. If alone, apply pressure to the wound and remind yourself that if you are capable of giving yourself first aid, there is a 97 percent chance you'll survive the wound. You didn't give up to the robber. Don't give up to your wound. Do not assume death automatically follows a gunshot wound because of what you see on television. Instead, will yourself to live because you will have to testify in court against the person who shot you. Both felons and victims routinely survive multiple gunshot wounds.

Know what shock is and anticipate you may suffer shock. You can sense you're going into shock and you can actually screw up the mental resolve to resist it long enough to call for medical assistance. It would be wise to organize a group of armed merchants, then contract with an appropriate medical expert such as an emergency medical technician (EMT), a paramedic, or a military medic or corpsman to learn first aid for gunshot wounds. The knowledge you gain can spell the difference between life and death.

Other Legal Stuff

Your worst nightmare has come to pass. You have just traded shots with a robber who is now lying on the floor. You can see blood and he is writhing with pain. You are shaking uncontrollably and your voice sounds like a Disney character. You may have involuntarily soiled your pants.

Before we get too deeply into this chapter, you should be aware that approximately three fourths of the world's lawyers live in the United States and law schools are spitting out lawyers as fast as American industry spit out Hellcats at the height of World War II. This shouldn't surprise you, considering we're the world's most litigious society. The problem is, for every ethical lawyer there seems to be a dozen Whiplash Willies and assorted ambulance chasers. Another problem is lawyers like to live well, make their first million before age thirty, marry a beautiful person, and drive a flashy car. That's where you figure in. Please read on.

In a Hollywood gun battle, the stud actor slays villains by the morgue full, then immediately performs the obligatory sex act before he gets around to the paperwork, if any. I'm sure after an epic gun battle, most of us would need to wait a few minutes before enjoying the pleasures of the flesh. Lightness aside, in reality, a deadly force confrontation is one of the most psychologically devastating experiences life has to offer. You may suddenly experience an overwhelming sense of pity, remorse, and compassion for the individual you have just shot. This is a normal reaction because you are a good human being who values life, and there before you is an individual whose life may be ebbing away from something you did.

Stop. Put on the brakes. The best thing you can do is to call for police and medical assistance. Be aware, at times, emergency medical personnel will not approach a fallen felon until he has been secured by the police. That is, disarmed and handcuffed if necessary. It would be difficult for you to assess whether or not the individual you have shot still has the means, present opportunity, and intent to cause you harm. Also, you are at risk from possible accomplices while your attention is fixed upon the individual you've wounded.

Avoid the temptation to rush to his aid. You must remain out of his kill zone because there still may be a lot of fight left in this individual. Even if you see blood, he may not be nearly as badly wounded as you think. Let's give credit where credit is due: the average street thug is more tenacious than the ordinary law abiding citizen. They're harder to stop and harder to keep stopped.

The emotion of remorse can also cause you to say some dumb things to arriving police officers such as "I didn't mean to do it" or "it was an accident." From a legal point of view, once you let it be known the shooting was somehow avoidable or accidental, you deny yourself the defense of justification. Consequently, **never try to transform a justifiable shooting into an accidental one.**

Within your value system, things which happen by accident are never as morally reprehensible as things done on purpose. Your father was more forgiving if you put a baseball through someone's window by accident than if it was a purposeful act. You also know, from life's experience, people don't usually go to jail as a result of an accidental death except with extenuating circumstances such as drunkenness or a reckless disregard for human life. It is understandable then, your act may seem more morally acceptable, in your mind, if you try to believe it was an accident rather than an intentional act.

Whatever mind games you want to play with yourself can cause you major legal problems. At a minimum, if you treat the shooting as accidental, it tends to lessen the severity of the crime committed by the felon, especially if he was armed with something other than a firearm. Automatically, the felon, or his estate, can sue you for injuries or accidental death. You may also be subjected to criminal charges which will consume your life's savings to defend yourself against.

While on the subject of dumb remarks, you must also refrain from impromptu, off the cuff retorts which could be subsequently exploited by an attorney. For example, you have killed a robber. A police officer, in checking the body says, "Gee, merchant, did you have to shoot him so many times?" Merchant—"I like to finish what I start."

Almost any response at this time is subject to exploitation. Also, the aftermath of a shooting is absolutely no time for humor. Don't try to minimize the situation or try to be cute or funny. Remember, you are under a microscope. The shooting is over. The confrontation is only beginning.

In some instances, a robber may freeze when you produce a gun, perhaps because his gun is a fake or because he's armed with a knife. Consequently, you'll find yourself in the so-called Mexican standoff. Do not issue any ultimatums such as, "Take one step closer and I'll shoot," or "Cross that seam in the floor and you're a dead man." In this situation it is more difficult to justify your actions because your primary reason for shooting appears to be geographic rather than to defend your life. In court, you will find yourself trying to explain yourself out of shooting someone for stepping over an imaginary line.

If you feel compelled to engage in dialogue with someone who would rip your guts out if given half an opportunity, simply state, "Stay where you are. Don't make me shoot you." The "line in the sand" should exist only in your mind. In a subsequent court action, your justification is the robber advanced upon you, possibly with the intent of disarming you. It makes for a cleaner defense.

Remember, attorneys like to win. If the person you've shot, or his estate, decides to sue you for a wrongful act, they will first obtain every scrap of evidence available. This includes the police reports, witness statements, recorded 911 calls, video tapes, autopsy findings, whatever. Then, the attorney will lock himself in a room and review the evidence with an electron microscope. If he can find absolutely nothing that can be exploited or shaded in favor of the plaintiff, he may advise his client to drop the legal action as there's virtually no chance of winning. Remember, it is **you** who will provide the encouragement for the other side to sue you.

While on the subject of statements, when police arrive, confine your statements to the absolute minimum necessary to establish who you are, it is your store, you were being robbed, and you are the victim. Then ask to call your lawyer and see a doctor. Invoke your right against self incrimination under the Fifth Amendment to the U.S. Constitution and do not answer any questions regarding the mechanics of the crime until you've had an opportunity to consult with your lawyer. Your minimized statement should never begin with or include phrases like "I thought", "I assumed," "it looked like," "I guess," "I wasn't really sure," "in my opinion," "the gun just sort of went off," "I don't even remember pulling the trigger." etc. Don't ask the police whether or not they think you were justified. You should already know this. These comments tend to introduce grayness into what you perceived the threat to be. They make you sound unsure, tentative, quick to overreact. Do not second guess yourself in the presence of investigators or beg for their forgiveness or understanding. Gray areas are a lawyer's dream. Some people suffer from diarrhea of the mouth. It's best to keepeth thy mouth shut.

When called to the scene, the primary mission of the police is to secure the scene in order to prevent further loss of life, make apprehensions if necessary, obtain medical aid for the wounded, and to begin gathering evidence. Judgement of your actions usually comes later. If the incident is assigned to a prosecutor or an assistant district attorney, he will review the evidence and also interview the officers who gathered it and obtained the witness statements. If those police officers fully believe you were justified in your actions, they may be able to dissuade the prosecutor from pursuing the matter any further. If the prosecutor becomes convinced your use of force was justified, he can then dissuade a grand jury from indicting you. Someone once said a district attorney has so much power and influence he could get a grand jury to indict a ham sandwich. The point is, your very first contact with the judicial system occurs when the first uniformed officer arrives on the scene.

Picture yourself on the witness stand, at trial, being questioned by a prosecutor or plaintiff's attorney. "Mr. Smith, you told arriving police officers you thought you were going to be robbed. What did you mean by, 'I thought'? Weren't you sure? You shot my client because you thought he was going to rob you? Since you thought he was going to rob you, is it possible he had no intention of robbing you, that you were mistaken? Is it possible my client had produced the knife merely to clean his fingernails?"

I think you get the picture. The next thing you should remember is you have committed a very serious legal offense for which you want to be excused based upon justification. Remember, innocent people are sometimes convicted for things they did not do, or because a justifiable act has become clouded by post incident verbal blunders, or by sloppy investigative work by detectives. Consequently, it is entirely possible for an innocent person to incriminate himself. Don't feel compelled to answer investigators' questions because you believe by doing so you will reinforce your innocence.

Some people equate invoking of Fifth Amendment rights with guilt. After all, you never see good guys invoking the Fifth on television. You're in the real world, not on television. A jury may not infer guilt by you invoking the Fifth Amendment. This is one of the constitutional protections or safeguards you enjoy. Be sure to use it until you've had an opportunity to consult with an attorney.

If you use your firearm against another individual, no matter how righteous or justified your actions, **you need a lawyer.** You probably don't need the guy who closed on your house or secured your certificate of incorporation, unless he's a former prosecutor. You need a skilled criminal attorney who will know how to present the facts to investigators and who can better rehabilitate you in the event you indeed said something you shouldn't have said. The lawyer may dispatch his own investigator to the scene to begin gathering evidence and statements to support you. Don't let your sense of moral outrage cloud your judgment. If you think our judicial system is anchored in ethics and fairness, you are sadly mistaken. The more liberal the area in which you live, the more likely it is they will attempt to find some fault with you.

At your convenience, call your lawyer, explain what I have said, then ask him to recommend one or two lawyers you can call in the event you must use force against another individual. Keep their phone numbers handy and call when it is safe to do so. For the moment, any lawyer known to you and is willing to leave a warm bed at 2 A.M. to come down to the local lockup to begin your initial representation is better than a highly skilled criminal lawyer who doesn't remember you and is not willing to leave his creature comforts at a moment's notice. Most civil lawyers will have enough legal sense to keep you silent until a lawyer with the proper expertise can be retained and brought into the picture.

More than likely, your first call for assistance will be to a 911 operator. As previously stated, these calls are recorded, consequently, you must select your words carefully. The utterance of a racial or ethnic slur can transform a justifiable shooting into a questionable one. An apparent lack of concern for the person you have shot calls your character into question and can lead to a blistering cross examination. You know when you're being cross examined in a blistering manner when your back side is trying to eat its way through the witness chair.

Those of you who harbor any animosities against a particular racial or ethnic group and habitually use racial slurs in conversation will most likely utter one without thinking. Racial or ethnic slurs recorded on the 911 tapes will come back to haunt you—guaranteed.

It is always better to leave no avenue of legal attack against you than to leave one wide enough for a truck to pass through, then hope your lawyer can save you. Consequently, you need to be very circumspect in ordinary conversation. Avoid making immature remarks or idle or vague threats regarding what you will do to an imagined adversary during a felonious emergency. Also, it would be wise to refrain from affixing any stickers or signs to anything you own which promises or implies an armed response upon any provocation.

Amazingly, the most innocent or inconsequential of remarks can find their way into the courtroom. If your justification is already weak, just a little additional legal damage can be enough to win an indictment or conviction against you. Attorneys hire private investigators specifically to find damaging facts which may be used against you. Once in the witness chair you may end up testifying against yourself.

Do not alter the crime scene. You may feel compelled to change something in order to strengthen you justification. For example, the robber did not fire his gun so you decide to fire a round from his gun, into the counter, to enhance your justification. Any intentional alteration of the facts will gravely weaken your legal position. Once justification is sufficiently eroded, you become vulnerable to criminal charges. Secondly, investigators can quickly detect alterations in most instances.

Let's try a hypothetical example, an individual walks up to your counter, displays a handgun tucked in his waistband and states that he'll shoot you if you don't hand over the register contents. Instead, you draw your own handgun and shoot the robber, who falls dead. You may feel an impulse to put the robber's gun in his hand to better justify shooting him. First, nothing was gained, legally, by the alteration. If you get your fingerprints on the gun or are observed handling it, the robber's family may allege you shot an unarmed man and the gun found in his hand was yours and you put it there to cover up a criminal act. I think I've made my point. Leave the crime scene untouched.

Yet another potential trap may await the storekeeper who has just defeated a robber in an armed confrontation: the media. You should be aware most of the media in this country, whether newspapers or the television networks, are owned or heavily influenced by the eastern liberal establishment which has been historically in favor of strong gun controls and against the individuals' right to self defense. These people are not your friends. Statements made to them may be used as incriminating evidence against you. Also, the media will not hesitate to sensationalize your statement or the events which occurred in order to increase its news worthiness.

The media isn't content to merely report the news. They also like to make news by introducing slants or angles which were not part of the confrontation. For example, a headline may read, "White Storekeeper Shoots Black Youth." The fact this particular black youth was armed and fired upon you is buried somewhere in the article. A more truthful and accurate headline would be: "Storekeeper Shoots Armed Robber." Unfortunately, the former headline will sell more newspapers in areas with large minority populations. The media never hesitates to fan the flames of racism, prejudice, or hatred if it will help them sell newspapers.

All inquiries by the media should be referred to your lawyer. Treat the media as a potential adversary. Also, the media does not have the right to enter private property. Consequently, you do not have to admit them to your store. Also, the police do not have the authority to admit the media upon private property against your will. Unfortunately, the media may enter your store with the cameras rolling, catching you by surprise and off guard. Any dialogue between you and them will be captured on videotape. Remember to conduct yourself in a courteous and professional manner when referring them to your lawyer. Don't utter any threats or ultimatums. Don't respond by putting your hand over the camera lens or by trying to push the cameraman out of the store. If your initial response is that of a raging lunatic, this footage will air on the news and again in court while you are undergoing character assassination. On the other hand, if you are fully cooperative with the media and use the opportunity to engage in a little chest pounding in public, chances are good you will inflict equal or greater damage upon your character.

Despite your best efforts at not making any moral, tactical, or legal mistakes, you may still find yourself facing criminal or civil charges. Let's take a look at the field of battle, namely, the courtroom. In one corner is the attorney. He's cool, pinstriped and wing-tipped, meticulous, polished, oozing professionalism, organized, and exudes confidence. In other words, he's a man-eater. In the other corner is you: fearful, ignorant, sweaty, nervous, apprehensive, shaking, and you think you need a restroom.

You should be familiar with some of the tactics trial attorneys use in order to get you to say something damaging. For example,

Attorney: "Mr. Merchant, how much money was in the cash register when the deceased attempted to rob you?"

Merchant: "Only about $10.00 and loose change. I had made a deposit earlier."

Attorney: "You mean you took a human life to prevent the theft of $10.00?"

Merchant: (first possible answer) "Well, it's my money and I worked for it!"

(second possible answer) "I didn't shoot him to prevent the loss of the cash in the register, I shot him because he had a gun (or whatever) and I feared he was going to use it against me."

If the first answer was given, the jury is left with the impression deadly force was used to prevent a property crime. Add a few more weaknesses and distortions in the case and the firm legal ground beneath your feet becomes quicksand.

Following this answer, the questioning would then go something like this:

Attorney: Speaking in a soft voice and facing the jury, "Mr. Merchant, is a human life only worth $10.00?

Your attorney: "Objection! Counsel is asking for an opinion."

Judge: "Sustained."

However, a great amount of damage has been done. The prosecutor or plaintiff's lawyer has made his point with the jury.

If this sounds outrageous, read on. In a recent case somewhere in the South, an intoxicated individual, following an earlier dispute with the defendant, came to the defendant's home with the intent of killing him with an edged weapon of some sort. In attempting to reach the would-be victim, he either turned over or kicked over a coffee table, at which time the defendant produced a firearm and mortally wounded his attacker. The local prosecutor decided he would not accept the defense of justification and charged the defendant with murder. During the trial, following a series of skillfully constructed questions, and after angering the defendant, he managed to get the defendant to state he shot the deceased because he had turned over the coffee table and no one can come into his home and trash his possessions. The fact the coffee table was knocked aside in an effort to reach the defendant no longer mattered. The defendant was led to tell the jury deadly force was employed as a result of property damage. The defendant was convicted of a murder charge when he should have walked free.

The set up: In order to get you to say something damaging, an attorney or prosecutor has any number of weapons available in his arsenal of tricks. He may deliberately misstate the facts to confuse or anger you and hope your attorney doesn't catch it and raise an objection. He may demand a yes or no answer to a question that can't be answered with a yes or no. He may also deliberately and repeatedly mispronounce your name to anger you. Just recently, we learned of a new weapon in the legal arsenal: the race card.

Another tactic I've seen used is something I call the spiral. The attorney begins at an easy pace with questions of a general nature. He is calm, almost friendly. As his questions become more specific, he begins to quicken the pace. He talks a bit faster, asks shorter questions, and tightens up the time between questions. As he speeds up, so will you. As a result, you may not be listening to his questions as carefully as you should and you're more inclined to respond without thinking about what you're saying, simply because you are trying to keep pace with him without realizing it. Once your state of anxiety is sufficiently aroused and he's got you on the ropes, he springs the key questions with the hope you'll say something damaging, something he can exploit.

Defending Against the Spiral

With any question asked of you, always listen very carefully to what you're being asked. Don't anticipate. Don't begin to answer before the attorney has finished his question. Make sure you understand the question before responding. Be especially careful with two part questions. If you're not sure of what you are being asked, tell the attorney you don't understand his question. As the pace of his questioning quickens, slow down your answers by talking slower. Take longer to think about what you were asked. Ask him to repeat the question if even the slightest hint of fuzziness is present. You and the attorney are at opposite ends of a leash. When he starts yanking on his end, you need to start yanking on your end. Not only are you throwing off his sense of timing but you also reduce the chance of making a damaging statement.

Perhaps the most common tactic employed against witnesses, including police officers who should know better, is to get the witness angry. Angry witnesses give emotional, rather than logical answers. Angry witnesses are far more easily confused, far more vulnerable to the spiral. Expect to be badgered (verbally beaten up). It is often said a rape victim is raped twice: once in the literal sense and again in court. If the attorney needs to portray you as a Rambo type, or even a racist, he will try to make you lose your composure on the stand. Also, angry witnesses are not credible witnesses. Take the verbal abuse. Swallow your pride. Don't fidget. Watch your body language. The best defense against an abusive attorney and the only way you may legally strike back and make him come unglued is to display the emotions of a cement block. Let the attorney unleash his entire arsenal of tricks. You must remain calm and unflustered, unaffected, serene. Never go tit for tat with the attorney. Expect he's going to bait you. Never display even the slightest hint of animosity or disrespect. Always look the attorney directly in the eyes. Never look away.

Avoiding eye contact is a sign of lying and a sign of weakness. And don't slink back or retreat into the witness chair.

Remember, conviction or acquittal can sometimes hinge on the most whimsical or seemingly insignificant fact, feeling, perception, omission, or emotion. It is vitally necessary you strike a sympathetic chord with as many jurors as possible. By words or deed, do not minimize the threat or circumstance created by the felon(s). This is not the time to be U.S. Marine tough. Don't sound tough. Don't act tough. Don't even look tough. Don't strut or swagger. Don't be sarcastic. You must convince the jury you were in fear of losing your life or suffering serious injuries, which is what motivated you to defend yourself. Remember, the good guys on television always overcome impossible odds and can push, punch, drive, or bully their way out of anything. The jury may expect the same of you.

It's not enough to merely say you were in fear. This must be reinforced by describing the physical changes you experienced during the confrontation. For example, your heart began to race, perhaps you had difficulty breathing, you began to sweat profusely, you were momentarily immobilized with fear, perhaps you soiled your pants, you were momentarily unable to talk. Everyone experiences fear sometime in their lives. By describing the physical manifestations of fear, you increase the likelihood of finding those sympathetic chords I mentioned earlier. Don't be embarrassed to share every last manifestation of fear with the jury. If you needed a change of clothing following the confrontation, the jury should know this.

Earlier in this chapter, I mentioned you should go to the hospital at the first safe opportunity following the confrontation. If you received medical treatment, perhaps for a spike in your blood pressure, or you received a mild sedative to calm you, these facts must be given to the jury. In some instances, victims suffer a heart attack in the hours following a robbery. If you are one of these victims, the jury should know this. Remember, fear, like love, is one of those emotions that is easier to define by example. In his summation to the jury, the plaintiff's attorney, or the prosecutor, will again try to weaken your justification by minimizing the circumstances leading to your use of force. If you don't describe HOW you were fearful, these very examples of fear may be given to the jury to demonstrate what fear is and they will be reminded you did not describe experiencing any of them.

When you're finally excused from the witness stand, you're still under the microscope. Do not show the slightest sign of relief. No sighs, no rolling of eyes, no shaking of head in disgust or relief, no dirty looks. Don't slither or skulk away. Stand upright and proud, offer a brief smile to both the jury and the attorney, and leave.

One last thing. The good attorneys already know the answers to the questions they are asking you. Therefore, if there's something in your past, or if you did or said something really stupid that's potentially damaging, you are your own worst enemy if you don't disclose this to your attorney. Never try to outsmart your own lawyer! He's on your side. If there's anything in your past that affects your credibility as a witness, it is always better to disclose the matter on direct examination, by your own attorney, than for the jury to first learn of it under cross examination. Under direct examination, the disclosure can be low key and matter of fact. Then, your attorney can rehabilitate you so as to maintain your credibility. If the situation is disclosed under cross examination, it comes as a revelation to everyone, especially you, who assumed the other side didn't know about it or wouldn't bother to look. Once the damage is done, your attorney must then try to rehabilitate you under re-direct examination. Often, damage that could have been avoided cannot be overcome. Had it been disclosed under direct examination, the matter is old news in the minds of the jurors and any attempt by the opposing attorney to capitalize on the disclosure will not be nearly as effective, if at all.

Conclusion

It is hoped by reading this book you have gained sufficient knowledge to understand winning an armed confrontation is far more than a matter of luck or owning a gun. You have also learned dozens of techniques which can tilt the odds in your favor. Gun battles are frequently won by the slimmest of margins, the slightest of advantages and indeed, sometimes by luck. We have discussed how law enforcement tries to avoid gun battles through proper tactical planning, and we have adapted police thought and practice to fit your circumstances.

Most of all, I wanted to impress you with the fact that merely having a gun is never enough. Being truly prepared for an armed confrontation requires much thought, knowledge, commitment, and preparation. First and foremost, you must make every reasonable effort to reduce the attractiveness of you and your store as potential robbery targets. It is always better to avoid a gun battle than to have to win one.

Having read this book, you may never look at your store quite the same way again. Hopefully, you now have a sufficient understanding of tactics to be able to evaluate your store regarding how it impacts upon your ability to defend yourself, and you will now have the knowledge to recognize potentially fatal traps which can benefit the robber, rather than you. In virtually every instance, minor, relatively inexpensive changes can be made to enhance your store's defensibility.

The material contained in this book is intended to help you reduce the likelihood of being robbed and to present you with the elements you must master in order to increase your odds of winning a confrontation you cannot avoid. Following the advice contained in this book should serve to reduce, but cannot eliminate, the possibility of being defeated during a robbery. No guarantee of victory should be assumed or expected, nor does the author state or imply, in any way, that following his advice will always cause you to win a confrontation.

CHAPTER THIRTEEN

AN INTERVIEW WITH A VICTIM

At 6:26 PM, November 5, 1993, Paul Pruzanski, a pharmacist, was in his pharmacy located in Brooklyn, New York, when an armed robbery occurred. Following are some questions I posed to Paul, together with his answers.

Q. How many workers were in the store at the time of the robbery?

A. Five.

Q. How many workers or partners were armed?

A. Just me.

Q. What were you armed with?

A. A 15 shot, Glock, 9mm.

Q. How many robbers entered the store?

A. I saw two but was told later that the robbery team consisted of four individuals.

Q. Did you see their guns?

A. I don't know how many were armed or exactly what kind of guns they were.

Q. How did they enter?

A. They entered through the front entrance. However, they separated upon entering and attempted to sneak up the aisles, undetected, to the cash register at the rear of the store.

Q. Did the robbers announce a robbery?

A. Not that I recall. The first shots were fired at about the instant I became aware of one or two of the robbers attempting to sneak up the aisle.

Q. Who fired first?

A. The bad guys.

Q. Why did they open fire?

A. Either they panicked or my partner at the register become frozen with fear and didn't move quickly enough.

Q. When did you return fire?

A. Almost immediately.

Q. Did you have a clear shot at the robber with the gun?

A. Not at the time I fired. I would have had a clear shot. However, a young store clerk was directly in the line of fire. I screamed at her to duck but she remained frozen in place and refused to move.

Q. Then what happened?

A. The guy with the gun moved behind a display. I didn't realize it but I could have hit him by shooting through the display. I didn't know that my bullets could have reached the robber through the display.

Q. Did you use cover?

A. No. I was trapped where I was and could not reach effective cover.

Q. How many rounds did you fire?

A. I think eight. I know I didn't hit the robber but my rounds prevented him from firing effectively. They also saved the life of a wholesaler who happened to be in the store. At the time, he was on the ground pleading for his life.

Q. I understand you were wounded?

A. Yes. As best as the detectives who investigated the robbery could ascertain, one of the robbers bullet's glanced off an adding machine and struck me in the jaw, doing considerable damage to my teeth and the surrounding bone structure.

Q. How long did the robbery last?

A. Two to three minutes.

Q. If you were to return to retailing, what would you do

differently?

A. I would keep a large dog in the store as a deterrent. Robbers don't like to mess with dogs. I would also insist that my partners be armed.

Q. Do you feel you had sufficient skills to take on an armed robber?

A. Definitely not. I should have gone for formal combat shooting lessons and learned not only combat skills but also what my guns and bullets were capable of doing. As I said, I had an opportunity to shoot him through a display. Had I done so, I don't think I would have taken a round.

Q. What advice can you offer other merchants and shop-keepers?

A. Learn from my mistakes. You must learn anti-robbery skills. Also, always keep your guard up. Always eyeball everyone entering your store. You should also learn the signs of drug abuse. If you see someone come in with track marks up and down his arms, get ready. I would also train my employees to obey my orders and to prepare them for a possible robbery. Had my clerk ducked as I'd ordered, I definitely could have hit the robber.

Q. What happened to the robbers?

A. I believe two were caught. The one that shot me, a youth of 16 years of age, was convicted of robbery and sentenced to 100 months in jail.

Author's note: Paul Pruzanski has since made a reasonable recovery from his physical wound.

APPENDIX A

FIREARMS SAFETY

Following are some range safety suggestions tailored for informal, commercial or gun club ranges. Upon visiting a range for the first time, you may see specific safety rules posted on a wall or bulletin board. You should read these rules and abide by them. Most private citizens use commercial ranges for target practice. Some of you may belong to a gun club that owns its own range or you may practice shooting on property you own if legal to do so. "Citizen" ranges generally are not as strictly regulated as police ranges. That is, the police officer does absolutely nothing unless given a command to do so while the private citizen, who rents an hour of range time, is essentially free to do as he pleases in accordance with common sense rules of gun safety. As a result, range safety rules will be different for police and commercial ranges.

Specific Range Safety Suggestions
1. Eye and ear protection should be worn at all times. Eye protection should be of wraparound or side-panel design of polycarbonate or other shatter resistant material approved for this purpose. You should also wear a baseball cap with brim to provide you with additional protection from ejected shell casings or fragments hitting your head or falling between the top edge of your safety glasses and your eyes.
2. Immediately upon picking up a firearm, lock the slide to

the rear or open the cylinder and visually check to see that the firearm is unloaded.

3. Check a second time.

4. Never take or give a firearm to or from anyone unless the slide is retracted or cylinder is open.

5. Load only at the range firing point.

6. Unload if instructed to do so by range personnel.

7. Keep the firearm pointed down range at all times.

8. Immediately cease firing and move away from the firing points if someone decides to go forward of the firing points for any reason.

9. Never draw/re-holster with your finger in the trigger guard or on the trigger. Keep your finger outside the trigger guard and off the trigger until your sights are on target and you intend to fire.

10. **NEVER HOLSTER A FIREARM WITH THE HAMMER COCKED**.

11. Never go forward of the firing points unless instructed to do so.

12. Never retrieve magazines, speedloaders, or anything which falls forward of the firing points without the assistance of range personnel.

13. Never make sight adjustments on a loaded firearm.

14. Pay strict attention to the range commands.

15. Never anticipate a command.

16. Notify range personnel of any unsafe range conditions, including improper conduct of others using the range.

17. Conduct a safety check of the firearm before and after a range session.

18. Be sure your ammunition is correct for the firearm you are using. Also, avoid having several different types of ammunition on the bench while firing.

19. If the gun does not fire when the trigger is pulled, it could signal a malfunction or a hangfire, a relatively rare cartridge defect in which a delay occurs between the time the cartridge primer is struck and the round fires. Keep the handgun under control and pointed down range. Discharges can

occur several seconds after the trigger is pulled and the primer has been struck. The best way to avoid hangfires is to avoid using very old ammunition.

20. Always clean your firearm after a range session, first making sure the firearm is unloaded.

21. Never clean or wipe a loaded firearm.

22. Everyone is responsible for range safety.

23. Never trust mechanical safeties.

Common Sense Rules of Gun Safety

The following rules of safe gun handling may be used for all firearms under any conditions. They apply whether you are a merchant, security guard, police officer, or deer hunter.

1. Treat every gun as though it is loaded.

Never assume a gun is unloaded. Never take someone else's assurance a gun is not loaded. Always check for yourself. The first step in handling a firearm is to open it and verify it is unloaded. If you do not know how to open or clear a particular weapon, leave it alone and have someone who is familiar with the firearm open it. Never pull the trigger when trying to clear a weapon. Engage the safety whenever possible in clearing the weapon. Magazine or clip fed firearms must always have their magazines removed first before proceeding any further.

2. Always point the muzzle in a safe direction.

It doesn't matter whether the firearm is loaded or unloaded. Never point the muzzle towards yourself or other people unless you are legally justified in shooting them. Do not allow anyone to point a firearm at you. If someone is inadvertently pointing a firearm at you, step away from the hazard and politely ask that person to point his firearm in a safe direction - one in which if an accidental discharge were to occur, there will be no human injury and, at most, minor property damage.

3. Unload guns when not in use.

Rifles and shotguns should never be stored loaded. With regard to handguns there are two opposing opinions. One theory holds that since most accidental discharges occur during the loading and unloading of firearms, we can reduce accidental discharges by leaving our everyday carry gun loaded. The second theory states that all guns should be unloaded when not in use. This theory has much merit at home, especially if you have children.

I recommend all firearms be unloaded when not in use. In order to safely load and unload your firearm you should identify a safe area at your home where, in the event of an accidental discharge, there is no possibility of the bullet going through a floor or wall to strike an unseen person. Safety can be further enhanced by filling a large, plastic laundry detergent container with dry sand and pointing the handgun directly it when loading and unloading.

A stack of tightly bundled newspapers, at least a foot thick, will also stop a single round from any commonly used self defense cartridge such as a .38 Special or 9mm. Magazines are even better than newspapers. Be sure to use the face of the stack and not the edge. When loading or unloading, point the muzzle at the face of the stack to contain the bullet should you suffer an accidental discharge. A masonry wall or floor should serve as a backstop to the bullet trap. Of course, you should be wearing safety glasses of some sort as a bullet impacting masonry is going to generate some shrapnel. Once your firearm is unloaded, it should be kept under lock and key and the ammunition stored separately.

4. Safeguard all firearms against theft.

Firearms should never be stored in the master bedroom. If you are the victim of a random burglary, the master bedroom is almost always the first place burglars look. Firearms and locked boxes, presumed to contain something of value, are prized finds for burglars. I recommend you invest in a gun safe and this safe be securely bolted to something solid such as a concrete floor.

5. Inspect the barrel for obstructions.

While most barrel obstructions occur while hunting (mud and snow), law enforcement officers sometimes fire their handguns with cleaning rod tips or cleaning patches stuck or forgotten in the bore. This can result in a burst barrel with possible injury to the shooter or bystander.

When shooting, if a particular gunshot or report sounds weak or different, cease firing immediately, wait at least 15 seconds, keeping the gun pointed downrange, completely unload the firearm, make double sure it is unloaded, then check the barrel for an obstruction. A defective cartridge (usually a cartridge without gunpowder) may have left a bullet lodged in the barrel. **Never attempt to shoot an obstruction out of a firearm.**

6. Whenever handling firearms for any reason, always keep your finger off the trigger and out of the trigger guard unless you intend to fire it.

7. Be certain of your target and what is behind it before discharging a weapon of any kind, for any reason.

Firearms in the Home

By extension, the law abiding merchant may have vague plans for defending his home and family against intruders. Regardless of whether or not such a plan exists, firearms are brought to the home from the store. Therefore, we must discuss firearms in the home. Home defense has just about been written to death in books and magazine articles too numerous to list. Consequently, I will confine my discussion to generic safety issues.

Ms. Donna M. Kirby Reynolds, the president of Personal Protection Unlimited Inc, and a nationally recognized expert and guest lecturer on women's safety issues states, "When you purchase a handgun, you have just become the parent of a child. You are responsible for that child. You have to protect it against abduction, keep it clean and make sure that someone who handles that child doesn't abuse it. The gun, just like the child, may save your life some day. Do not put that child into jeopardy. You are and must remain a responsible parent."

First and foremost, the gun owner must safeguard his firearms against unauthorized access by children, adult family members, and guests. Some years ago, a personal friend, a member of a local police department, commonly left his service and off duty revolver in a nightstand. While on a business trip, his wife hosted a small party for old high school friends, one of whom showed up with a date, a man she'd just met. During the course of the evening, this individual asked to use the bathroom off the master bedroom as the main bathroom was occupied. No one became suspicious when he closed the bedroom door. Subsequently, both firearms, together with jewelry and other valuables, were discovered missing. Fortunately, these two firearms were recovered but not the jewelry.

As previously mentioned, the master bedroom is almost always the first room searched by the random burglar. Firearms left in night stands or in locked boxes anywhere in the bedroom are likely to be found by burglars. Stolen firearms remain with the criminal element and are seldom recovered except during the commission of a crime.

In order to properly safeguard your handgun you must be willing to undergo some inconvenience. My handgun is in the master bedroom only when I'm at home. If I'm leaving for any reason and not carrying the handgun, it goes into my safe, elsewhere in the house.

Guns not being used should be stored unloaded and under lock and key. Better yet, you should strongly consider purchasing a safe large or heavy enough to prevent two thugs, fresh from a weight training regimen at your state prison, from being able to lift or manhandle it out the door. Serious safes should weigh at least 600 pounds or more. However, guns intended for felonious emergencies must be readily accessible. At your discretion you may consider leaving your primary defense handgun accessible, provided you can eliminate unauthorized access with 110 percent certainty.

Most law enforcement officers do not unload their carry gun at home. Unfortunately, this has sometimes led to tragedy when the gun was found by a child or the child's friend. It should be noted, in the case with autoloaders, and assuming you have been practicing correct loading procedure, autoloaders can be loaded so quickly, even in total darkness, there's little advantage to keeping the handgun loaded. Consequently, you must weigh the slight time advantage of having a loaded gun against the potential of a loaded gun getting into the hands of a family member or house guest. The decision is yours. However, if it is your decision to keep a handgun loaded at all times, I recommend it be kept in a locked container of some sort. Secondly, you must take the added precaution of affixing a tag to it which plainly states "loaded." You must allow for the possibility that if something were to happen to you, you haven't left a booby trap for your next of kin. Related to loading and unloading guns, you should be aware this activity, particularly with autoloaders, is a leading cause of accidental discharges. Consequently, if you leave the gun alone, it will leave you alone.

Be aware, in typical residential construction, most any bullet can easily reach the living quarters with lethal force when fired in the basement or garage. Typical floorboards, whether 3/4 inch plywood or one by four pine, will not stop a bullet. Ordinary wall board, even tiled on one side, will not stop a bullet either.

Try to establish consistent procedures for handling guns in the home. For example, I doubt if there are any law enforcement officers who, after 20 years, have not forgotten their handgun on the toilet tank at least once, if only for a moment. If the bathroom beckons while wearing a handgun, consider storing your handgun in a safe place before using the facilities. Gun carelessness usually doesn't occur when you first obtain one. People get careless through complacency when, after years of carrying or owning a gun, the gun becomes second nature and its owner treats it no differently than his wallet, house keys, and eyeglasses.

Never store firearms in your automobile even for the briefest period of time. If the car is stolen, the gun goes with it. Vehicle storage may seem like an easy way out when you have children. The gun that gets stolen, along with your chariot, may someday be used to kill another merchant or a police officer. As a law abiding citizen, you must do your part in preventing firearms from reaching criminal hands. Besides, it's not a wise idea for people to see you putting guns in the car or removing them. This makes it easier for a brain equipped robber to neutralize you when he strikes. Some of them are indeed intelligent.

Many states are granting citizens the right to carry firearms for personal protection. I'm all in favor of the individual right to carry concealed firearms provided some sort of training program accompanies it. You should be aware even through you are legally armed, you may face serious criminal charges if you carry a handgun in the following locations: courthouses, schools, federal buildings including post offices, local governmental buildings in some states, and certain portions of airports. In some states you may not carry firearms in any bank or establishment where alcoholic beverages are served. Other states grant private businesses the right to restrict the carrying of firearms on their premises. Violators can be subject to prosecution depending on how the state law is worded. **Learn and follow the laws of your state.**

Last but not least, we need to talk about handguns and minor traffic violations. Your home state or the state in which you are traveling may have guidelines regarding whether or not to inform a police officer you are armed in the event you are pulled over for a traffic infraction. These guidelines should be followed.

If the officer asks you to step out of your vehicle and you feel doing so may reveal you are armed, you should inform the officer you have a concealed weapons permit or license (if applicable in your state) and you are armed. In highly restrictive states such as New Jersey (where even retired police officers and federal agents are not trusted with handguns), the officer may have never seen his state's handgun license. You can expect to be disarmed and detained until the officer can verify your handgun license or permit is genuine. Full cooperation with the officer and lack of "attitude" on your part is always the safest course to follow.

If the officer elects to check your handgun against your handgun license, slowly turn your gun side to him and offer that he remove it from the holster. If he asks you to do it (which I highly doubt) remove it with two fingers, not your regular shooting grip. If the officer unloads the handgun, leave it unloaded until he leaves and until you can find a safe place to reload. Remember, every motion must be slow and deliberate. Do not show the slightest disrespect to the officer (a good policy whether or not your're armed). The least terrible thing that can happen is you'll get off with a warning. The second least terrible thing is a summons for a traffic infraction. Anything after that and you'll need a lawyer. Armed individuals must at all times be polite, respectful, non-combative, and in control of their words, actions, and emotions.

APPENDIX B

FIREARMS & DEFENSIVE TACTICS TRAINING FACILITIES

Following is a listing of well known firearms and defensive training academies that were kind enough to grant permission to be listed in this book. There are several other academies. However, they did not respond to my request to include them here.

Bill Rogers
Institute of Advanced Weapon Craft
1736 St. John's Bluff Road
Jacksonville, FL 32246

Chuck Taylor
American Small Arms Academy
PO Box 12111
Prescott, AZ 86304
(602) 778-5623

Modern Warrior
711 N. Wellwood Ave
Lindenhurst, NY 11757
(516) 226-8383

Green Valley Rifle & Pistol Club
formerly the Chapman Academy
4350 Academy Road
Hallsville, MO 65255
(573) 696-5544

Thunder Ranch
HCR 1, Box 53
Mt. Home, TX 78058
(210) 640-3138
Attn: John S. Farnam

Defense Training International Inc.
PO Box 917
Laporte, CO 80535
(970) 482-2520
(970) 482-0548 (fax)

Tactical Guard Training Center
PO Box 1817
Kingston, NY 12402
(914) 339-3440
http:\\www1.mhv.net\~cavan\tht.htm

Donna M. Kirby-Reynolds
Personal Protection Unlimited Inc.
PO Box 1186
Groton, CT 06340
(401) 596-3909

Paxton Quigley Enterprises Inc.
9903 Santa Monica Blvd #300
Beverly Hills CA 90212
(310) 281-1762

Front Sight Firearms Training Institute
PO Box 2619
Aptos, CA 95001
(800) 987-7719

The Firearm Training Center
9555 Blandville Road
West Paducah, KY 42086
(502) 554-5886

Gunsite Training Center
PO Box 700
Paulden, AZ 86334
(520) 636-4565

Emanuel Kapelsohn
Peregrine Corp.
PO Box 170
Bowers, PA 19511
(610) 682-7147

Smith and Wesson Academy
2100 Roosevelt Ave.
Springfield, MA 01102

SIG Arms Academy
Corporate Park
Industrial Drive
Exeter, NH 03833
(603) 772-2302

Heckler and Koch Academy
21480 Pacific Blvd
Sterling, VA 20166-8903
(703) 450-1900

Massad Ayoob
Lethal Force Institute
PO Box 122
Concord, NH 03301
(603) 224-6814

APPENDIX C

BALLISTIC COMPARISON CHART

Threat Level	Bullet Type	Barrel Length	Velocity (FPS)
Type I	.22 cal. 40 grain LR	6"	1050
	.25 cal. auto 50 grain FMJ	2"	810
	.32 cal. auto 71 grain lead	3"	905
	.38 cal. auto 86 grain JHP	4"	990
	.38 cal Special 158 grain lead	6"	850
	12 gauge #4 lead shot	18"	—
	.38 cal. Special 158 grain SWC	6"	850
Type IIA	.22 Mag. 40 grain solid point	6"	1180
	12 gauge "00" buckshot	18"	—
	.38 Special 125 grain SJHP+P	6"	1028
	.38 Special 158 grain lead +P	6"	1090
	.38 Special 110 grain JHP+P	6"	1235
	.45 cal. 230 Grain FMJ	5"	810
	.357 Mag. 158 Grain JSP	4"	1250
	.357 Mag. 158 grain lead	4"	1250
	.357 Mag. 158 grain SWC	4"	1250
	.41 Mag. 210 grain lead	8 3/8"	1080
	9mm 95 grain JSP	4"	1250
	9mm 100 grain JHP	4"	1250
	9mm 124 grain FMJ	4"	1090
	9mm 115 grain JHP	4"	1130
	9mm 147 grain sub-sonic	4"	1129

	9mm 124 grain Hydra-Shok	4"	1027
	9mm 124 grain Hydra-Shok+P+	4"	1145
	9mm 147 grain Hydra-Shok	4"	1100
	9mm 115 grain Silver Tip HP	4"	1131
	10mm 155 grain Hornady JHP	5"	1301
	10mm 180 grain Federal JHP	5"	1103
	10mm 180 grain Norma JHP	5"	1124
	40 S&W 180 grain Win. JHP	4"	1145
Type II	.41 Mag. 210 grain JSP	4"	1300
	.44 Mag. 240 grain SJSP	4"	1180
	.44 Mag.240 grain lead	4"	1200
	.44 Mag. 240 grain JHP	4"	1212
	.44 Mag. 180 grain SJHP	4"	1400
	.357 Mag. 125 grain JHP	4"	1450
	.357 Mag. 110 grain JHP	4"	1550
	.357 Mag. 148 grain JSP	6"	1395
	.357 Mag. 158 gr. JSP Hornady	6"	1445
	.357 Mag. 158 grain lead	8 3/8"	1410
	9mm 124 grain FMJ	5"	1175
	9mm 123 grain FMJ Geco	4"	1195
	9mm 115 grain FMJ Israeli	4"	1160
	9mm 115 grain Silvertip HP	4"	1170
Type IIIA	.44 Mag. 240 grain SWC	6"	1400
	9mm 124 grain FMJ	9 1/2"	1400
	9mm 123 grain FMC Geco	16"	1310
	9mm 115 grain FMJ Israeli	16"	1300

GLOSSARY

Autoloader: Any firearm which relies on the energy developed by the fired cartridge, either in the form of gas or recoil, to remove the fired shell casing from the firearm and to insert a fresh cartridge into the chamber.

Autoloading: The act of extracting and ejecting a fired casing from the chamber and introducing a fresh cartridge into the chamber utilizing energy produced by the fired cartridge.

Barrel: The portion of a firearm through which the bullet is fired.

Battery: A term used to describe the position of a bolt or slide when it is fully and correctly in its forward-most position and which allows the firearm to be fired.

Birdshot: Lead or steel shot, normally loaded in shot shells and for use in shotguns, designed or intended for use on birds, waterfowl, and small game. Birdshot is available in many sizes, from coarse to fine.

Bolt: The portion of a rifle or shotgun which contains the firing pin and locks the cartridge to be fired in the firing chamber.

Brass: A slang term used to describe fired shell casings which are most often made of brass.

Breach: The particular portion of a firearm where the loading, unloading, and removal of fired shell casings occurs. This term is not commonly used with revolvers.

Buckshot: Large, coarse lead shot, normally loaded in shot shells for use in shotguns, designed or intended for use against big game animals, such as deer, at close range.

Bullet: The portion of the cartridge which is fired from the gun towards its target.

Butt stock: The rear or back end of a rifle or shotgun stock that is held to the shoulder when firing.

Carbine: A shortened version of a pre-existing rifle. Today, most often used to describe rifles with barrels 20" or less and often chambered to fire handgun cartridges.

Cartridge: A fully loaded round of ammunition, ready for firing, consisting of a shell casing, primer, powder charge, and bullet.

Case mouth: The opening at the top of the shell casing through which the powder charge is inserted and which holds the bullet in place.

Casing: The fired, empty, or expended portion of a cartridge after it has been fired.

Chamber: The portion of a firearm that holds the cartridge to be fired. It is sometimes referred to as the firing chamber.

Chamber mouth: The opening or entrance to the chamber.

Choke: A constriction at the muzzle of a shotgun designed to regulate the degree of spread of the shot.

Clip: A device used to quickly recharge a magazine or for use in a firearm designed to be clip fed, such as the M-1 Garand. Often, clip and magazine are used interchangeably. However, they are different mechanical devices with similar functions.

Cycle: The act of taking a fresh cartridge from the magazine and feeding it into the chamber and/or removing the fired shell casing by using the mechanical features or parts of the firearm intended for this purpose.

Cylinder recess: A step machined into the rear face of a cylinder so as to allow the extractor star to seat flush with the cylinder face.

Eject: The act of expelling fired shell casings or live ammunition through the ejection port.

Ejection port: The opening in a firearm through which fired casings are ejected and through which loaded cartridges may also be removed. Generally, the term is most often used with auto-loading, lever, and pump action firearms.

Extractor: Most often a hook-like device, attached to the bolt or slide which grips the rim or extractor groove of the shell casing for the purpose of removing it from the chamber.

Extractor star: The star-like end of the ejector rod of a revolver which simultaneously raises all cartridges and shell casings contained in the cylinder for ejection or removal.

Firing pin: The pin-like device which strikes the cartridge primer.

Full metal jacket: A bullet in which the jacket material extends all the way to the bullet tip.

Frame: The main portion of a handgun upon which all other parts are attached or assembled. Under federal law, possession of a frame is the same as possession of an entire firearm.

Hammer: The hammer-shaped protrusion at the rear of a pistol which, when released, strikes the firing pin, sending it into the cartridge to fire it.

Hang fire: A potentially hazardous condition in which there is a perceptible delay from the time the firing pin strikes the primer until the cartridge fires.

Hollow point: A cavity at the tip of a bullet designed or intended to speed expansion of the bullet upon striking its target.

Magazine pouch: A leather or nylon container, worn on the belt, designed to hold one or more extra magazines.

Magazine: A spring loaded device designed to hold cartridges in position for successive feeding into the chamber.

a. Detachable magazine: A magazine designed to be inserted and removed from a firearm.

b. Self contained magazine: A magazine which is actually part of the firearm and not removable.

c. Double stack magazine: A magazine which holds two columns of cartridges and which alternately feeds ammunition from each column into feeding position.

d. Staggered magazine: Same as double stack magazine.

e. Single stack magazine: A magazine with one row of cartridges.

Magazine lips: The curved metal structures at the top of a magazine which hold the next or topmost cartridge in position for feeding.

Magazine well: The portion of a firearm in which a magazine is inserted.

Malfunction: A general term used to describe a failure of the firearm to perform one or more of the various functions it was designed to perform.

Muzzle: The forward end of a firearm's barrel.

Pistol: A semi-automatic handgun designed to be fired with one hand although two hands may also be used.

Primer: The cup-like device, most often silver in color, which when struck by the striker or firing pin, produces a hot flame to ignite the main powder charge.

Pump action: A type of mechanical action requiring a pump-like motion to cycle fresh rounds through the chamber.

Purchase: The ability to quickly and efficiently grip something in order to perform a mechanical function or to maintain control of it.

Rack: A slang expression referring to the act of retracting the slide of a semi-automatic handgun, then releasing it to travel forward under its own power.

Return spring: A heavy spring, either surrounding the barrel or located just below the barrel which provides the force necessary to return the slide to battery. It is also known as a rebound spring.

Revolver: A firearm, most often designed to be fired with one hand, which contains a revolving cylinder that successively brings fresh ammunition into alignment with the barrel and firing mechanism.

Sear: A mechanical stop or lever which holds the spring

loaded firing mechanism in a position to fire the chambered cartridge.

Semi-automatic: An autoloading firearm designed to fire one cartridge for each pull of the trigger.

Semi-wadcutter: A bullet having two essentially flat surfaces, one at the tip of the bullet, and a second near, or at, the case mouth and about at the mid-point of the bullet.

Shell: (or shell casing) The portion of a cartridge or shotgun shell holding the primer, powder charge, and projectile.

Short cycle: A human error in which an individual, firing a shotgun, fails to allow the reloading mechanism to travel fully rearward before again returning it forward to battery.

Shotgun operating handle: A small, curved extension from the side of the bolt on autoloading shotguns.

Slide: The upper or topmost portion of a semi-automatic handgun which travels or slides forward and rearward on the frame.

Slide release: A mechanical stop which automatically holds the slide to the rear when the handgun has fired its last cartridge and which may also be used by the shooter to release the slide so it may return to battery.

Slide stop: Another name for the slide release.

Slide stop lever: Another name for the slide release.

Speedloader: A cylindrical device designed to simultaneously load all chambers of a revolver.

Speedloader pouch: A container, worn on the belt, designed to hold a speedloader.

Stack: (or stacking) A condition where a trigger becomes progressively heavier and more difficult to pull within its range of motion.

Stock: The portion of a rifle or shotgun which is held against the shoulder and may extend to the muzzle.

Stoppage: Used interchangeably with "malfunction" but more closely associated with the failure of a semi-auto or full automatic firearm to perform one or more of the functions it was designed to perform.

Strong hand: The right hand of a right-handed person or the left hand of a left-handed person.

Striker: Usually called a striker assembly, this refers to the mechanism which moves forward to fire the chambered cartridge in pistols not equipped with a conventional hammer.

Sub-machine gun: A fully automatic firearm designed to fire handgun ammunition.

Velocity: The term most often used when referring to the speed of a bullet.

Wadcutter: A flat nosed bullet in which the flat surface is the full diameter of the bullet and which is designed to cut neat, clean holes in a target for ease of scoring.

Weak hand: The left hand of a right-handed individual or the right hand of a left-handed individual.